EVEN DARKNESS MUST PASS

A Long Journey to Trust:
Discovering God's Rule and Rest

B.R. THIGPEN

EVEN DARKNESS MUST PASS
Copyright © 2025 by Frontline Media

ISBN 979-8-9935064-0-1 (paperback)
ISBN 979-8-9935064-1-8 (hardback)
ISBN 979-8-9935064-2-5 (Ebook)

Published by Frontline Media
P.O. Box 908951
Gainesville, GA. 30501
brttrm2@yahoo.com

Cover and interior formatting by KUHN Design Group | kuhndesigngroup.com

This book is dedicated to:

WADE HAMPTON THIGPEN

March 19, 1991—August 21, 1994

"...By and by..."

CONTENTS

PREFACE

If I could gather all the Christians in the world together in one place and speak to them all at the same time, first of all, that would be a logistical disaster. Think about it: If you've ever tried organizing a church function with more than three people involved, you already know the chaos. Now multiply that by several billion. Someone would demand we start with hymns; someone else would want fog machines and a laser show. The chanters would be circling the edges with incense pots. And don't even bring up Bible versions unless you're ready for a theological slugfest. Regulating the room temperature alone would require an act of Congress, a senior lady wearing a shawl, and probably a miracle—or at least one very stressed-out deacon with a thermostat app.

But if we ever managed to get past the worship wars and thermostat debates, here's the message I'd deliver: **the sovereignty of God**. And that's exactly what this book is about. His sovereignty and my journey to accepting it.

After we come to God for salvation, the most important thing we can do is not just learn about His sovereignty—but actually live like we believe it. Without that anchor we drift. Trust me, I've tried navigating life without directions (both spiritually and geographically), and the results are somewhere between inefficient and mildly catastrophic. A life without a settled understanding of God's sovereignty is like using a paper map in a hurricane. You may feel like you're making progress, but it's mostly flapping and confusion. Bonus points if the map is not upside down.

I've seen this struggle up close. Years working among the Slavic people—Belarus, Russia, Ukraine—showed me how deeply people believe in all kinds of things. There is this one tradition in Russia that goes like this: Before any trip, you're supposed to sit down for a moment on anything close enough that will support you to ensure good fortune on your journey. I don't know if it's the act of sitting or the pause before chaos that's supposed to help, but it's taken very seriously by many. Then there are folks who follow GPS instructions with cult like devotion. I've been in a car where someone drove miles out of their way because "the voice" said so. That's the kind of trust we need in God—**except He actually knows what He's doing**.

Becoming a Christian means putting your faith in Christ for salvation, yes—but then what? That initial faith isn't a lifelong autopilot. It's more like joining a gym: You got in the door with a membership, but your biceps aren't going to show up without effort. Faith grows through daily trust. And trusting God's sovereignty is like lifting spiritual weights. It doesn't always feel good, but it builds something deep inside you. Unfortunately, there's no protein shake for spiritual maturity.

So why a book about a subject most people can't spell? Because I've lived through enough pain, confusion, and wrestling to know that trusting God isn't automatic—and that God's sovereignty doesn't always make sense and will not completely unfold for us until we get to heaven.

I'm not writing this because my life is some heroic spiritual high-light reel. It's not. I don't even think my story is that unique. You can probably find more inspiring tales in the waiting room of your local hospital. But I'm writing this because my story might help *you* make sense of *yours*. I'm not baiting you for sympathy or giving spiritual clichés. I'm offering a mirror—and maybe a flashlight. Possibly a snack.

Truth is, I thought I'd write this book years ago. But, as you know, life has a way of fast-forwarding the calendar. One moment you're saying, "I'll do it soon," and the next your favorite band is now doing reunion tours, your jeans don't fit, and you've lost your car in the parking lot so many times that you come to expect it.

Looking back, I wasn't ready to write it years ago. I was too hurt, too confused. If I had written this book back then, it would have been pages of emotional soup flavored with confused conjecture. Later, I was still in the middle of learning the lessons I now hope to share. And writing about lessons you haven't learned yet is like giving financial advice when you're still getting calls from debt collectors.

Also, honestly, I failed to write because of—**pride**. Pride has a way of convincing us that we've got it all figured out. And God, being God, is not especially moved by our self-confidence. He teaches through patience, not popularity. Sometimes it takes years of missed exits and spiritual flat tires to realize that His hand has been steady the whole time.

Let me be clear from the beginning: This isn't light reading. This isn't a feel-good devotional for quiet mornings and cinnamon rolls. This is for the struggler—the griever, the questioner, the one staring at the ceiling wondering if God is really in control. If you're reading this while sipping a latte with soft jazz in the background, I admire your optimism. But chances are you're not. Chances are you're in the thick of something more serious. And if you are, I wrote this for you.

And if you haven't gone through that dark season yet—**hold on, it's coming.** Not because I'm a pessimist but because I've read the Bible. Suffering isn't optional; it's promised. But so is grace.

As we go forward, I want you to know something: **Even in your hardest seasons, God's sovereignty is not on pause.** You might feel like He's gone silent or worse—absent. But the silence of God is never the absence of God. Sometimes He is doing His deepest work when you hear Him the least.

I don't know where you are in your journey. You don't either. That's the wild part. There's a reason David wrote, "There is but a step between me and death." (1 Samuel 20:3) Our time is short, but it is meaningful and should be enough. Whether you're just beginning, somewhere in the middle, or seeing the final chapters on the horizon, the truth of God's sovereignty can reframe everything.

Someone once said that life is like a coin—you can spend it any way you want, but you can only spend it once. If you've received His grace and forgiveness, you are blessed. But if you've come to trust His sovereign hand through pain and mystery—you are *most* blessed.

For me it took suffering. It took loss to bring me to understand and accept God's sovereignty in my life. For you it might take something else entirely. But maybe—just maybe—God in His mercy brought you to this book at just the right time. And if these words nudge your heart a little closer to trusting Him, then this book has done what it was meant to do.

So wherever you are in your journey, may His providence guide you. May His hand steady you. And may you see His sovereignty—even in the darkness.

Because even darkness must pass.

INTRODUCTION

Frodo: *"I can't do this, Sam."*

Sam: *"I know. It's all wrong. By rights we shouldn't even be here. But we are. It's like in the great stories, Mr. Frodo. The ones that really mattered. Full of darkness, and danger, they were. And sometimes you didn't want to know the end, because how could the end be happy? How could the world go back to the way it was when so much bad had happened? But in the end, it's only a passing thing, this shadow.* **Even darkness must pass.** *A new day will come. And when the sun shines, it'll shine out the clearer. Those were the stories that stayed with you. That meant something. Even if you were too small to understand why. But I think, Mr. Frodo, I do understand. I know now. Folk in those stories had lots of chances of turning back, only they didn't. They kept going. Because they were holding on to something."*

Frodo: *"What are we holding on to, Sam?"*

Sam: *"That there's some good in this world, Mr. Frodo...and it's worth fighting for."*

SAM'S SPEECH TO FRODO FROM
The Lord of the Rings: The Two Towers[1]

---

1. J.R.R. Tolkien, *The Two Towers* (Boston: Houghton Mifflin, 1954), T*he Lord of the Rings: The Two Towers.* Directed by Peter Jackson. New Line Cinema, 2002.

I've loved the Tolkien tales since I first read them decades ago. Just as Frodo ventured into the unknown carrying a terrible burden, I too have walked through seasons of darkness carrying a weight I didn't ask for. And like him, I often wanted to turn back—or at least lie down and let the story pass me by.

Jordan Peterson says that life is the story of our journeys. I've found that to be deeply true. This book is about one of mine—the long walk toward understanding and embracing God's sovereignty. There was a moment not long after the tragedy I'll share later in these pages when I quietly echoed Frodo's words: "I can't do this."

I truly believed that happiness was gone forever. That my story had fractured beyond repair. But somehow, by the grace of God, I survived. And slowly I came to see what Sam saw: *even darkness must pass*. There is still good in this world—more than we sometimes dare believe—and when seen through the lens of God's sovereign hand, it's not just comforting. It's worth holding on to.

CHAPTER 1

WADE'S STORY—PART 1

The Hinge in My Life

*"And we know that all things work together for
good to them that love God, to them who are
the called according to his purpose."*

ROMANS 8:28

No one ever wakes up expecting *this* to be the darkest day of their life. Most mornings, we rise in neutral—or if you're like me in reverse and end up right back under the covers negotiating with the alarm clock like it's a hostage situation.

I've heard people say their first waking thoughts are spiritual, lofty, and inspired—"This is the day the Lord has made!" I've never seen these people when the alarm goes off, but I imagine they also floss after every meal and keep a journal for their garden. My mornings usually begin somewhere between "Where's the coffee?" and "What day is it?"

I can't recall exactly what I was thinking on August 21, 1994. But if it was like most mornings, I was focused on getting dressed, corralling the family, and making sure no one left without shoes. We were preparing for a short trip to a small town in North Georgia— about eighty miles away—but it felt bigger than that. This was the beginning of a new chapter for our family. We were heading toward a life of ministry in Eastern Europe.

The Iron Curtain had fallen. Nations once sealed tighter than a Tupperware lid in the freezer were suddenly wide open. After seventy years of state-sponsored atheism, the Gospel could be preached freely again. I believed then—and still do—that it was one of the greatest mission opportunities in the history of the modern church. We had volunteered to go and were ready. At least we thought we were.

There was excitement, a little nervousness, and a sense of awe. This was going to be a defining moment for our family.

What I didn't know was that *this* would also become the hinge upon which my entire life would swing.

· · ·

Obviously there were miles to go and much to do to make that mission happen. What surprised me was how few people seemed to be chasing this incredible opportunity. The doors were flung wide open, but the hallway still felt empty.

I passionately wanted to do my part in this enormous work. But before we could board a plane or pack a single box, we had to go through the process known in church circles as "deputation." Why we call it that, I still don't know. I've looked up the word, and the etymology is as foggy as an early morning mountain road.

For those unfamiliar with the term, "deputation" means you travel from church to church, meeting to meeting, person to person, sharing your mission, your calling—and yes, asking people to support you.

That's the polished version. The unpolished version is that we had to ask people for money. Now, we never said it quite like that. "Would you support the work?" sounds nobler than "Would you mind writing us a check?" But let's be honest—support meant finances, and the process was long, exhausting, and humbling.

Though I don't remember all my thoughts on that first day of beginning our mission, I do know this: My motives and my heart were as pure as I knew how to make them. No one was forcing me to go to Eastern Europe. In fact, no one was even asking me to. There wasn't some spiritual draft pulling me from Georgia to the other side of the world. There was no booming voice, no handwriting in the sky, and no guilt trip from a missions committee.

I wasn't running from something—I was running *toward* something.

It's not lost on me that I was thirty-eight at the time. That's the age when some people buy a boat or start playing pickleball; I decided to move to a country I'd been taught was the enemy as a child. I didn't know the language. I didn't know the culture. And I certainly didn't know how many ways I would be humbled in the years ahead.

But I saw a need—and someone once said that a need recognized is a call received. Whether you chalk it up to a divine calling or just a man willing to say "Yes" when the door opened, I stepped forward. I offered what I had, trusting that somehow God would do something with it. It didn't feel heroic. It felt right.

What could possibly go wrong? That's not just the name of a country song—it's also a great way to tempt fate. I genuinely believed blessings would follow obedience. I had no hidden agenda, no ulterior motives, no pressure from anyone twisting my arm. I honestly and deeply loved God—and still do—and I was walking forward with as much sincerity and trust as I could muster.

I didn't think the road ahead would be easy. But I assumed it would at least be paved with some sense of assurance, of purpose fulfilled. I hoped we'd be effective. I prayed we'd be fruitful. And I expected—naively maybe—that the days would unfold with favor.

What I did *not* expect was what would unfold later that very day. And nothing could've prepared me for it.

* * *

Mornings—especially Sunday mornings—are their own kind of chaos in most homes. Ours was no exception.

At some point along the parenting journey, I had adopted the gloriously irritating tradition of waking my boys with ridiculous "Good morning!" songs. I'm convinced that everyone—deep down—enjoys silly songs, especially children. And if they say otherwise, they've probably just decided to be crotchety people...or they're teenagers.

I had a few of these tunes in my arsenal, and I'd sing them until the boys either got up or pretended to be in a coma. Honestly I'm not sure if I pulled out the "Rise and Shine" setlist that particular morning, but it would've been like me. Humor, after all, is a good way of nudging joy into the day. Even on days that feel weighty, it's how I tried to lighten the load—especially for my kids.

My youngest son at the time, Wade, was three years old and shared a room with one of his older brothers. He woke up that morning and true to his routine toddled to the top of the stairs, turned himself around, and slid down the carpeted steps backward on his stomach like a tiny, determined sled.

He caught himself at the bottom, gave his eyes a good rub, and began his mission to locate his mama—and his breakfast.

All my sons at that age wore nightshirts to bed—essentially

oversized T-shirts that doubled as uniforms for everything from sleeping to sprinting to spontaneous indoor wrestling. The best kind of garment, really. Especially because those shirts gave me just enough fabric to grab during our ferocious living room wrestling matches— no rules, no points, just all-out joy. If one of my wild little creatures made a run for it, I had the nightshirt as my lasso.

We spent literal hours in the kind of father-son roughhousing that should be listed in parenting books under "vitamin joy." To this day, I believe fun is one of the most underrated virtues of family life— and I tried to serve it up as best I could.

All our kids had been born blond-headed—except Wade. He was our dark-haired boy with a dimple just like mine and a brightness in his eyes that you couldn't help but notice. He was a beautiful little guy.

At three Wade was just stepping into that delightful age of sweetness and curiosity, the kind of innocence that makes you pause and think, *If only we could bottle this.*

If I had to pick an age I've most enjoyed with my children—just for the sheer fun of it—I'd probably say three. Of course, every age has its moments, from first steps to first eye rolls. But age three? That's the golden hour of childhood.

That morning, like many others, their clothes had been laid out the night before. After breakfast the older boys could get themselves dressed without much fuss. But Wade? He got the royal treatment. His mom helped him get ready, brushed his teeth, and made sure he looked just right.

This Sunday wasn't like any other they'd known. No regular church routine. No familiar friends or classrooms. Everything was new. Different.

And let's be honest—different isn't always easy, especially for a child.

What goes on in the heart of a three year old when his world suddenly shifts? We can only guess. But I imagine it's pretty simple: They want to be safe, they want to be happy, and they want waffles if possible.

Honestly, we all want that—no matter how grown up we pretend to be.

I think my family was like that. I know I wanted us to be.

We all grabbed our Bibles (These were the days when you carried a hard copy and not a smartphone version—because, brace yourself, there were no smartphones.), did last checks for hair, and made the final round of "Does anyone need to go to the bathroom?" calls. That sacred Sunday tradition.

Once everyone was reasonably presentable and reasonably relieved, we loaded into our full-sized van. Wade got the VIP treatment in his all-world-approved, NASA-endorsed, fort-knox-level car seat. (I literally despise these things. I can never get them in the vehicle without battling them.) I backed out of the driveway of the house where he had literally been born and pointed us toward the road that would change everything.

We didn't know it, but this was the beginning of a journey we wouldn't return from—not really. Regular sameness was ending; a new kind of different was about to take its place. As the house shrank in the rearview mirror, none of us knew Wade would never walk back into it again. He was going to a different home. A better one. One not built by human hands.

It was a good-looking August day in Georgia—sunny, quiet, and deceptively normal—as we drove from Gainesville to the tiny town of Resaca. If you've heard of Resaca, it's probably because you're a Civil War buff. The Battle of Resaca was part of Sherman's march north toward Chattanooga. Other than that bit of trivia, Resaca is the kind of place you pass through without realizing you've passed through it.

It took about two hours to wind through the foothills of the Blue Ridge Mountains, and the drive was blessedly uneventful. If you've traveled with kids, you know that "uneventful" is right up there with "miraculous." There were no spills, no squabbles, no unexpected biology experiments. Just peace.

We weren't speaking in the church that morning. We were simply attending—another family in the pews, chasing obedience, holding hope.

I had known the pastor for many years, and he had once told me, "Drop in and be in service with us whenever you can." This happened to be the first day that I could. The church had a long history and a solid reputation in that part of Georgia. The pastor was something of a legend in our denominational circle—a sincere, devout man who had preached an old-fashioned tent revival at our church several years earlier. He was known for supporting men who felt called to serve in other countries. That was me now. So naturally this felt like a good place to start.

We were always, as we say in the South, "a sight," when walked into a church somewhere. A parade of people, Bibles, and diaper bags. This day was no exception. As we slid into a pew near the back, people began to trickle over to greet us and figure out who we were. And as church people often are, they were kind, curious, and appropriately nosy.

My kids were model citizens that morning—either from an early baptism into childhood holiness or from a healthy fear of what would happen if they weren't. Likely both. They sat wide-eyed in this new church environment. Wade was tucked in beside me. I remember clearly that I had some 3x5 cards in my Bible—standard equipment for jotting down notes, thoughts, or sermon one-liners worth stealing—and an ever present pencil tucked in the back.

Wade let me know that he wanted to draw with the pencil and cards, and I remember glancing down to see what he was working on. It didn't take long to realize that whatever talent he had, it probably wasn't in the arts. The drawing offered undeniable proof: This child had inherited his artistic skills from me. In other words, there weren't any. Still, he scribbled with the focus of a budding genius, unaware that the paper was a battlefield of confusion.

Every now and then, he'd lean his head against me and just…be. That simple leaning brought back memories of when I was a little boy in church, resting against my own mother without any grand thoughts or anxious plans—just existing in the quiet safety of someone else's care. I think that's what Wade felt that day: not the weight of a sermon or the stirrings of a calling but the comfort of being near someone who made him feel safe.

I couldn't tell you what the sermon was about that day. Honestly, I wasn't really listening. My mind wandered in and out of thoughts, making lists of things to do and scanning through all that lay ahead. When the service ended, we lingered just long enough to talk with a few folks and make sure the pastor knew we had been there—and more importantly, why we were there. Once that was done, we all climbed back into the van for the winding drive home.

From the rearview mirror, Wade sat right in the center of my view—wide-eyed, alert, soaking in the newness of it all. He was simply being three. And that in itself was sacred.

◦ ◦ ◦

It was after noon, which meant it was time for lunch—or past time, really—and so began the great and ancient family debate: Where should we eat? This particular topic has always baffled me. If you've ever tried to pick a restaurant with more than two people, you know it's less about hunger and more like trying to broker a peace deal in the Middle East. Everyone has strong opinions, no one agrees, and somehow someone ends up slightly offended.

Over time I've learned a trick. The best way to resolve the lunch standoff is to just pick a place and start driving there. Inevitably once you're in the parking lot, everyone mysteriously finds something they're willing to eat. Of course this approach also comes with consequences—namely being labeled as insensitive and possibly excommunicated from the sacred order of "considerate fathers and spouses." But eventually you have to choose your martyrdom.

That day we landed on McDonald's. There were no mobile phones, no GPS, no comforting voice saying, "Turn left in half a mile." I simply remembered seeing a McDonald's earlier that morning on the way to church, and I figured I could retrace our steps. Our route home took us through Gilmer County, through the charming little mountain town of Ellijay, Georgia—famous for its apples and annual fall festivals. At the time I didn't know anyone from there and had no real connection to the place.

But after this day Ellijay became something else entirely.

It's strange how a place can become branded in your memory, not because of what it is but because of what happened there. That little town didn't do anything wrong—its streets didn't betray me, and its hills didn't curse me. But it became the backdrop for a moment I would never forget. Etched into my memory not with a gentle touch but with a cold, unfeeling chisel. Everyone has a place like that—a location that unexpectedly gets assigned to your pain. Mine, as it turns out, will always be a McDonald's in Ellijay, Georgia.

It sat up on a little hill just off the highway we were on, and as we pulled into the parking lot, we spotted the ever-present and universally loved kids' playground out front—the colorful jungle of plastic tubes and slides where dreams and germs collide. As we walked toward the entrance, we did the usual parent shuffle: head counts, hand-holding, and sharp turns to keep the littlest ones from veering off into shrubbery.

Ordering at a fast-food place like McDonald's followed a familiar and mildly chaotic script. Mom or I would gather intel from each child—what they wanted to eat, how they wanted it prepared, whether today was a ketchup day or a mustard-only day—and then I'd step forward to the counter and translate those wishes into fast-food speak. It was like being a culinary diplomat at a drive-thru summit. And inevitably I got something wrong.

Someone wanted a Dr. Pepper, and I ordered a Coke. Someone wanted fries, and somehow onion rings appeared—though I still don't know where those came from because McDonald's doesn't even serve onion rings. But the most repeated, most classic blunder was with my oldest son.

He hates cheese. I know this. It has been stated plainly, publicly, and repeatedly. And yet, against all odds, I somehow always ordered a cheeseburger for him. From the deepest places in my heart, I promise I wasn't doing it on purpose. It just happened—as if the Lord Himself were gently nudging my son toward the joy and sanctity of melted American cheese.

To me cheese is sacred. It's not just a food group; it's the cornerstone of culinary civilization. A burger without cheese is like a sermon without hope—it technically counts, but it leaves something vital out. My son, however, sees it differently. And while I tried to respect that, my subconscious clearly believed it was a phase he'd grow out of by the time he turned thirty. It was not.

That was our routine back then. A thousand tiny moments like these, stacked and woven into the fabric of our family story. We were younger, funnier, and slightly less tired than we are now—but those were the days that built the scaffolding of who we would all become.

o   o   o

On that noteworthy day we were all bunched around the Maccounter, going through the familiar ritual I just described. I don't recall it being particularly busy—no long lines, no impatient strangers breathing down our necks. That small grace meant we could take our time, which, as any parent knows, is a luxury.

We were careful parents. Possibly too careful. If there are moms and dads in this world who have loved and watched over their children more intentionally than we did—and still do—then those kids are among the most blessed on earth. Our children never had to wonder if someone was watching. They never had to earn our affection or guess if they mattered. We hovered. We shepherded. We tried, imperfectly, to love them well.

Sometimes I see kids darting through restaurants or grocery store aisles like little wild banshees, their parents miles behind them in both distance and awareness. I don't mean to judge—I really don't—but I marvel at how casual some folks seem with their kids' well-being, like they're letting them grow up via spontaneous combustion. I suppose we were the counter-example, maybe to a fault.

People would often comment as we traveled or ate in public on how well-behaved our boys were. That always meant a lot to me. Not because we needed the praise—we certainly made enough parenting mistakes to keep us humble—but because it meant our efforts to guide and guard them were bearing some kind of fruit.

I say all of this not to set us on a pedestal. As I said, we were far from perfect. But I want to be clear about something: The catastrophe that was about to unfold wasn't the result of neglect. It wasn't carelessness or indifference. Maybe it was a lapse. But it was never a lack of love or vigilance.

Sometimes in the fast-food-ordering process there's a quiet tension that creeps in—the kind that only parents recognize. It comes from small voices asking with increasing urgency whether there will be enough time to play on the playground. That playground in Ellijay was nothing extraordinary—just your standard, sun-faded plastic fortress that dots so many roadside restaurants. But Wade loved it, as only a three year old can love anything with a slide.

Deep within every father who truly loves his children is a God-given compulsion to protect. It's part instinct, part divine wiring—the reason some men go to war and why all of us would throw ourselves in front of a moving train without a second thought if it meant saving one of our own. Ask any good dad, and he'll tell you without hesitation, without calculation that he would give his life to spare his child.

Sometimes this protective impulse is shaped by a strong upbringing. Other times it rises in spite of one. I've seen it in men who grew up with no guidance, no warmth, and yet something awakened in them the moment they held their child. I've spent years working with boys from orphanages—kids who came from places of deep neglect—and I've watched some of them grow into fiercely loving fathers, transformed by the very responsibility they were once denied.

This isn't to suggest that mothers don't share that same urgency—they absolutely do. But I believe there's a unique weight placed on fathers both in Scripture and in the fabric of how the world works. In the divine order of family everyone has a sacred role to play—but when it comes to protection, the first line and the last line of defense is Dad.

These convictions weren't abstract to me that day. They weren't something I'd heard in a sermon or read in a book. They were a living part of who I was—as I stood at that counter and slowly realized that my Wade had wandered away.

* * *

The following hours and events on that day are the hinge on which my life swings. There is life before these moments and life after—and things would never, ever be the same again. In the years since when I try to remember that day, those first few minutes move slowly, like a shadowy, low-budget stage play flickering across the back wall of my memory. The key players are still clear, their movements retraceable. But the others—those secondary people standing nearby—appear as blurred silhouettes. Careless witnesses it seemed to the most horrific scene any father can endure.

And then the moment.

My wife came running toward me. Her voice broke the air with words that have echoed in my soul ever since: "Something has happened to Wade."

At that precise moment the world shrank. Everything else fell off the edge of the map. Nothing else in life was even remotely important. My singular instinct was simple and primal: I had to get to him. Whatever it was—whatever had happened—if I could just get to him,

I believed I could fix it. That's what men like me think. That's what pride does. There is this inner belief, built over years of solving problems and holding things together, that nothing can truly be broken if you're fast enough, strong enough, or close enough to intervene.

The distance from the counter to the place where Wade lay was no more than fifty feet. Just fifty feet. But it became the longest, most crushing stretch I have ever run. Time bent, and the air thickened. And every step forward carried me farther away from the world I once knew.

The moment I saw him, something very deep in the God-regions of my soul told me this was more than anything I'd ever faced. It wasn't a whisper. It wasn't a nudge. It was a thunderclap in my spirit—a certainty that what I was seeing would divide my life into two parts: everything before and everything after.

No one saw exactly what happened. There is no eyewitness account, no clear sequence of events to explain why my son was lying motionless on the asphalt parking lot outside that McDonald's in Ellijay. We can only guess. Maybe he'd slipped away toward the playground—drawn like all little boys to the plastic adventure just beyond the glass. Maybe he was doing what boys do—balancing on the curb like it was a tightrope in the circus. And maybe at that same moment a young teenage boy turned the corner in his small pickup truck, simply trying to get lunch. It was a horrible perfect storm.

They met in that terrible instant.

* * *

Wade was struck—his upper body, including his head—by the front tire of the truck.

I've been asked over the years whether I blame the young man driving that truck. Whether I believe he was careless or distracted or somehow responsible for the tragedy. But I don't. I truly don't. From everything I've learned—and everything I felt even in that moment—I don't believe he was reckless. He wasn't speeding. There were no phones in his hand, no music blasting. He was just a kid on a normal day who suddenly found himself in a moment that would mark him for life. According to the report, he told the officer he didn't see Wade in time. And I believe him.

There's no fault to assign here. No villain to drag into the light. Just a sorrow so sharp it slices through reason. Everyone involved that day would trade almost anything to change what happened.

Every dad wants to be the rock when the storm hits. The stable one. The steady voice. The strong arms. And as I ran toward Wade, I desperately wanted to be that man. I wanted to kneel beside my son and radiate calm and strength, to be the presence he needed.

But I wasn't.

I don't claim to be a hero. But I'm not a coward either. And yet on that day—in that moment—I was entirely unprepared. Emotionally ambushed. Crushed in body, mind, and spirit in a way I had never experienced before.

There was no manual. No script. No brave music swelling in the background.

Just a dad, broken open in the parking lot of a McDonald's, trying to reach his little boy in time.

I wouldn't want to repeat—or wish on anyone—that precise moment when you realize the disaster you thought only happened to other people has now arrived at your doorstep. In one micro-moment it sucks the breath from your lungs and the logic from your brain. It evacuates your senses. Everything that makes you human is suddenly frozen.

That was me.

I was locked in place. My emotions had short-circuited, my body suspended in a fog of disbelief. I couldn't move. I couldn't speak. And even if I had, nothing would've made sense—not to me and certainly not to anyone else standing nearby. It's hard to describe, but the best I can offer is that—for those first awful seconds—life was a void. No people. No sound. No thought. Just emptiness.

Wade was lying on his back, struggling to breathe. I will always be grateful—forever—that though his upper body had been crushed, there was only a trickle of blood coming from his nose. That small mercy is one I've never forgotten.

I should've reached for him. I know that. I should've dropped to my knees, spoken his name, done something—anything—to help, to comfort, to make it right. But I didn't. I couldn't. My mind had gone completely blank. There was no clock ticking in those moments, no comprehension of how long I stayed in that paralyzed state. It couldn't have been long—seconds, maybe—but it felt eternal. A slow-motion moment that marked me permanently.

And then somehow in that void—through the thick silence, the paralysis, the unformed prayers—something broke through. The presence of an angel.

CHAPTER 2

WADE'S STORY—PART 2

In the Presence of Angels

What I want to explain to you next is something that for me is the most helpful and most believable—*but only in the way I will describe it.* I repeat...*for me.*

You must decide how to interpret the events in your life—sifted through what God shows you in His Word and His ways. So please don't try to talk me out of what I believe or run it through your grid of rational analysis to make it all neat and tidy in your mind. I'm not looking for logic here. I want no part of that.

And definitely—*please*—don't try to correct my theology so it makes better sense to you. What I've come to believe about the next moments of that day has been spiritually life-giving for me. It's how my heart, mind, and soul received it. So in all your well-meaning rationality...don't try to take that away from me.

As I looked down at my son, his small body was struggling to pull in oxygen through lungs that had collapsed. His eyes were closed, and

29

as far as I could tell, he was unconscious. Then suddenly I noticed someone kneeling beside him—a woman, precious and calm—who had appeared from I don't know where and disappeared just as mysteriously once it was over.

She was gazing directly and lovingly into Wade's face, her voice barely more than a whisper: "Breathe, Wade. Just breathe."

As she spoke, she spoke to him as if they were well acquainted. This was obviously not the first time she'd met him. She gently rubbed his head and tended to him with such tenderness; it was as if she had known and watched over him for every one of his few days on this earth. "Everything will be okay, Wade. Just breathe," she repeated softly.

It seemed as though she *knew*—deep down in a place beyond explanation—that no matter what happened next…all would somehow be okay.

There are voices on earth that settle us at times like nothing else will. There is no rasp in these voices as well as no doubt. Whatever that voice says, you want to believe. Even if there is little hope, this kind of voice brings at least a little for you to cling to. If that voice says all will be good, then maybe it will be. That voice is what voices in heaven must sound like. It will be how we talk to each other in perfect surroundings someday. The tone is perfect, and the rhythm is exactly appropriate to the space around it. And…it probably has a British accent.

Her voice had that quality. The tone was perfect. The rhythm— exactly right for the space it entered. It was as though her words didn't just comfort—they *willed* him to breathe. They carried on a frequency deeper than sound.

And here's the strange thing: In comforting him, I believe she was reaching me too. Somehow her presence, her voice, was helping steady my soul in its free fall.

·   ·   ·

I've studied angels. I certainly believe they exist. The Bible is full of stories where they've made themselves known to ordinary people—sometimes bold, sometimes hidden. Scripture even warns us to treat strangers well because we might be entertaining angels without even knowing it. (Hebrews 13:2)

So was the woman who knelt beside Wade that day an angel? We've all heard of guardian angels. We've all hoped for them. Was she Wade's? Was she as heartbroken as I was that her charge had fallen?

Was she an angel?…Yes. She was.

She did her job in a way that was both magnificent and unmistakably supernatural. God knew—and, therefore, she knew—that I was handcuffed, physically and spiritually, in my son's darkest moment. So in whatever form or explanation you want to assign, I believe this: God sent an angel to attend to Wade.

As quickly as she arrived, she was gone. I never saw her again. But I will.

I want to spend at least a little bit of eternity listening to her voice.

·   ·   ·

At some point in all of this I broke away and crossed the parking lot until I found a small hedgerow. There was a space between two of the boxwoods, and I fell to my knees there—covered my face with my hands and buried my head into the cedar mulch beneath them.

It wasn't a time for deep, composed prayer. It was a time for crying out.

This was David, prostrate on the ground, weeping for his sick son through the night (2 Samuel 12).

There's a deep and wide chasm between crying and weeping. Crying is loud. Weeping is *deep*. It comes from the well of the soul—the part of you that doesn't know how to use words. And when you weep like that, the weeping *is* the prayer. God hears it more clearly than language.

I wept as I had never wept before. The only words I could push through the tears were, "God, please don't let my boy die." That one request, over and over again, poured out from that now sacred spot between those two bushes.

• ◦ •

Eventually I walked back across the parking lot to where Wade was. By then a small crowd had gathered around him. I bent forward, hands on my knees, looking down at him—and from the corner of my eye, I saw his brother approaching.

This was the one he shared a room with. The one he had a sweet, almost inseparable bond with. He had been inside the McDonald's this whole time, along with the other boys, not fully aware of what had happened—certainly not of how serious it was.

As I noticed him coming, I looked up in time to stop him. "Don't come out here," I told him. "Go back inside."

Days later he asked me why I did that. The best answer I could give was that I was trying to protect him. Even in the middle of my collapse—even as a crumbled mess—I was still trying to shield him from the worst of it.

Someone had called 911 right after everything happened, and now the paramedics had arrived. The angel had gone, and the professionals took over, doing the best they could.

And to be honest, it's not easy to follow an angel. But they did their job well. They loaded Wade into the ambulance and took him to Gilmer County Hospital just a couple of miles away.

*   *   *

Thanks to the kindness of some nearby strangers, our family followed and made our way to the hospital too. The staff found a space for us to wait, and the good folks from the McDonald's stayed to help look after the other boys.

We knew Wade was alive—but that's about all we knew. And it's *these* kinds of hours that are the hardest for me. The hours of not knowing.

It's a strange kind of waiting. You're wondering, but you don't even know *how* to wonder—because you have no information. If there's a problem and I know what it is, then at least I can work on a plan. Start figuring it out. But in that waiting room at Gilmer County Hospital, there was nothing to figure out. Nothing to solve. Just…wait.

Eventually someone came and told us they'd be transporting Wade to Erlanger Children's Hospital in Chattanooga—about two hours away. And that meant one thing to me: He was still alive. And there was still hope.

We weren't allowed to see him, and that not seeing added a layer of fear that logic can't reach. They would take him by helicopter, and we'd have to get ourselves there some other way.

But what about my other boys? That's the question that suddenly echoed in my mind. And then—grace.

There are times when the evil of this world threatens to swallow us whole. But there are other times when the goodness of people… catches us. Holds us up.

Some of those same strangers who'd been with us at McDonald's came to the hospital. They offered—without hesitation—to stay with our children until someone could come for them. I've never forgotten that.

Because sometimes angels arrive with wings. And sometimes… they show up with car keys and kind eyes.

It was then that I called my dear friend back in Gainesville—the one I knew I could call in *any* situation. The kind of friend who doesn't ask a lot of questions—just shows up.

I told him what had happened and what we were doing, and without hesitation he stepped in. I knew he'd make sure my other boys got home safely. These are the people God gives us for the days when we can't carry things on our own. He was that person for me.

· · ·

We arrived in Chattanooga later that evening, but the trip itself was a hazy fog. I had hope—but it wasn't the confident kind. It was more like "maybe there will be a miracle" kind of hope.

The kind of hope you might cling to if your parachute didn't open. You're falling; you're bracing, but there's still that irrational sliver of belief that somehow you'll be the one in a million who survives. Hurt, yes. Broken, definitely. But alive.

All throughout that drive, and even long before it, I kept repeating my deepest, most desperate prayer: "God, don't let him die."

I begged for an exchange. If there were any deal to be made, any divine trade possible, I pleaded for it. "Take me instead."

That wasn't poetic sentiment. It wasn't a noble gesture. It was the most sincere and guttural request I could make.

In the most certain, unshakable place in my soul, I *knew* I would have been genuinely joyful—*happy*—if I could trade places with my son.

I believe those are the kinds of thoughts that rise from the very core of who we are in desperate moments. Even though we know they can't come true, we wish for them with everything in us.

Wade had arrived at the hospital long before we did, and I could already sense that the outcome had been settled in those couple of hours before we got there.

They led us to a waiting area—but it wasn't like any waiting room I'd ever seen. It was more like a service corridor. Isolated. Away from people. Quiet. Cold.

My wife and I sat there nervously and impatiently waiting. That room will always stay with me—not because of what happened in it but because of what it lacked. There was no comfort in that room. It was the coldest, most sterile, most antiseptic place I've ever been. No germs could have survived in there. But neither could peace.

The wait wasn't long.

When the doctor entered, I stood. It felt like standing before a judge—awaiting the verdict. One that would either set my soul free… or condemn it to a depth of pain I couldn't begin to imagine.

She didn't waste words. And maybe she couldn't. I imagine she had said it a number of times before, in rooms just like that one. I tried to read her face, but there were no answers there.

Then came the words: "We did all that we could…but we could not save him. Wade is dead."

CHAPTER 3

WADE'S STORY—PART 3

Parents Should Not Outlive Their Children

"When I lay these questions before God I get no answer. But rather a special sort of 'No answer.' It is not the locked door. It is more like a silent, certainly not uncompassionate, gaze. As though He shook His head not in refusal but waiving the question. Like, 'Peace, child; you don't understand.'"

C. S. LEWIS[2]

I n a choking, guttural voice I let out a cry so raw, so alien, it hardly felt human. It came from somewhere deep—way past words, past logic, past whatever part of your soul is supposed to hold together during a moment like this.

What came out of me wasn't coherent, but it was real. Over and over again, I could only manage the same words spilling out like a broken faucet: *"I'm sorry. I'm sorry. I'm so sorry."*

It wasn't a calculated apology. It wasn't even clear whom I was addressing—though I knew in my heart it was Wade. But it was also

---

2. C.S. Lewis, A Grief Observed (New York: Harper One, 2001)

my family, every one of them. Somehow I had failed them all. And when a man feels like he's failed the ones he's supposed to protect, it goes right to the bone.

I wasn't sure how I could ever face them again, much less lead them. What kind of husband or father loses the one thing he was entrusted to guard? I had dropped the most sacred ball a dad can carry. And when you do that, there's no locker room speech that fixes it.

This, for me, was the valley of the shadow of death. And death, death sounded better than this. It was all so final. He was not coming back. I would never see him again in this life. He was really gone.

It's clear to me now that from that moment until I finally found some relief over Wade's passing, I was walking a tightrope over madness. I didn't just feel broken—I felt like someone trying to balance grief, responsibility, and guilt all while the floor was giving out. I couldn't stand to look at myself in the mirror. I hated the sound of my own voice. And let's be honest: When even *your own voice* irritates you, you're not exactly thriving.

. . .

There were decisions to be made—many, in fact—and I was in no shape to make them. I was barely coherent. Thankfully, people around us, again, were incredibly kind. They did their best to comfort us, and we lacked nothing in terms of physical help or material needs. If something was needed, it was handled almost invisibly.

One of the strongest shoulders I leaned on during those days was the dear friend from Gainesville I have already mentioned. He was huge in helping us find a place to bury Wade and walking through all the funeral arrangements with us. And the thing is—we already shared a bond forged in heartbreak. Just a few years earlier I had walked beside him as he buried his precious daughter after a long battle with cancer.

Back then I had tried to be there for him in his pain. And now without a word, without needing any prompting, he showed up and quietly carried me through mine. There are some things in life that feel so sacred you know you'll never be able to repay them—not because anyone asked for payback but because the gift itself is priceless. It's the gift of comfort. Of love. Of loyalty.

Because I was barely functioning, he simply stepped in and handled things. He knew what I couldn't say. He did what I couldn't do.

I'll never forget it.

I've been on the other side of these moments. I've stood with families at the bedside when a loved one passed. I've led funerals, offered prayers, and tried—often fumblingly—to say something helpful. That's what we pastors and professional comfort-givers try to do. We learn to be careful with our words. Timing matters. Tone matters. And sometimes silence is the most pastoral thing in the room.

But when it was my turn—when I was the one needing comfort—no words, no matter how wise or sincere, could reach the depth of the place I had fallen into. It's not that the words were wasted. They just couldn't get past the surface. They stayed skin-deep, like a bandage on a wound that needed surgery.

Part of the problem is that when someone speaks to you, there's usually an expectation of a response. A nod. A word. A smile, even. But I didn't have the capacity to respond. It's like my brain forgot the choreography of human conversation. All I could do was stand there and hope I didn't look as lost as I felt.

Oddly enough the thing that helped most in those days wasn't a phrase or a passage of Scripture—it was a hug. Just a simple, warm embrace. That more than anything was a healing balm. A hug felt like a cool cloth on a fevered forehead. And if it came with silence? Even better. No pressure. No performance. Just presence.

. . .

Of course, I know I'm not the only one who has ever been through something like this. People all over the world face loss every single day. I'm not unique in that. And everyone processes grief in their own way. Personality, upbringing, emotional wiring, faith—all of these play a part in how we hold up or fall apart.

I was a man of faith. Still am. But I'm also inviting you behind the curtain of that faith—showing you what it actually looked like in those days. And I'll admit, it might not have looked like faith to you. If you had seen me during those hours—greeting guests, attending the funeral, walking to the graveside—you might have just seen a grieving dad doing what grieving dads do. Tears, yes. Sadness, of course. But also handshakes, small talk, maybe even the occasional half-smile that looks more like muscle memory than joy.

I was speaking. I was functioning. I was, as they say, "holding it together." But only just enough to get through it—and maybe to help others get through it too. Because sometimes the thing that keeps you standing is the knowledge that other people need you to stay upright.

What I've tried to describe in these last paragraphs is the man who was trapped inside that body. I wrote earlier that I am no hero—and I meant that. But I do believe there comes a point where emotion must give way to responsibility. That's what held me up. Crumbling into complete, unmovable ruin would've only compounded the loss for my family. If I had collapsed, what would they hold on to? Duty, I've learned, will make your feet move even when grief has your hands in handcuffs.

Sometimes you drag yourself through the thick, sludgy fog of pain—not because you feel strong but because there's something you're supposed to do. You move not by faith, not even by hope, but by obligation. For me the formality, the ceremony, the honoring of Wade—those moments didn't flow from great spiritual strength. They came from raw, stripped-down responsibility.

As strange as it sounds, there was actually some relief in having a funeral to plan. As dysfunctional as I was, my mind could escape the nightmare for moments at a time by focusing on logistics. There were guests to greet. Tasks to be done. Even though I couldn't fully engage, people were graciously present, and duty gave me something to do—something outside of the spiral.

But I knew it wouldn't last. In the back of my mind there was this looming awareness: It's all going to stop. The service would end. The people would leave. The food would be packed away. And then I'd be alone again. The dread of that silence was worse than the noise.

On the day of the funeral as we drove to the church, I stared out the car window at the world around me. And something rose up in me that surprised even myself: anger. Not just irritation—actual, red-blooded anger. People were out shopping. Kids were laughing in parks. Someone was jogging. People were driving as if—get this—*life was still happening.*

Didn't they know? Didn't they care that my world had just imploded?

Of course they didn't. But at that moment it felt like they should.

Like somehow the entire planet should pause out of respect or at least sympathy. If I was crushed, shouldn't the earth have the decency to sag just a little?

Now logically I know how unfair that is. I didn't think in terms of fairness at the time. But deep down there was this feeling that grief should be a shared experience—like emotional jury duty. If one person is devastated, shouldn't everybody feel it?

I wasn't being rational. But grief doesn't ask your permission before it rewires your expectations of the world.

* * *

Many people attended the funeral. Many good and right things were said. Then we went to the graveside.

The Alta Vista cemetery in Gainesville has more than its share of Georgia history. A couple of governors rest there. So does a famous Civil War general, James Longstreet. As you drive in, you pass all of them—until you reach the place where Wade now rests. That day I remember thinking how oddly fitting it was that Lee's old warhorse, General Longstreet, would be just up the hill from my little boy. Not that it made anything better, but there was a strange, historical dignity to it.

We all gathered around the freshly dug grave, said more good and right things, and then—just like that—it was time to go.

But then another horrible thought added itself to the ever-growing heap of horrors already cluttering my mind: Wade was going to be under that black sod alone. Now I knew better. Theologically, I knew he wasn't there. He was with the Lord. I knew the angels had been present, and I knew he was safe—truly safe.

But knowing something in your heart and accepting it in your bones are two different things. He was still *physically* close to me. Too close for me to cut those earthly apron strings. And that grave—dark, deep, final—felt like such a terrifying place for a little boy.

I walked over to it, knelt down, and wept again. I reached into the flowers that surrounded it, trying as best I could to comfort him. I hadn't been able to hold him as he drew his last breaths in that parking lot. But now? Now I wanted to hold him with everything I had left. To protect him one last time.

* * *

After the funeral there was a reception at my house.

Now if you've spent any time in the South, you'll understand this next part: Everything—*everything*—revolves around food. Birthdays? Food. Anniversaries? Food. Thanksgiving, Christmas, Groundhog Day, a college football win or loss? Food. And of course—death calls for food.

Southern churches are uniquely equipped for these moments. There's usually a committee of ladies (and don't you dare underestimate them) who can mobilize a potluck army faster than FEMA responds to hurricanes. And let me tell you, when tragedy hits, they don't ask—they *show up* with casseroles, banana pudding, and that one mysterious dish everyone eats but no one can identify.

And thank God for them. Because the last thing a grieving family wants to do is prepare food for a lot of well-meaning people who come through the door. So they did it for us. And a lot of people came. And yes—we ate.

Now I hadn't eaten much of anything since that tragic Sunday afternoon. In fact, I wasn't hungry at all. I didn't understand it then, and I still haven't researched the biology behind it. Maybe trauma shuts off your appetite like a blown fuse. But for whatever reason, I just wasn't hungry. Still, there was food. And people needed to be fed.

I honestly believe there's something sacred—*spiritual*, even—about God's people gathering around food. I mean, think about it: It was food that got Adam and Eve into trouble in the first place. Israel spent half their wilderness journey complaining about food—*even the food that literally fell from heaven.*

Jesus often taught while breaking bread. He performed miracles around it. And on His last night before the cross, He didn't preach a sermon—He hosted a supper.

And one day—when all of this is over—when pain has passed and tears are wiped away? We'll sit down again. Together. At a table. At the Marriage Supper of the Lamb. I think we'll all be hungry then.

And at that time no one will go home empty.

. . .

The people who came to comfort us were incredibly kind, and again I was grateful to not be left alone with my own thoughts. Silence in those moments can feel like a canyon. So the presence of others— just the noise of life around me—was a kind of grace.

There was a moment during that day when I pulled aside the wife of my close friend—the same friend who had walked through the valley of losing his own daughter. I asked if we could talk. She's a quiet, reserved woman—genuinely timid by nature—so I knew this wasn't easy for her. But in her gracious way she said "Yes."

And I only had one question.

"Will I ever smile again?"

That may sound dramatic, but I really meant it. I hadn't smiled since Wade died, and somewhere deep down I was convinced I never would. Not a real one, anyway. Not the kind that starts in your gut and works its way to your face.

She looked at me gently and answered, "You will. But it will take time."

Just a few words. But they gave me something I hadn't felt in days: hope.

Soon after that conversation the last guests left, and it was just us—our family, together but now forever changed. That was a strange feeling. The house had been full of movement and people and casseroles. And now…quiet. Just us.

I was face to face again with my family. With the finality of it all. With the closing chapter of Wade's earthly life.

And now I had to face God.

Or maybe more truthfully—I had to wrestle with how I felt *about* God. And whether peace could ever find its way back into that conversation.

CHAPTER 4

EVERY JOURNEY
HAS A FIRST STEP

People have been asking why for as long as they've been walking this earth—especially when pain shows up and refuses to leave. Philosophers, poets, prophets, and plenty of ordinary folks have spilled ink or tears or both, trying to make sense of suffering. Even Jesus, hanging on the cross, cried out to the Father with that haunting question: "Why have You forsaken Me?" (Matthew 27:46). So no, asking why isn't wrong. In fact, it might be one of the most honest things a person can do.

Did I ask why when Wade died? Maybe. I know others asked it for me. Well-meaning people often tried to offer explanations or theological comfort, even when I wasn't looking for either. I might've whispered the question to God at some point, but if I did, I don't really remember it.

For reasons I still can't fully explain, I never found myself angry with God—not in the shaking-my-fist-at-the-sky. "Lieutenant Dan," kind of way. (If you know the reference…you know.) That doesn't mean I haven't known anger. I have. Anger and I go way back. It's been an unwelcome companion through many chapters of my life, usually dragging pride along with it. I've learned the hard way that anger often just builds walls that love has to spend years tearing down.

But when it came to Wade's death, I didn't feel that kind of anger. Maybe some very smart psychologist or theologian could sit me down and make a compelling case that I *was* angry with God and just didn't realize it. Maybe. But honestly, I don't want to be convinced.

What I do know is that the grief sent me into a deeper search—not for a reason but for a Person. My journey wasn't about demanding an explanation from God; it was about trying to find His face in the darkness. It was not about asking— "Why did You let this happen?"—but rather, "Who are You really when everything falls apart?"

And slowly, quietly I began to see His hand.

Let me try to describe what my days looked like in the first couple of weeks following Wade's funeral. To really understand those long, heavy days, I need to start with the nights that came before them. I didn't want to sleep. I was afraid I'd see Wade in my dreams. That might sound strange to some—comforting, even—but for me it would have been a nightmare. My heart wasn't ready for even a dream-version of him. Maybe it was my brittle psyche or maybe just my body trying to protect me from more pain, but sleep felt like something to resist.

And yet when sleep did come, I didn't want to wake up. Because the waking brought back the crushing guilt. The sharp, gut-punching realization that Wade was gone—and that my own perceived failures had something to do with it. Whether or not that was true, it's what I felt. Guilt has a way of becoming your narrator if you let it.

But life doesn't hit pause, even for grief. Family, responsibilities, and the steady ticking of the clock all conspired to drag me out of bed and into another day. I moved through the mornings like a character in *Pilgrim's Progress*, burdened with an invisible weight that no one else could carry.

The memories came uninvited. Some were sweet, but most opened the floodgates. I didn't break down like I did in those first hours after Wade's death, but tears were still my closest companion. After getting through the basics of the morning, I'd sit at my desk and open my Bible. And I mean literally open it—set it down and let it fall open to whatever random page it chose. That was my spiritual strategy: desperate, Bible roulette.

And one day it worked.

* * *

The first flicker of relief in all that darkness came from Scripture. It shouldn't surprise anyone who's spent time in the Book—it's built for days like those. The Bible has an otherworldly ability to bring calm to a storm-tossed mind, assuming that mind can slow down long enough to actually read the words.

That day, my unscientific method landed me on 1 Peter 4:12–13. And God met me there and very clearly said to me:

> *Buddy... think it not strange concerning the fiery trial which is to try you, but rejoice, inasmuch as you are a partaker of Christ's sufferings; that, when His glory shall be revealed, you will be glad with exceeding joy.*

I don't remember how many days had passed since Wade died. But I do remember this: For the first time since the worst day of my life, a flicker of hope sparked in my heart. Maybe—I dared to believe—I might actually smile again.

No one preached a sermon to me. No one gave me a theological outline. But the message of that verse came through loud and clear: This pain wasn't mine alone. It wasn't unique. It wasn't some strange anomaly that had managed to slip past the divine radar. Suffering has been stitched into the human story since the fall, and I—like so many before me—was simply walking the same road.

Really, why should I be spared from pain when some of God's greatest saints had suffered so much more? Thinking I was somehow singled out or uniquely targeted by God wasn't just unhealthy—it was prideful. I'm no better than any other person who has grieved, questioned, or wept their way through life.

But then a really strange word appeared—*rejoice*. I saw it, and my heart tilted sideways. That was not the word I expected to find that morning. Sadness, pain, guilt, maybe even endurance—but *rejoice?*

It felt out of tune with the melody I'd been living. That word rang like a sharp, minor chord in a song written in the key of lament. Still, there it was—undeniable and loud, like a billboard off I-85 in downtown Atlanta.

And somehow as I sat with it, that word began to shift. It blended slowly with the sorrowful notes I'd been carrying, forming something richer, something like harmony. What had seemed discordant began to soften.

Because *rejoice* didn't mean denial—it meant companionship. It meant that I wasn't just linked to the suffering of others who had walked through fire before me. I was being drawn into the suffering of Christ Himself. A shared sorrow. A sacred nearness.

Christ suffered more than anyone. And yes, even God the Father suffered.

And I—somehow—I was being invited into that fellowship.

It was around that same time that another realization settled in— quiet but weighty. The thought of God's Son dying suddenly carried new meaning for me. I had known it my whole life as doctrine. Now it had become personal. For the first time I could relate to God the Father—not in theory but in lived experience. He and I were both fathers whose sons had died.

Not everyone, thankfully, can say that. But I could. And so could God.

That realization opened the door to a new kind of relationship with Him. One not built just on reverence or obedience—but on shared grief. It may only make sense to those in this sorrowful fraternity. You may have your own grouping with God—your own place of tender knowing—but this was mine. Not by choice. Not by merit. But by grace and loss.

And then woven into that revelation came another whisper from the Word: That all of this—this ache, this wreckage, this tragedy— was not the end. There would come a day when His glory would be revealed and what was hidden would finally make sense.

I took this day that Peter writes about to mean the return of Christ. The day when everything wrong would be made right, and every tear would be dried. And on *that* day He promised I would be glad with a joy that would not only match but also surpass the sorrow I had known on that dark August afternoon.

Not just glad—exceedingly glad. A joy so radiant, so consuming it would make this current grief seem like a shadow by comparison.

As I sat there with my Bible still open, I breathed in something that felt like heaven's air. Just a trace. But it was enough. And with it came a smile—not a wide or confident one but a small, perfect one. The first in a very long time.

And that, I now know, was the real beginning of my journey. The day I first stepped into the land of His sovereignty.

· · ·

Soon after that day, a second ray of hope shone through. It came in the form of an old-fashioned "snail mail" letter I received from a dear man who had been my pastor during my college years. After leaving that church he became the president and editor of a Christian newspaper in Tennessee. At the very time we were walking through fire, he was in the midst of his own—a battle with cancer that would soon usher him home to heaven.

He had been my mentor, and I had come to love and deeply respect him. On the day Wade died, he was hospitalized himself. But as soon as he was well enough, he sat down and wrote me this letter:

Dear Buddy,

When I heard about the early home going of your precious son, I wanted to write to you immediately. However, I was unexpectedly taken to the hospital, and after a ten-day stay, I finally came home last night.

I need not tell you, my dear, dear brother, that God makes no mistakes, even though sometimes we do not understand Him. His blessed sovereignty means that He can do what He wants to, when He wants to, for whomever He wants to, for as long as He wants to, for whatever reason He wants to— and He doesn't owe us an explanation. But we may always rest assured that God does best for those who love Him. That is the promise of Romans 8:28, and I have never one time doubted that wonderful promise.

Several years ago, I met some missionaries. You may not remember, or may never have read about, the great preacher R. E. Neighbors of yesteryear. The missionary I met was his daughter. They lost a son in an accident. When I heard her story, we published the book here at the Sword of the Lord. I'm enclosing a copy of the book, which I hope will comfort your hearts at a time that some people think is a great loss. But remember, as long as you know where something or someone is, it is not lost; and we both know where your precious Little General is residing today.

God bless you forever. Keep making soul-winning your main business, and may God use you in a mighty way in the land of Russia. May we see many born-again Christians in Heaven who are won to Christ through your ministry as they gather from around the world to surround the throne of God and sing His praise, how He "redeemed us to God by His blood out of every kindred, and tongue, and people and nation."

Your friend in Christ,
Curtis Hutson

With all reverence and no comparison to Scripture, reading that letter felt divinely timed—like it had been written just for me. Just as I felt myself slipping toward a spiritual abyss, I read these words:

"His blessed sovereignty means that He can do what He wants to, when He wants to, for whomever He wants to, for as long

as He wants to, for whatever reason He wants to—and He doesn't owe us an explanation. But we may always rest assured that He does best for those who love Him."

I gripped those words. Not with full understanding but with raw, desperate hope. I didn't yet grasp all they meant, but I clung to them like a handhold on a cliff.

And little did I know—those words wouldn't just break my fall; they would keep me upright.

Even now, they still do.

CHAPTER 5

WHEN THE
HEART BELIEVES

I had heard about God's sovereignty since I was a young Christian. It always sounded noble—like the kind of word that deserves to be written in calligraphy or carved into marble. *Sovereignty.* It had weight to it, like something you'd say right before taking off your shoes on holy ground. When pastors or seminary professors brought it up, they'd pause just slightly—like they were handling a rare and sacred antique. Naturally I nodded along. I understood. Of course God is sovereign. He's the Creator, the King, the One who runs the show. It's His world; we're just using His place.

I mentally filed the concept in the "Important but Currently Not Urgent" drawer—right next to "how to interpret Revelation" and "what exactly cherubim are." I figured I'd get around to it when I needed it—kind of like flossing or reading the terms and conditions.

The truth is, I had never really studied sovereignty. Not in the slow, honest, soul-wrestling way. It was more like I had inherited it. Theological hand-me-downs from good teachers, sermons, and the occasional late-night debate with friends who were trying to sound more Calvinist than the other guy. I picked up the lingo and added it to my Christian vocabulary toolkit. "God is sovereign" became one of those phrases I could toss into conversation to sound spiritually mature, especially if I tilted my head and added a reflective pause.

Let's be honest—we Christians have our own dialect. A kind of spiritual slang. "Christianese," I call it. We pick up these theological terms like recipes on old 3x5 cards and stick them in the card box of our minds whether or not we've ever actually cooked with them. They sound right, they feel right, and in church settings they work. We say things like "traveling mercies" or "hedge of protection," and no one bats an eye—even though most of us wouldn't know a hedge if it blocked our driveway.

But here's the thing: There's a massive difference between words I can recite and truths that have taken root in my soul. Between what I say I believe and what I *actually* believe when the floor drops out and the doctor walks into the room looking like she's about to change your life.

That difference is everything.

○ ○ ○

Maybe that's just how it works. Maybe real belief transfers from head to heart only when life hands you something that knocks the wind out of both. For me the journey toward understanding God's sovereignty wasn't a gentle hike through theological ideas—it was a plummet into the deep valley of death's shadow. Actually forget the shadow. I was in the valley's basement.

It was there in the raw ache of losing Wade that God's sovereignty moved from something I *knew* to something I *needed*—the only thing that kept my mind from unraveling. It became the anchor I didn't even know I'd thrown overboard.

That "aha" moment—that realization—I've come to call "The Disciples Effect."

You know the disciples I'm talking about: Peter, James, John, Matthew…and those other guys. (Judas, of course, doesn't make the cut. He flunked out of the program early.) What strikes me is how differently each of them came to Jesus. Peter and Andrew were busy fishing—just trying to make a living, probably complaining about taxes—when Jesus shows up and says, "Follow Me," and they say, "Okay." James and John were hanging with their dad, fixing nets, and suddenly they were in. Matthew was literally out there collecting money and dirty looks.

They had different jobs, different personalities, different emotional settings—introverts, extroverts, likely a couple of outcasts in the bunch—but the common thread was this: Jesus came for them. And just like that they became "disciples."

Now let's not pretend they had their theology worked out. They knew the Law, sure. They had probably heard some version of "the Messiah is coming" every Sabbath since they could walk. But I doubt they had a clear grasp on what was unfolding. If I had to guess, I'd say most of them were in "let's see where this goes" mode. Honestly, some of the questions they asked along the way were…well, bless their hearts.

They followed Jesus for three and a half years. They witnessed miracles, soaked in sermons, lived in the presence of God Himself—and still, so many of the lessons He gave them seemed to bounce off their foreheads like pickle balls. Some of the teachings landed on their eyeballs and sat on their eardrums but never even made it to the brain. Others went in one ear and got lost somewhere in the Sea of Galilee.

Those truths, though not nestled in the heart, had been heard and seen and felt. These lessons were divine, of course, coming from the God-Man, Jesus Himself.

Yet it wasn't until they went through the trauma of the cross that all the layers of truth they'd taken in with their senses—the teachings, the parables, the divine tone in Jesus' voice—finally melted into their souls like snow in the morning sun. Over those three and a half years, it had been accumulating little by little, like snowfall on a rooftop. But the resurrection? That was the sunrise. The warmth of that impossible morning melted the layers and sent them flooding into their spirits. And that's when they truly became disciples—not just in name but in essence.

Real disciples. The kind that gave up everything and never looked back. The kind that one by one laid down their lives for the One they finally knew was who He said He was.

Jesus had told them plainly that He was God. They heard it. But you can hear a lot of things without really believing them—like when the dentist says, "This won't hurt." Sure, Jesus had done miracles. Sure, He walked on water (which, let's be honest, probably was top story at every party). But still…what if He was just a brilliant illusionist? What if it was some first-century version of David Blaine? There were other guys running around Galilee claiming to be divine. There always are.

So for three and a half years, they followed—but often confused, often clumsy, often missing the point. Jesus even called them out for it: "Oh you of little faith," or my personal favorite, "How long must I be with you?" You get the sense that Jesus was running the first small group in history where the Leader knew the answers and the members just brought snacks and blank faces.

But here's the grace in it: Jesus knew it would take time. He wasn't recruiting theologians; He was forming disciples. They weren't shallow because they were stupid—they were shallow because they were human. They believed enough to follow but not enough to die.

Until they did.

What they once heard with their ears, they finally understood with their hearts. And once it got there—once it sank into the deepest places of who they were—it changed everything.

Just like it did for me.

To make the point even clearer, consider Thomas—the disciple with the world's most unfortunate nickname. "Doubting Thomas." Poor guy. One sentence, one moment of honest skepticism, and boom—branded for all eternity. If heaven has name tags, his probably says, "Hello, I'm Thomas…Yes, *that* Thomas."

Honestly, I've often wondered what my eternal nickname might be if someone recorded all *my* spiritual blunders. I've had front-row seats to God's grace and provision and still managed to miss the point on more occasions than I care to count. If we're handing out titles the way we did for Thomas, I could easily be "Buddy the Dullard." A cautionary tale in Sunday school flannelgraph.

Back to Thomas. He wasn't there the first time Jesus showed up after the resurrection. (No idea where he was—maybe running errands, maybe just needed a day off from all the trauma.) But when the others told him Jesus had risen, Thomas went full skeptic: "Unless I see the nail marks…and put my finger where the nails were…I will not believe" (John 20:25).

You've got to give him points for honesty.

And soon after that Jesus shows up again—this time with Thomas in the room. He doesn't shame. He doesn't lecture. He simply invites: "Go ahead, Thomas. Touch. See" (John 20:27).

And in that moment doubt dissolved. Truth collided with experience. Thomas fell to his knees and gave one of the most beautiful declarations in Scripture: "My Lord and my God!" (John 20:28).

That's the moment it all became real for him. Not theory. Not hearsay. Truth. Personal, undeniable truth. It was in this moment that Thomas' doubt was transformed into a profound belief in the resurrected Lord.

That's what happens when grace meets honesty. When God doesn't just show up *in general* but shows up *for you.*

Let's think about this for a moment. Hadn't Jesus been talking about this resurrection thing for literally years? Didn't Thomas listen? Of course he did—but listening is not the same as connecting the dots. Thomas had the data; he just didn't install the software. And that made him a skeptic.

Doubt does that—it sneaks in through the side door when you've got more questions than confidence. And often it drives you to isolation. Thomas wasn't in the room that day with the others. He'd gone AWOL—maybe sulking, maybe scared, maybe wondering if he'd just spent the last three years following the wrong carpenter. Whatever the reason, he missed the miracle.

And that's how it goes for a lot of us. Uncertainty strips us of our footing. Even when we've heard truth. Even when we've seen God move. When the storm hits hard enough, the teachings we once nodded along to can feel suddenly like suggestions instead of anchors.

Thomas had watched the horror of the crucifixion from a distance and then—radio silence. No Savior, no plan, no idea what came next.

So he did what many of us do when hope gets pulverized: He disappeared into fear. It's possible, even likely, that Thomas would've stayed there for good had there not been a resurrection and a Savior who came back just to let him touch the truth.

And here's where Thomas becomes more than just a cautionary tale—he becomes a map. A guide to the way many of us come to faith: slowly, honestly, and sometimes through a door labeled "pain."

See, Thomas's process wasn't punished—it was *honored.* Jesus gave him exactly what he needed, not what everyone else needed. The others in the room had seen Jesus and believed. Thomas needed more. So Jesus gave him more.

Some people hear truth and leap. Others crawl their way to it, dragging doubts behind them like carry-on luggage. And you know what? Jesus meets both types.

Call it maturation if you want—but I think it's more than just time passing. I've seen people sit in pews for decades, nodding at all the right moments, stacking up spiritual information like old church bulletins in the back of a Bible—and still be spiritual infants. Bloated with truth they've never digested.

What Thomas needed wasn't more time—it was *encounter.* That sacred collision of divine presence and human honesty.

And that, my friend, is where belief becomes real.

* * *

No one would describe childbirth as a modest, tidy progression—like it's just one more event on the family calendar right between "oil change" and "buy bananas." Something profound happens between a mother and her child over those nine months. It's a sacred bond, a surrender, a mysterious kind of soul connection that only mothers can fully explain. She gives of herself so fully that when the child finally arrives, it isn't just a baby being born—it's a whole new life entering the world through sacrifice.

The baby moves as she moves, feeds as she feeds, lives as she lives. And then at just the right time—when all is ready—life pushes forward. But not without trauma. Not without pain. Because nothing beautiful is born without something breaking open first.

And when the birth is complete? That child is free to grow into all they were meant to be.

It's not just maturation. It's transformation. It's something deeper and more disruptive. And so it is when new life enters the soul.

Spiritual birth doesn't come without seeds being planted. It takes time. It often takes some kind of soul-quake—an event that rips through our assumptions and pride and makes room for truth to grow roots. For me it was an August day in Ellijay, Georgia.

Now hear me—your experience may not need to be as dramatic as mine. Some people, it seems, have souls made of soft soil. They listen early, learn quickly, and don't need to be dragged to the brink before surrendering. Bless them.

Then there are others—people like me. The prideful, the self-reliant, the ones who nod in church but secretly like having the steering wheel. For us the crust around the soul has thickened over time, layer after layer of independence and distraction. And when the crust is thick, the hammer required to break through has to be heavier.

Looking back, I suspect God tried to get through to me long before He finally did. Maybe there were whispers, nudges, moments when heaven leaned in—but I wasn't listening. I can't recall the specifics, but I'm sure they were there. I just wasn't paying attention.

It's like being in the same room with someone but completely checked out. They're trying to tell you something important—life-changing even—but you're thinking about your grocery list or your next meeting. You nod, maybe grunt a little affirmation, but your mind is on autopilot.

Then they pause, waiting for a response…and nothing. So they say your name—gently at first, then louder. Still nothing. Finally, they shout your name, and it startles you. You blink, flustered, realizing you've missed half the conversation.

Only then can you truly hear them. Only then can you receive what they're trying to give. That was me. That might be you. And sometimes it takes a divine shout to finally wake us up. In my story, Wade was the explosion that finally got my attention.

God may have tried to gently share this lesson—and others—with me for years before Wade died. But I was busy. Doing the next thing. Planning the next meeting. Fixing the next problem. I wasn't ignoring Him out of rebellion; I was just distracted. Like a man staring at his calendar while God whispers eternity into the room.

C. S. Lewis famously said that "God shouts in our pain." And it's true. For me, it wasn't an angry shout—it was more like a fire alarm that finally went off after years of smoldering warnings. It was loud enough to stop me cold. To get my full attention. And while I wish I'd listened sooner, I can say without a doubt: This was the moment His sovereignty was born in me.

Make no mistake—God doesn't *only* use tragedy to get our attention. He's not a cosmic drill sergeant who only shows up during boot camp. As I've said, the thicker the crust around our hearts, the heavier the hammer needed to break through. But it doesn't always have to be this way.

Sometimes God reveals Himself in the happiest moment of your life—if you're listening.

Take John 9, for instance. There's this man, born blind, who spent his days begging in the darkness. The Pharisees had probably walked past him for years with their robes swishing and their eyes averted. They couldn't help him. They didn't try.

But one day Jesus came by.

And in one miraculous moment He gave the man sight. Can you imagine that? The first thing he ever saw—*ever*—was the face of the Son of God.

This should've been the happiest moment of his life—and it was. But it also stirred up trouble. Because grace always disrupts things.

The Pharisees weren't having it. They pulled the man aside and basically said, "This can't be real. Jesus is a sinner. And besides, He did this on the Sabbath, so we've got paperwork to do."

But the man didn't get tangled in theology. He hadn't taken Systematic Theology 101. He just said, "Look, I don't know about all that. All I know is—I was blind yesterday. And now I see."

Simple. Honest. Unarguable.

When Jesus heard that this man was being harassed, He circled back. That's Jesus for you—He always circles back for the ones who get pushed to the margins. And He spoke to the man again.

And in that second encounter the man didn't just see *physically*. He saw *spiritually*. He confessed, "Lord, I believe" (v. 38). And he worshiped.

It happened in a time of absolute joy. Not sorrow. Not crisis. Not trauma.

. . .

So what will your path to the revelation of His sovereignty be?

Maybe you're reading these words and nodding along. They make sense. They seem wise. But maybe they're just bouncing off for now—like water on a duck's back. That's okay. I've been there. Many of us have.

Of course, we'd all prefer that our "I believe" moment comes through joy. Through a wedding, a sunrise, a healed friendship. But it doesn't always work that way. It depends on your openness. Your posture. Your willingness to hear Him whisper before He has to shout.

And it depends on what He's trying to show you.

For our purposes here, let me say plainly. The lesson God was trying to show me—the truth that changed everything—is this: **His sovereignty.**

Again, in my opinion, it is the single most important truth He wants His followers to truly understand. It's the key that unlocks peace in chaos, faith in darkness, and steadiness both on the mountain and in the valley. It won't answer all your questions. It's not a tidy solution. But it will hold you together while the questions remain unanswered.

His sovereignty is what tells me: Even when I don't understand the story, I can trust the Author.

Even when I don't see the outcome, I know the One who holds it.

And even when life breaks my heart, I can believe—deep in my bones—that He still has me in His hands.

CHAPTER 6

CAN WE REALLY UNDERSTAND GOD'S SOVEREIGNTY?

Try this sometime—type "God's sovereignty" into a search bar. Within seconds your screen will explode with more debates than a Presidential primary. Nearly every link launches you into a theological steel-cage match: Calvinists vs. Arminians, Traditional-ists vs. Everyone Else, and probably a few angry seminary bloggers who haven't seen daylight since 2007.

Now imagine being the average layman—just trying to make it through your Sunday school quarterly without pulling a spiritual hamstring—and suddenly you're knee-deep in discussions involv-ing predestination, foreknowledge, irresistible grace, and about six-teen other words that could double as obscure vitamins. After hours of reading, you're more confused than when you started. The end is worse than the beginning. Like putting kids' Christmas toys together with a flashlight and no instructions.

And here's the thing: Many of the things of God are actually sim-ple. Beautifully simple. But many theologians have a spiritual gift of making the simple complicated—usually with charts and graphs. Now I don't fault those who sincerely want to explain the glory of spiritual things. May they live long and prosper. But I confess—I long for simplicity. For teachers who can take the vast, dazzling mysteries of God and explain them without needing subtitles. If you find such a person, sit at their feet. Take notes. Cancel your lunch plans. They're rare.

To be clear, I believe we absolutely need our deep-thinking theologians. Their job is to journey deep into the caverns of Scripture, pick up the glistening gems, and show them to the rest of us without sounding like they're auditioning for *Jeopardy!: Theology Edition*. Back before the internet turned every phone into a digital seminary, I had shelves stacked with thick, dusty volumes written by these brilliant minds. Now they teach me through podcasts and Kindle books. Same wisdom, less shelf space.

I've listened to them since I was young. Still do. But I never quite learned to speak their language. As intellectually towering as they were, I was…well, not. I tried. But sometimes I felt like I was reading theology through a fogged-up shower door.

So over the years I had to whittle these lofty, PhD-level truths into something that would fit inside a bachelor of science brain. And that's okay. Some of us aren't meant to be theological architects—we're the guys trying to read the blueprint without flipping it upside down.

In my opinion, the greatest gift in teaching is this: to be able to grasp the deep wonders of God and then lay them out so clearly and gently that people like me—who sometimes forgets why they walked into the kitchen in the first place—can actually understand them. That's a rare talent.

One man who had that gift was Dr. Elmer Towns—professor,

prolific author, co-founder of Liberty University, and longtime champion of the Sunday school movement. He was also my professor, mentor, and friend. For years he was America's expert on Sunday school before churches gave up on the idea altogether and decided to just meet in coffee shops and call it "community." But to me Dr. Towns will always be the gold standard: a genius who never acted like one. He talked to fledgling young wannabe theologians like me in a way that made us feel not just smarter—but seen.

I remember sitting in early morning theology classes with twenty or so other poor souls, many of whom had just worked the night shift. Some of us were barely holding it together with nothing but stale coffee and the vague hope of graduation. As we crept into the classroom like nocturnal rodents, we passed the front-row zealots— the "sons of the prophets"—who were already flipping through their Greek New Testaments before the bell rang.

We, the weary few, took our place in the back row. Always the back row. Two reasons: First, it was easier to hide behind the people in front of you if (when) you dozed off. Second, you were statistically less likely to be called on. The back row was more about surviving than thriving.

Some of those theology lectures were more endurance sport than education. I'd glance down our row and count who was still upright. Sometimes we lost a few early in the "introduction to the introduction." And look, I'll admit it—theological concepts like "hypostatic union" made me flinch. "Anthropocentrism"? I think that's when your foot falls asleep.

Meanwhile, the front-row guys were practically levitating. They lived for this. And yes, some professors opened their mouths with such academic firepower that we back-row zombies checked out before the amen. If we even made it to the amen. Some of those lectures were miracles in themselves. (And yes, I do know the Greek words for miracle—*ergon, teras, dunamis,* and *semion.* Boom. Representing the back row!)

In those days professors taught to the front two rows. The third row doodled. The fourth row drifted. The back row occasionally snored. But not with Dr. Towns. He saw us. He engaged us all. He didn't teach watered-down theology. He taught the same deep stuff as the others—but he knew how to deliver it to real people. He would walk to the back, look us in the eye like we were equals, and talk about God like He was someone who could ride shotgun on your morning commute.

I believe he thought it was better to help students understand truth than to impress them with his vocabulary. And that made all the difference.

This is a bit of a soapbox for me, but I get a little twitchy when people make faith more complicated than it needs to be. Yes, there's a danger in oversimplifying—but the goal should be clarity, not confusion. The best kind of teacher knows how to take the precious gems of Scripture and place them on the bottom shelf where anyone can reach them—even the guy who barely passed Greek.

Jesus said we need faith like a child. That doesn't mean childish—it means clear, uncluttered, honest. That's the kind of faith I'm after. That's what I want to say, simply and plainly: **Understanding the sovereignty of God is possible.** Even for back-row guys like me.

CHAPTER 7

WHEN GOD SPEAKS, LIFE BEGINS

If you've ever tried to explain the wonders of God to someone—whether in a classroom, a sermon, or just across a kitchen table—you've probably realized something quickly: The Almighty isn't always easy to summarize on a napkin. Making the complex simple should be the goal of every teacher, preacher, scholar, or parent. Unfortunately, some people take this as a challenge to do the exact opposite. They treat clarity like it's optional—like seatbelts in the '70s.

And when it comes to the incredible things of God, the complexity meter tilts into the red. Here's why.

Isaiah 55:8-9 reminds us: "For my thoughts are not your thoughts, neither are your ways my ways, saith the Lord. For as the heavens are higher than the earth, so are my ways higher than your ways, and my thoughts than your thoughts."

Translation: God is God, and we are very much not.

After thousands of years of brilliant minds trying to unpack what He meant, most of us are still just doing our best with what I call *holy head scratching*. Faith, it turns out, is not just a comforting word—it's

our life jacket in the sea of divine mystery. It's okay—even commend-
able—to say, "I don't fully get this. But I trust the One who does."

I've walked with Christ for more than fifty years, and I'm still regularly blindsided by how much I don't know. It's like playing a game
of theological whack-a-mole—every time I think I've nailed something down, a new truth pops up and surprises me.

Have you ever tried to count how many sermons you've heard
in your lifetime? I did once. (Which may say something about how
exciting my Saturday was.) Between Sunday mornings, Sunday nights,
Wednesday nights, revivals, conferences, special meetings, and services around the world, I estimate I've heard at least ten thousand
sermons. That's not an exaggeration—that's just Baptist math.

And yet even now I'll be sitting somewhere minding my own
spiritual business when someone shares a passage I've heard a hundred times…and boom—something new hits me like divine déjà vu.

God's Word isn't just information. It's living. It's active. It doesn't
wear out or fade like that pair of jeans I keep forgetting to replace.

* * *

Here are just a few of the verses that remind us of its power:

> **Proverbs 30:5**—"Every word of God is pure: he is a shield
> unto them that put their trust in him."

> **Isaiah 40:8**—"The grass withereth, the flower fadeth: but
> the word of our God shall stand forever."

> **Matthew 24:35**—"Heaven and earth shall pass away, but
> my words shall not pass away."

Hebrews 4:12—"For the word of God is quick, and powerful, and sharper than any twoedged sword, piercing even to the dividing asunder of soul and spirit, and of the joints and marrow, and is a discerner of the thoughts and intents of the heart."

Joshua 1:8—"This book of the law shall not depart out of thy mouth; but thou shalt meditate therein day and night, that thou mayest observe to do according to all that is written therein: for then thou shalt make thy way prosperous, and then thou shalt have good success."

2 Timothy 2:15—"Study to shew thyself approved unto God, a workman that needeth not to be ashamed, rightly dividing the word of truth."

Psalm 119:105—"Thy word is a lamp unto my feet, and a light unto my path."

Revelation 1:3—"Blessed is he that readeth, and they that hear the words of this prophecy, and keep those things which are written therein: for the time is at hand."

God's Word doesn't change. It doesn't go out of style. And though none of us will ever fully grasp it or live it perfectly, we're still called to pursue it. Study it. Teach it. Share it—as the Holy Spirit opens our understanding.

Scripture is often described as being full of "nuggets of gold." But the fact is that no one just kicks a gold nugget down the sidewalk. If you want treasure, you've got to dig. And yes, digging is hard. But hard isn't the same as impossible.

Truth—especially the truth of God's sovereignty—usually lives a little deeper down. It doesn't just lie there on the surface, waving at you like a parking lot attendant. Most folks dig in for a while, hit some rocks, and quit. But if you press a little further—go beyond the surface clichés—you may just strike something rich.

If you Google "sovereignty," as I suggested earlier, you'll probably get a definition like "supreme power or authority." That's not wrong, but it feels like calling the Grand Canyon a "hole." Accurate but not exactly awe-inspiring.

In the Bible God's sovereignty is bigger than a definition. It's the thread that holds the whole story together. It means God is God and nothing catches Him off guard. He doesn't panic. He doesn't pace. He doesn't lose track of the plan because He *is* the plan.

* * *

Here are a few passages worth slowing down for. Don't skim. Linger. Let them speak to your questions—and maybe even to your fears:

> **Colossians 1:16-17**—"For by him were all things created, that are in heaven, and that are in earth, visible and invisible, whether they be thrones, or dominions, or principalities, or powers: all things were created by him, and for him: And he is before all things, and by him all things consist."

> **Psalm 115:3**—"But our God is in the heavens: he hath done whatsoever he hath pleased."

> **Romans 11:33**—"O the depth of the riches both of the wisdom and knowledge of God! how unsearchable are his judgments, and his ways past finding out!"

Ephesians 1:4-6—"According as he hath chosen us in him before the foundation of the world, that we should be holy and without blame before him in love: Having predestined us unto the adoption of children by Jesus Christ to himself, according to the good pleasure of his will, to the praise of the glory of his grace, wherein he hath made us accepted in the beloved."

Jeremiah 32:17—"Ah Lord God! behold, thou hast made the heaven and the earth by thy great power and stretched out arm, and there is nothing too hard for thee."

Matthew 19:26—"With God all things are possible."

Proverbs 19:21—"There are many devices in a man's heart; nevertheless the counsel of the Lord, that shall stand."

James 4:14-15—"Whereas ye know not what shall be on the morrow. For what is your life? It is even a vapor, that appeareth for a little time, and then vanisheth away. For that ye ought to say, If the Lord will, we shall live, and do this, or that."

1 Chronicles 16:31—"Let the heavens be glad, and let the earth rejoice: and let men say among the nations, The Lord reigneth."

Revelation 4:11—"Thou art worthy, O Lord, to receive glory and honour and power: for thou hast created all things, and for thy pleasure they are and were created."

One of the life-altering truths I learned from the back row of Dr. Towns's classroom was this: *Light brings more light.*

When you receive truth—really receive it—it multiplies. If you start to see God's hand in history or in nations or even in the chaos of your own life and if you can say by faith, "Lord, I believe this is from You," then more light comes. Not necessarily clarity about everything but certainly a stronger sense of purpose and peace. By the same token, if you reject light, darkness lingers and grows.

Understanding God's sovereignty brings spiritual stability. And stability brings effectiveness. You're no longer tossed around by every gust of anxiety or wave of circumstance. Instead, you begin to walk with a quiet confidence—not in yourself but in the unshakable, unchanging character of the One who reigns. And sometimes when you least expect it, you realize: The words of God really are life-changing.

CHAPTER 8

THE WORD THAT BOTH WOUNDS AND HEALS

"I wish the ring had never come to me.
I wish none of this had happened."

FRODO

"So do all who live to see such times, but that is
not for them to decide.... All we have to decide
is what to do with the time that is given to us."
Gandalf, being Gandalf, and also being right

J. R. R. TOLKIEN,
The Fellowship of the Ring[3]

There's a word in Scripture that has an odd effect on people. It can either strengthen your legs in the middle of a storm or feel like someone just handed you a fortune cookie that says, "Hang in there!"—after your world collapsed.

That word is *good*. And the verse is Romans 8:28:

---

3. J.R.R. Tolkien, *The Fellowship of the Ring* (Boston: Houghton Mifflin, 1954)

*And we know that all things work together for **good** to those*
who love God, to those who are the called according to his
purpose (emphasis added).

This is not your average refrigerator magnet verse. It's more like
an electric charge wrapped in cotton. Soft to the touch, but it carries a jolt. It's bold—almost mocks you—when you're in the middle
of loss. And yet…it might be the anchor verse for anyone standing
knee-deep in grief, pain, or just general chaos.

I opened this book with it because *this*—this one sentence—is
where God's sovereignty and our sanity often meet. At least for me it
was. It's the verse that seems to glow on the page, like it's been set in
Georgian font bold and italic and with a bright yellow divine high-
lighter. You don't really need to be a Hebrew scholar to understand
it. You just need a pulse, some patience, and enough faith to believe
it even when your life looks nothing like it.

Which brings me to the catch: It's not hard to *read* this verse. It's
hard to *believe* it.

Before we buried Wade, I had heard dozens of sermons that quoted
Romans 8:28. I could probably have written a decent essay on it for
a Bible college class. But it's one thing to *teach* the truth. It's another
thing to *need* it so badly that it's either true or you can't breathe.

People use this verse all the time for comfort purposes. In reality, however, it lands differently when it comes from someone who
has only ever lived on the outside of pain. I don't mean that criti-
cally—just truthfully. It's like someone giving you a pep talk about
skydiving while they're still standing on the ground. Helpful? Maybe.
Reassuring? Not really.

Evangelist Ron Dunn, who lost his eighteen-year-old son to suicide, once said that you don't have the right to yell, "Praise the Lord," at a funeral unless it's your loved one in the casket. That's a raw truth, but it's real. And it's exactly what makes Romans 8:28 either the most comforting or the most offensive thing you could ever say in a hospital room or at a graveside.

I don't call this my life verse. That always felt a little too cute for a verse that I've wrestled with in the dark. But I *have* studied it more than almost any other passage in the Bible. And here's what I've found: It's not a theory to me. It's personal. I've lived it. I've fought it. And I've finally come to believe it.

There's a deep certainty in these words. Paul doesn't say, "We hope all things work out." He says, "We know." There's no footnote. No asterisk. Just an unwavering statement of confidence that God—sovereign, wise, patient, and somehow still good—is actively working **all** things (yes, even *those* things) together for our good.

And let's not miss this: Paul says *all things*, not *some*, not *most*, and definitely not *just the things we like*. It's not a spiritual "greatest hits" album. It includes the stuff we'd rather skip. The fights. The layoffs. The losses. The diagnoses. The weeks that feel like a hundred years.

And still—*we know.*

But we don't know this because we're naturally optimistic. We know this because the Spirit helps us hold on to truth that feels, at times, out of reach. We know this because Jesus didn't avoid suffering—He went straight through it and promised He'd never leave us alone in ours.

The first lesson to notice—maybe painfully quickly—is that while all things will *work* for good, not all things will *feel* good. Paul doesn't say that whatever happens to believers is *good*. That would be a strange, borderline delusional claim. (If you've ever stubbed your toe in the middle of the night, you already know not all things are good.)

What the verse *does* say is that things will be worked *out* for good. And there's a difference—like between "This house is beautiful" and "Right now it's a pile of lumber, nails, and one guy named Ralph with a tool belt on." One is finished. The other is faith in progress.

The things God allows—or sometimes orchestrates—aren't guaranteed to boost your comfort level. In fact, some of them will do the opposite. If you're expecting this verse to be an eternal feel good message, it'll let you down. Paul's speaking of good as *God* sees it. His definition of good often has a lot more to do with refining than reclining.

And note: These things aren't just randomly roaming around in the universe, bumping into each other until something nice happens. This isn't a mystic version of "oh my, look how that worked out!" Paul says *God* is the one who is working. He's behind the scenes, stitching together pain and joy and ordinary days into something ultimately good.

Here's the part we often breeze past: Who is this promise for? "To those who love God, who are called according to His purpose." This is not a fortune cookie for the whole world. It's a covenant truth for believers. For those who reject God there's no ultimate guarantee that *anything* works out for good. Not even eternity. Without Him suffering is just suffering. And a broken world stays broken.

For the believer the good doesn't happen by luck or probability. It's not a gamble. God Himself—who sees what we can't and knows things we'd frankly rather not deal with—is weaving it all for good. Not always immediately. Not always visibly. But always intentionally.

There is a real danger though. Some of us have heard Romans 8:28 so many times it's become spiritual elevator music. We hum along without really listening. It plays in the background of sermons, devotionals, bumper stickers—and we've tuned it out like it's the sixth time through the same old music.

But this isn't background noise. This is life-saving truth. So turn it up. Listen to it like it's the first time you've heard it. Let it be real to you. Because if we can really hear it—if we can really believe it— it will change everything.

• • •

It is vitally important to place this verse on its proper foundation. Romans 8:28 doesn't just float around like a free agent promise, hoping to land somewhere meaningful. It's built to sit on something solid—specifically, the deep, unwavering love of God. Think of it like a lighthouse: strong on its own, yes—but only because it's anchored into a rock that doesn't move when the waves come crashing. Without that foundation, it's just a poetic sentence. With it, it's a lifeline.

Like all of God's most powerful truths the foundation of Romans 8:28 is His unshakable love. Read the verses around it—don't skim them. Let them breathe. They're not just theological filler. They're a declaration. God wants you to *know* the extent of His love—not theoretically but in the middle of your real, messy life:

> And we know that all things work together for good to them that love God, to them who are the called according to his purpose. For whom he did foreknow, he also did predestinate to be conformed to the image of his Son, that he might be the firstborn among many brethren. Moreover whom he did predestinate, them he also called: and whom he called, them he also justified: and whom he justified, them he also glorified. What shall we

then say to these things? If God be for us, who can be against us? He that spared not his own Son, but delivered him up for us all, how shall he not with him also freely give us all things? Who shall lay anything to the charge of God's elect? It is God that justifieth. Who is he that condemneth? It is Christ that died, yea rather, that is risen again, who is even at the right hand of God, who also maketh intercession for us. Who shall separate us from the love of Christ? shall tribulation, or distress, or persecution, or famine, or nakedness, or peril, or sword? As it is written, For thy sake we are killed all the day long; we are accounted as sheep for the slaughter. Nay, in all these things we are more than conquerors through him that loved us. For I am persuaded, that neither death, nor life, nor angels, nor principalities, nor powers, nor things present, nor things to come, Nor height, nor depth, nor any other creature, shall be able to separate us from the love of God, which is in Christ Jesus our Lord. (Romans 8:28–39)

Can you see how determined God is to drive this point home? This isn't subtle. This is Paul with a bullhorn. And the message is simple: God's love is the unshakeable foundation beneath every promise.

* * *

Let's spotlight two massive truths:

First, God has always loved us, and He will never stop—*for any reason*. (Yes, even that reason you're thinking about right now.)

This matters especially when we walk through trauma because one of the first things we tend to do is blame ourselves. The guilt rolls in

like fog: *Maybe this wouldn't have happened if I had prayed more....*
Maybe it's punishment.... Maybe Job's friends had a point.

But Paul slams the door shut on that thinking. "Who shall lay
anything to the charge of God's elect?" Translation: Who dares accuse
one of God's kids? Who's going to march into the courtroom of
heaven and point fingers when Jesus is your defense attorney—and
your judge—and already paid the sentence?

So when tragedy strikes and the critics get loud, remind them:
God's love hasn't left the building. He's not pacing nervously in heaven
wondering what to do with you. He's close. He's constant. He loves
you, past, present, and future. No expiration date.

Second, we ask: *How can God love me and still let this happen?*
It's a fair question. A hard one. But these verses answer it not with
theory but with a promise: *nothing*—not suffering, not heartbreak,
not unanswered questions—*nothing* can separate us from His love.

Romans 8:28 doesn't just float in the clouds. It stands firmly on
this list of brutal, real-life experiences: tribulation, distress, persecution,
famine, nakedness, peril, sword. (That's not just poetry. That's been
a week for some people.) And the promise remains: *He still loves you.*

So what does "all things work together for good" actually mean?
It means that God in His long view wisdom is taking all of it—the
messy, beautiful, disappointing, painful collage—and shaping it for
our good and His glory. Even when it looks like chaos now.

And if you want Exhibit A, look at Joseph. Genesis 37–50 gives
us a masterclass in divine plot twists. Dysfunctional family? Check.
Betrayal? Pit. Slavery? Prison. Misery? For years. And then—just when
it looks like the credits are about to roll—God lifts Joseph up to second-in-command in Egypt and uses him to save nations.

Joseph's mic-drop moment comes in Genesis 50:20 when he looks at the brothers who sold him like a garage sale treadmill and says, "You meant evil against me, but God meant it for good"

That wasn't luck. That was Romans 8:28 in slow motion.

Paul wraps it all up with verses 38–39, piling on every imaginable threat—death, life, angels, demons, present, future, heights, depths—and ends with this thunderous truth: *Nothing can separate us from the love of God in Christ Jesus our Lord.*

Paul is daring you—daring all of us—to try and name a circumstance where God's love runs out. Spoiler: You can't.

So yes, you're being carried. Through the good. Through the worst. Through the unexplainable. And if *that's* how He loves you, then you can trust that He is absolutely working the best possible plan for your life.

CHAPTER 9

THE STORY OF JOB

When God Shows Up in a Storm and Brings the Thunder—Literally

I'll refer to Job often throughout this book because no one in Scripture better illustrates what it means to live fully in the midst of God's sovereignty.

The story of Job is one of those biblical moments that starts off sounding like a Sunday school flannel board story and ends with you staring into space whispering, "Wait—what just happened?" It's God's thunderous reminder that He is sovereign—ruling not just the stars and galaxies but also the lives of real people. People with mortgages and back pain. Nothing happens outside His knowledge, and no suffering enters our lives unless He allows it. That's not always comforting—but it is deeply true.

Now let's not sugarcoat it: This story is rough. Job was a good guy. Not the kind of good guy who pretends to be good—he actually was good. He was a great husband, loving father, reliable friend, and the sort of neighbor who doesn't let his dog bark past 10 p.m. He was wealthy, respected, and righteous. If he lived today, he'd have really nice yard, a fully funded retirement plan, and his streaming services would all be bundled. The man even prayed for his kids in case they sinned (Job 1:5). Not because they did—just in case. That's next-level parenting. That's like packing an umbrella for a hike on a sunny day—just in case.

Then—bam. In one day Job's life collapsed like a condemned building when the blasts go off. Livestock gone. Servants gone. Kids gone. Health gone. And worst of all? God didn't give him a heads-up or an explanation. No divine text message. Just silence.

If you're anything like me, your reaction is probably somewhere between outrage and confusion. "Hold on—Job didn't even get a warning, and God just let this happen? Isn't God supposed to be better than that?" At first glance it looks like Job is nothing more than a pawn in a vast wager between God and Satan. It's a heavenly courtroom drama, and Job's the one getting hit with the gavel.

So how do we wrap our heads around this? Why would God allow suffering—especially to a super good person? If He's all-powerful and loving, why not just step in with a miracle and a speech? These are not small questions. They are the cry of every hospital room, every grave site, every sleepless night. And Job asked them too.

But when God finally answered—it was not the answer Job expected. Or the one we usually want. It came in a whirlwind. Literally.

JOB'S LIFE FALLS APART—LIKE, SPECTACULARLY FALLS APART

Like we said, Job had it all. Then in one day he didn't anymore.

On that day messengers sprinted to him, each one somehow breathless and worse than the last:

"Job! Your oxen and donkeys were stolen—your servants were killed!"

"Job! Fire fell from the sky and burned up your sheep and shepherds!"

"Job! Raiders took your camels and murdered your workers!"

"Job…" (At this point, Job had to be thinking, *Surely that's it, right? Please let that be it.*)

"…All of your children were crushed when their house collapsed in a storm."

Everything. Gone. In. One. Day.

I don't know what Job was thinking at that moment, but I imagine it was something like, *God…what is happening?!*

I know that on the worst day of my life—the day we lost Wade—my thoughts were mostly about how I could make it all stop. I couldn't breathe, couldn't think. Just pain. But Job? Job didn't panic. He didn't curse God. He didn't even yell. He fell to the ground in grief—and worshiped.

He said, "The Lord gave, and the Lord has taken away; blessed be the name of the Lord" (Job 1:21).

That may be one of the most stunning lines in all of Scripture. Because that kind of faith doesn't come from having an easy life. It comes from knowing that even when life crumbles into rubble, God is still God. And He is still good.

AND THEN SATAN GOES FOR ROUND TWO

But Satan wasn't done. He went back before God, basically saying, "Sure, Job didn't crack—but that's only because he still has his health. Take that away, and he'll go down like a folding table at a church pot-luck with one too many casseroles." And—amazingly—God allowed it.

Soon Job was covered in painful sores from head to toe. Not like a paper cut or a pulled muscle—this was the kind of affliction that makes you question all your life choices, starting with birth. He sat in ashes, scraping his skin with broken pottery. Which honestly raises a lot of questions. Why pottery? Was this a prescription from an ancient urgent care doctor? Like, "Here's your clay shard and ashes—apply as needed."

And then Job's wife enters the scene. We're not sure how much time passes but long enough for Job to gather his pottery tools, rip his clothes, and find a good ash pile to sit in. She walks out, sees her husband looking like he crawled out of a chimney wearing beggars clothes, and says, "Curse God and die."

Now before we all pile on Mrs. Job, let's pause. She just lost every-thing too—all her children, her security, her sanity. She's grieving. She walks outside and sees her husband in full ash-and-pottery mode, and it's all just too much. The words come flying out.

And yes, she gets a bad rap for that line. But if the truth be told—some of us have snapped over an airline losing our luggage. She just lost her entire life. In that moment, grief spoke louder than faith.

Job, meanwhile, is sitting there—covered in sores, emotionally shredded, surrounded by ruins. He looks up, and with stunning clar-ity and steadiness, says, "Shall we accept good from God, and not trouble?" (Job 2:10).

That's not just a quotable verse. That's leadership. That's faith in full-blown ashes-and-pottery reality. Job didn't pretend everything was fine—he just refused to give up on the God who had never given up on him.

ENTER JOB'S FRIENDS—THE WORST INTERVENTION TEAM IN HISTORY

Three of Job's friends came to visit. When they saw him, they were so shocked they just sat in silence for seven days. And honestly? That was probably their best move.

Most of us aren't great at comforting people. Someone tells us their life is falling apart, and we panic, not knowing whether to hug them or bring food. So seven days of silence? Not a bad call.

But then they opened their mouths—and it all went downhill from there.

> Friend #1: "Job, let's be real—you must have sinned. Nobody suffers like this for no reason."

> Friend #2: "Bad things don't happen to good people. You did something wrong."

> Friend #3: "Just admit your guilt, and maybe God will fix this."

At this point Job was probably rethinking their entire friendship.

Finally, he snapped. "Why was I even born? Why does God let the wicked succeed while I suffer? I've lived an honest life, yet I've lost everything! If only I could stand before God and ask Him why this is happening!"

And just as Job finished pouring out his grief and confusion—a storm rolled in.

The wind howled. The sky darkened. And from the middle of the storm…God spoke.

GOD SPEAKS FROM THE STORM (JOB 38-42)

God Says, "Let's See How Smart You Really Are."

Somehow, someway, Job—still sore-covered and ash-sitting—found himself in the presence of God.

And then the questions started:

"Who is this questioning Me without knowledge? Stand up like a man. I have some questions for you, and you will answer Me. Where were you when I laid the foundations of the earth? Tell Me, if you know so much. Who marked off its dimensions? Who stretched out a measuring line across it? Who told the oceans how far they could come? Do you command the morning or set the boundaries of light and darkness? Have you explored the depths of the sea or walked in the recesses of the deep? Do you know where I store the snow? Can you summon lightning with a shout?"

At this point, Job was probably thinking, *I should've stuck with silence.*

And then God really ramped it up. He brought out Behemoth.

"Look at Behemoth," He said. "It eats grass like an ox but has strength like no other. Its bones are iron. Its muscles are cables. You can't trap it. You can't tame it. Don't even try."

Then Leviathan.

"Can you catch Leviathan with a hook? Will it beg for mercy? Good luck. It breathes fire. No sword or spear can touch it. It laughs at your weapons. If you're scared of Leviathan—and you should be—why aren't you more in awe of the One who made it?"

This goes on for four chapters. Divine mic drop after divine mic drop.

And then God said, "Will you discredit My justice and condemn Me just so you can be right?"

At this point, Job was done. Absolutely undone. He sat there, surrounded by ash, clay, and the overwhelming reality of God's glory. And he said:

> I know that You can do all things. No purpose of Yours can be stopped. I was talking about things I didn't understand, things too wonderful for me. I had only heard of You before, but now I've seen You with my own eyes. I take back everything I said. I sit here in dust and ashes. I repent. I have no answers.

And then...the storm stopped. The winds quieted. The sky cleared. God had spoken.

And after all of it—after the pain, the loss, the silence, and the storm—God restored Job. Everything. Tenfold.

EPILOGUE: THE HAPPILY EVER AFTER

So after God dropped His thunderous four chapter monologue on Job, He turned His attention to Job's three so-called friends—and let's just say...they were in trouble.

God speaks directly to Eliphaz the Temanite and basically says, "I am NOT happy with you or your two buddies. You've been out here flapping your gums, misrepresenting Me and misjudging Job, while he—sitting in a heap of ashes and heartbreak—actually got it right."

Now picture Job in that moment. He's still emotionally scorched, physically wrecked, probably still peeling dried clay off his arm—and then he hears God say, "By the way, Job was right this whole time." I like to think he slowly turned his head, looked over at his friends (and probably at his wife too), and gave the smallest, most righteous smirk in biblical history.

But that's not the end of it. God says to the three friends, "Here's what's going to happen. You're going to bring seven bulls and seven rams for a sacrifice. And then—wait for it—Job is going to pray for you. And I will listen to him."

This is one of the all-time great human dynamics in all of Scripture. If I were in Job's sandals, I'd have been incredibly tempted: "Oh, so *now* you need me to pray for you? Because last week you were telling me I was trash and God was punishing me. But sure, let's pray. Just let me finish scraping this sore real quick." I might have been tempted to pray that they get a gentle smiting—just enough to make them rethink their career in comfort-giving.

But Job was a better man than me. He didn't gloat. He didn't lecture. He didn't make them grovel. He simply prayed. And God listened.

God accepted Job's prayer. And just like that, the three friends who had completely fumbled their attempt at comfort were spared from God's judgment—by the very man they had condemned. Talk about grace!

JOB'S BIG COMEBACK

Right after Job prayed for his friends, something incredible happened—God restored everything. And not just restored—doubled it.

Job got back twice as much as he had before. Imagine checking your bank account one day and realizing you suddenly have twice the money in there. I don't know about you, but I would need some time to just sit there and process this windfall.

And then—this part really gets me—all of Job's family and friends suddenly showed up. They came over to his house to eat. Question: Where were they before? I mean, Job was sitting in ashes, covered in sores, scraping his skin with a broken plate, and none of these people started a sign-up sheet to bring over a meal. But now? Now they were all there, showing up at his house like, "Job! So good to see you, man! Hey, glad everything worked out; we've been meaning to stop by!" And to make it even weirder—each one of them gave Job a piece of silver and a gold ring. Which is nice…but where was this generosity when Job was broke?

Imagine Job in the receiving line, and he's thinking, *Oh, great, NOW you all have money to spare. How convenient for you.*

God didn't just give Job back his wealth—He overloaded him with it. After what he went through, I don't begrudge him a single camel.

- 14,000 sheep
- 6,000 camels
- 1,000 oxen
- 1,000 donkeys

Which raises the question—what do you even do with 6,000 camels? I mean, what is the daily maintenance on that? Did Job have a full-time camel manager? Job had to be the biggest employer in the county. Dung hills were famous back in that day, so I'm sure Job cashed in on their popularity. Don't know if I would have wanted to live across the street, however.

And then Job had ten more kids. It's worth pausing here for a minute because this is a big deal. Losing his first children was devastating. I remember more than one person saying to us when Wade died that it was good we had other children to replace the one we lost. No, Wade could never be replaced. But just as I discovered, having more kids didn't "replace" the ones Job lost, but it shows that God was restoring Job's life.

And apparently these kids were something else. His daughters were so stunning that the Bible specifically points out they were the most beautiful in the entire land. Now this is so interesting to me because the Bible doesn't often comment on people's looks. But here? We're given a beauty pageant ranking.

It even mentions their names:

- Jemimah (really?)
- Keziah
- Keren-Happuch (which, if you're looking for baby name ideas)

And in a huge twist Job does something that wasn't normal for that time—he gives his daughters an inheritance along with his sons. Which basically means Job was ahead of his time. The guy went through the worst suffering imaginable, met God in a storm, came out wiser, and decided, "Yeah, my daughters are getting land too." No mention of his wife in the will by the way. Just saying.

After all of this Job lived another 140 years! That means Job was probably well over 200 years old when he died. Now I don't know if Job was thrilled about that, but I know he probably just got tired at some point. Imagine trying to keep up with four generations of family members. Great-great-great-great-grandchildren all at the same family gatherings. Maybe he put them to work with the camels? That would have been a plus, but on the other hand, that's a lot of birthdays. And it's a lot of remembering names. I can tell you for sure I would have struggled with that. At some point Job had to be like, "All right, God…I think I'm good now. I'm ready to come home." And finally Job passed away, full of years.

THE ANSWER TO JOB'S SUFFERING AND THE MYSTERY OF HOW IT WORKED FOR GOOD

Job's story isn't just a "happily ever after" fairy tale. It's a reminder that suffering is not the end of the story. That even when life falls apart in ways we never expected—God is still in control. That the pain we go through will not last forever and that God restores. And if we truly trust Him, we will find that what is ahead of us is far greater than what we left behind.

As I said, Job's suffering is hard to look at. I want to dismiss it and refuse to think about what happened to him. It looks random, unfair, and, honestly, seems like a terrible way to spend a season of life. But God was not being cruel—He was showing Job, and through him all of mankind, that His ways are higher than ours.

Now unless I miss my guess, you're like me that when you hear, "God's ways are higher," you start thinking, *Okay, well…how much higher? Are we talking just out of reach, or like I need the Webb Space Telescope to even get a glimpse?* Sometimes I'd really like a little insight into the plan, wouldn't you? Just a hint. Just a Post-it® note from heaven that says, *Hey, this is going somewhere good, no joke, I promise.*

But Job didn't get that. And neither do we. I suddenly realized as I was writing this that Job never did get to see or know about God's conversation with Satan. For all we know, he just figured God had chosen him arbitrarily for these life lessons. Don't we all feel like sometimes we're the only ones in the world who go through what we go through? And don't we often think *why me?*

But another thing Job couldn't see was that his suffering became a testimony for all generations. Job never knew that thousands of years later people would still be reading his story, preaching about his patience, and turning to his life as proof that God is still in control during tragedies. He didn't see it, but we do. And in that we realize something huge—Job's suffering was not just for himself; it was for us.

Now I can tell you from my own experience that it would not have made him feel better at the time knowing this would be for good later. I doubt sitting in a pile of ashes, scraping sores off his body, he was thinking, *You know what? Someone's really gonna benefit from this one day.* But he didn't need to see it for it to be true. And if that's true for Job, then it's true for us too.

Through Job we learn something that changes everything: Suffering does not mean abandonment from God. I don't know what you've been through. I don't know how many nights you've laid awake wondering if God sees you, if He hears you, if He even cares. But I know this: Job sat in the dust and thought the same thing. And then God showed up.

He did not explain Himself. He did not apologize. He did not hand Job an itemized breakdown of why everything happened. Instead, He revealed His power. And when Job saw who God really was, somehow, he didn't need the why anymore.

JOB'S STORY WAS A PREVIEW OF
THE GREATEST SUFFERING TO COME

One more thing—Job's suffering was not just about him; it was also pointing forward to someone greater. Because one day another innocent man would suffer. One day another blameless man would lose everything. One day another man would cry out in agony, abandoned by those who loved Him. One day another man would sit not in ashes but in Gethsemane, pleading with God. But unlike Job, this man would not be restored in this life. This man would die. Not just to prove a point. Not just to be an example. Not just to show us how to endure suffering well. But to take on the suffering we actually deserve.

Job lost everything, but Jesus took on everything. And when He rose again, it wasn't just His own story that was restored—it was ours.

GOD WORKS ALL THINGS FOR GOOD—
EVEN WHEN WE DON'T SEE IT

Here's the truth Job never saw but we get to know: God works all things for good—not just for our good but for His glory. Even when life is dark and even when suffering seems unbearable. Even when we cannot fathom why this is happening, God is not absent. He is not indifferent. He is not powerless but in control. God is good. He is sovereign. He is worthy of trust.

And one day, like Job, we will see Him for who He really is. And in that moment all our questions will fade away.

Blessed be the name of the Lord.

CHAPTER 10

THE MYSTERY OF GOD'S RULE AND MAN'S CHOICE

This is the part of the story when people start leaning in and saying, "Wait a second…if God is in control of everything, then what in the world am I doing with all these decisions, consequences, and stress headaches?" Welcome to the theological Bermuda Triangle: God's sovereignty meets human free will. And yes, it's as tricky as it sounds.

Honestly, this is the moment when many people smile politely, back away slowly, and go back to watching YouTube videos about how to peel boiled eggs. Because trying to sort out divine sovereignty and personal responsibility feels about as tangled as Christmas lights coming out of the box you so neatly put them in last year.

The way Romans lays it out it kind of sounds like everything is already mapped out, right? Like God has the whole game planned, called, and scheduled down to the minute—like the divine NFL. So people naturally ask: "If it's all going to happen anyway, why does it matter how I live?"

That's not a new question. It's not even a Millennial or Gen Z thing. It's ancient—like scroll-and-goat-hair ancient. Theologians have been arm wrestling over this for centuries. And here's what we've come to: Both are true. Yep. Somehow in God's infinite wisdom (which is still way smarter than your friend who says he could fix the economy if they'd just let him) both truths stand.

In the Bible when it comes to how God's sovereignty plays out in real life, you're free. You're responsible. And your choices absolutely matter. Nobody's standing behind you with a divine cattle prod forcing your hand. You make real decisions. You bear real consequences. And yet—here's the twist—everything you do, all of it, fits perfectly into the sovereign plan of God. Without Him needing to rig the system or manipulate you like a puppet.

Let's look at a couple of verses that help shine some light without melting our mental circuits:

> **Proverbs 16:9**—"A man's heart deviseth his way: but the Lord directeth his steps."

> **Proverbs 16:33**—"The lot is cast into the lap; but the whole disposing thereof is of the Lord."

Translation? You make the plan. You pack the bag. You even buy the plane ticket. But God's the one who ensures the flight lands where it needs to. Or, if we're being honest, He might redirect you to the scenic route through Helsinki when you swore you were going to Paris.

In verse 9, Solomon says we're the ones mapping out our way. But what happens to that map, where it ultimately takes us—that's God's department. Then verse 33 gives us the ancient version of rolling dice or flipping a coin. You make the toss. God calls the landing. That's not divine trickery—it's divine orchestration.

So yes—you are free. Yes—you are responsible. But also yes—God's plan never breaks a sweat. The beauty is that your story with all its twists, tears, triumphs, and regrets is already being woven into something greater. And it's being written by a sovereign God who doesn't need to micromanage to make it meaningful.

God works all things out and doesn't violate your free will. Is that possible? Hard to grasp? You're not alone. J. I. Packer waded into this same deep end and came up holding a word that sounds like something your dentist might say before numbing your jaw: *antinomy.*

He discusses the concept of *antinomy* most notably in his classic book *Evangelism and the Sovereignty of God.*

You'll find it in chapter 2, "Divine Sovereignty and Human Responsibility," where he explains an *antinomy* as "an appearance of contradiction between conclusions that seem equally logical, reasonable, or necessary."[4]

Packer uses the term to describe the relationship between God's sovereignty and human responsibility in Scripture—two truths that seem to conflict, but must both be held as true because the Bible affirms them.

Packer said that when it comes to divine sovereignty and human responsibility, the answer is—brace yourself—both. He put it like this: The Bible speaks unapologetically of both. Not one at the expense of the other. It's not a contradiction, but it sure looks like one from our side of the cosmos.

---

4. J.I. Packer, *Evangelism and the Sovereignty of God* (Downers Grove, IL: InterVarsity Press, 1961)

An *antinomy*, he explained, is when two principles stand side-by-side, apparently irreconcilable, yet both are undeniable. Like light. Is it made of particles? Yes. Waves? Also yes. It's like trying to figure out whether a taco is a sandwich or a hot dog—science just throws up its hands and says, "Yes."

The total quote from Packer :"An antinomy exists when a pair of principles stand side by side, seemingly irreconcilable, yet both undeniable. There are cogent reasons for believing each of them; each rests on clear and solid evidence; but it is a mystery to you how they can be squared with each other."[5]

We don't fully understand how it works, but we know it works. The same goes for God's sovereignty and our free will. They're both true, both real, and both functioning even if our brains occasionally overheat trying to hold them in the same mental container.

So does man have free will? Absolutely. Is God sovereign? Completely. Not either/or but both/and. God isn't overriding your free will like some divine override button. He's actually working through your choices, not despite them. Our decisions are the very threads He uses to weave the tapestry of His purposes.

And here's the jaw-dropper: Your choices matter. Not in a participation trophy kind of way—but in a real, divine, eternal purpose kind of way. You make real decisions that carry weight. And somehow—beautifully, sovereignly—they fit into God's perfect ending.

* * *

The Bible isn't shy about showing this dynamic in action. Take Genesis 3:15, the first whisper of Jesus on the way: "I will put enmity

---

5. J.I. Packer, *Evangelism and the Sovereignty of God* (Downers Grove, IL: InterVarsity Press, 1961)

between you and the woman…He shall bruise your head, and you shall bruise His heel" (Genesis 3:15). From that moment God declared that the Messiah would come—and come He did. But not without a long line of messy, dramatic, and sometimes flat out disastrous human choices along the way.

Still, despite all the detours, delays, and disobedience—Jesus came. The plan was never in jeopardy. The same is true for your life.

Want another example? Enter Jonah—the prophet who turned a simple assignment into a nautical nightmare. God told him to go to Nineveh. Jonah heard that and said, "Cool…but what if I don't?" And he booked a ticket in the *exact* opposite direction.

God didn't stop him. Jonah made that choice. But God—being sovereign and fully aware that He had some rather persuasive fish on standby—allowed Jonah to run.

Cue storm. Panic. Ancient dice-rolling ritual. Jonah overboard. Ocean calm. Whale Uber.

Even in all that chaos, God was not absent. He orchestrated the storm, guided the dice, and summoned the great fish—all to bring Jonah back on course. Jonah wasn't forced into obedience. He was escorted—with intensity.

In that messy story we see both Jonah's free will and God's sovereign plan playing out like an improv show that somehow sticks to the script. Jonah chose rebellion. God chose redemption. The mission was accomplished, the message delivered, and the prophet—well, he had one unforgettable fishing story.

The broader truth? God's eternal purposes will prevail—globally and personally. We might zig when we should zag, take detours, or even run away from Nineveh. But God in love and wisdom redirects, redeems, and weaves even our wanderings into His masterpiece.

Sure Jonah could've skipped the whale belly chapter altogether by just saying yes from the start. But then again, we wouldn't have this wild, messy, grace-filled story. And sometimes that's what makes the journey unforgettable—for us and for others watching the story unfold.

CHAPTER 11

WHY GOD PERMITS WHAT HE DOESN'T PREFER

I'm afraid that this chapter is one of those you'll need to slog through in order to get to the next one. It reminds me of those days sitting on the back row in theology class. The front-row guys were furiously taking notes and asking the right questions while my brow was furrowed as I drew stick figures and creative doodles. The professor was not wrong; it's just that the words did not immediately penetrate my skull like it did the others. That is until I needed them to. What I found was that if I applied myself, I could understand anything if I thought it was important enough. The concepts in the pages of this chapter will be "stodgy" for sure. *Stodgy* is a word I learned while watching *The Great British Baking Show*. In baking terms it means dense or heavy. In a literary sense it means dull or uninteresting. Stodgy or not, the next pages are important to our complete understanding of how God practically works in the universe as well as in our personal lives.

When we talk about God's sovereignty, it is good to remember that God allows many things to happen that are confusing to us and that would not have been allowed in the newly created perfect world. He allows them in order to accomplish His long range, big picture, perfect will. This is called God's permissive will.

When God created the universe, He created it all perfectly, part of His perfect plan. We cannot say for certain why or when He created it. What we can say for sure is that when He was finished with creation, it was "very good," as stated in the Creation story in Genesis. Within that perfect work, He created spiritual beings with a will and the ability to make decisions. Otherwise, He would have only manufactured robots, not people. Because of this ability to exercise free will, humans chose disobedience, at which point sin entered into God's perfect universe. Of course, sin brought along with it death, suffering, disease, and all the other consequences we have come to expect in life. God allowed these things to happen because of His permissive will.

It was not as if God lost control of His creation; that would eliminate Him from being God at all. We come to the edge of our ability to understand God when we stand at this precipice of the world's story. It is a strain to see but possible if we have the right perspective on who God is compared to who we are.

God is omniscient and sovereign over all things. His omniscience means He knows all things that have occurred and all things that will occur over all time. His sovereignty means He must permit all events and all happenings for all mankind for all time. It is not possible for Him to be mistaken. So we see that He intentionally made humans with the ability to make their own decisions and placed them in the garden where He also placed the Tree of the Knowledge of Good and Evil, even though He knew Adam and Eve would willingly choose to disobey. Within God's sovereignty, He chooses to allow many things to happen that He takes no pleasure in—the fall of man is one of them. Lest you think this is totally contrary to good fathering, don't we do the same thing with our own children? Sometimes we allow them to make mistakes because there is no better way to teach them. That is not bad fathering; in fact, there is an argument to be made that it is the best kind of parenting.

God does not force us to carry out His commands. Rather, in His permissive will God allows us to make decisions—even bad decisions that are not God's best for our lives. For certain, we can choose not to follow God's commands, but we cannot choose the consequences. That's like choosing to eat a dozen donuts and expecting to lose five pounds. It doesn't work that way.

For example, there's a story in 1 Samuel 8 where the Israelites really want to have a king. They go to Samuel, the prophet at the time, and demand that he make it happen. This is not what God wants for them, and Samuel warns them against it. However, this doesn't matter to the people, and in 1 Samuel 8:19–20, their response is recorded like this: "But the people refused to listen to Samuel. 'No!' they said. 'We want a king over us. Then we will be like all the other nations, with a king to lead us and to go out before us and fight our battles'"

It's like a bunch of toddlers demanding candy for dinner. "We know what's best, Samuel! Give us a king!" And God in His permissive will essentially says, "Okay, but don't come crying to me when this guy raises your taxes, drafts your sons, and confiscates your vineyards."

So God allows them to have what they demand, giving them a king like the other nations. What would have happened if they had listened to God's Word through the prophet Samuel? Well, it'll be an interesting topic for some millennia in eternity. We can pull up a heavenly recliner and ask Samuel himself.

What we are promised is that even in this detour from God's perfect will into His permissive will, it worked within and according to His divine plan.

We graciously experience God's permissive will every day as He allows us to make our own decisions based on how we choose to live and whether we want to acknowledge Him or not. When we wake up, what we eat, where we go, who we go with, who we marry. Some of our choices have lifelong consequences, while some won't. (Like whether you wear socks with sandals. That one's mostly just socially damaging.) But whatever the consequences, the choices are ours to make.

It is important to remember that whatever choices we make, God is not just randomly hoping all will work together for our good in spite of our decisions. No, He is actively aware and guiding your ship through the waters you have chosen to the destination He has in mind for both you and all of His creation.

It is an awesome thought to think about how omnisciently powerful our God is. He will always be enthroned, never shaken, and will never lose control. No matter how devastating we think things are.

I have often heard the question from doubters in a sovereign God that if He is so good and powerful and if He has our best interests in mind, then why does He allow evil to exist? It's one of those tough questions that seems tailor-made to be asked while someone's holding a cup of coffee and answered by someone with a pipe in their mouth. It's real. And it's fair.

So yes, within God's permissive will, evil is indeed allowed to function. However, that doesn't mean God is at fault or turns His eye from those who suffer through it. Ultimately, we live in a broken world of our own making. The evil that exists is the evil that we chose in Eden and, indeed, choose in our own individual lives. Though that evil exists, God's perfect plan triumphs every time and will prevail as time is fulfilled.

An example of this can be seen in the famous story of Joseph. An amazing man this Joseph was. As we read the stories of other characters in the Bible, the distracting warts they have become visible over the discourse of their life story. It's hard to find those flaws in Joseph, though they surely existed. To our point, God allowed Joseph to be kidnapped and then enslaved. God could have stopped that process at any time, but He "permitted" it to happen. A very important point to see here is that God's permission to allow this evil did not and never will counteract His sovereign overarching plan. As the story unfolds, we see that God allowed the evil acts of Joseph's brothers in order to bring about a far greater good—the rescue of the entire known world!

Another example can be seen on the night that Jesus was arrested. He told those who came to take Him, "This is your hour, and the power of darkness" (Luke 22:53). What Jesus was saying is that at that moment and in the following hours as He made His way to the cross, evil had been granted a window of time to work, and darkness was loosed to do what it would. That was indeed a horrendous time, but the end result was the salvation of all mankind for all time. **God only permits that which leads to His sovereign will being accomplished.**

The concept of God's will has intrigued theologians, philosophers, and believers for centuries. When discussing God's will, a distinction often made is between His "active will" and "passive will." These two aspects help provide a framework for understanding how God interacts with creation, human choice, and the unfolding of events in the world. By delving into these two aspects of divine will, we gain insights into how God's sovereignty, love, and justice are manifested, even in complex or challenging situations.

UNDERSTANDING ACTIVE WILL

God's active will refers to what God directly wills, initiates, or brings about. This encompasses actions, events, and outcomes that align directly with God's purposes and intentions for creation. When God's active will is at work, we see instances where He intervenes or commands specific outcomes to ensure His divine purposes come to pass. Scripture often illustrates God's active will in instances of miracles, judgment, divine guidance, and the fulfillment of prophecy.

For example, in the Bible God's active will is seen in Creation itself, as Genesis 1:1 states, "In the beginning God created the heaven and the earth." Here, God initiates Creation through His active, perfect will, bringing everything into existence with purpose and order. Similarly, in the story of Israel's deliverance from Egypt God's active will is seen in His intervention through Moses to liberate the Israelites. He performs miracles—sends plagues, parts the Red Sea, and leads His people with a pillar of cloud by day and fire by night (Exodus 13:21–22). These actions were not random but intentional, directly serving God's purpose of rescuing His chosen people.

God's active will can also be observed in the life and ministry of Jesus Christ. The incarnation itself—God becoming flesh in Jesus— was an act of God's active will. As described in John 1:14, "The Word became flesh and dwelt among us" indicating God's direct intervention in human history to bring about salvation. Jesus' teachings, miracles, and ultimately His death and resurrection all reflect God's active will to reconcile humanity to Himself, as stated in 2 Corinthians 5:19: "God was reconciling the world to himself in Christ, not counting people's sins against them"

However, it's important to recognize that God's active will is not always aligned with human desires or plans. His active will can bring about difficult situations or outcomes that challenge human understanding, especially when God's judgment is involved. An example of this is seen, once again, in the story of Job. (I told you I'd refer to him a lot). Though Job was a righteous man, God allowed him to endure severe trials to test his faith and refine his character (Job 1:8–12). While it might not align with Job's desires, God's active will in this case served a greater purpose, revealing His sovereignty and Job's eventual growth in understanding of God's nature.

UNDERSTANDING PERMISSIVE WILL

Now on the other side of the coin (probably one of those ancient Roman ones with Caesar's profile), we have God's permissive will. This is what God allows to happen, even if it's not His first choice or direct command. It's the kind of thing He says yes to—not because He's thrilled about it but because He honors the free will He built into us. It's kind of like when your kid wants to eat cold pizza for breakfast—you allow it, but you're quietly questioning your parenting choices the entire time.

God's permissive will includes the things that arise from human free will, natural consequences, and the brokenness of a world that's been limping since Eden. He allows them—not because He's checked out or distracted but because He sees how even the messiest parts can be folded into a larger redemptive story.

A classic example? Sin and suffering. God didn't create the world with pain and sin preloaded like apps on a new phone—those showed up later, courtesy of human choices. He created everything good—very good, actually. But He also gave humans the ability to choose. And we did. Poorly. In Genesis 3, Adam and Eve chose disobedience, and just like that, pain, death, shame, and mosquitos entered the world. God permitted it—not because He wanted it but because He wouldn't revoke our freedom every time we veered off course. And let's be honest, if He did that, we'd have missed eight-track tapes.

Then there's suffering. God doesn't delight in it, but sometimes He allows it. Why? Well, He sees the end from the beginning. Like Romans 8:28 reminds us, "And we know that in all things God works for the good of those who love him" That means even the worst stuff—the waiting room news, the sleepless nights, the unreturned calls—none of it is wasted. God can repurpose it. He shapes us in the furnace, not on the recliner with a sweet tea in hand.

Take Pharaoh. God didn't create Pharaoh just to be stubborn. But when Pharaoh kept resisting God, the Lord said, "Okay, I'll let that stubbornness grow legs." The hardening of Pharaoh's heart (Exodus 9:12) is a wild example of permissive will at work. Pharaoh's refusal led to plagues, loss, and eventually, Israel's liberation. God didn't force Pharaoh to be a villain—but He used the story anyway, and the credit still goes to Him with His glory on full display.

THE RELATIONSHIP BETWEEN PERFECT AND PERMISSIVE WILL

Understanding the relationship between God's perfect and permissive wills helps illuminate the complex nature of God's sovereignty and human responsibility. While God's active will ensures that His ultimate purposes are achieved, His permissive will allows for human choices, natural processes, and even the presence of evil to play a role in the unfolding of history.

This dynamic shows up big time in the concept of free will. God's permissive will gives humans the freedom to choose between right and wrong. He doesn't force anyone to love or obey Him—He invites, He calls, but He doesn't twist arms. In Deuteronomy 30:19, God says, "I have set before you life and death, blessings and curses. Now choose life, so that you and your children may live" God's perfect desire is for life and blessing, but He permissively allows each person to make that call.

And here's where it gets wild: Even when we make lousy choices, God's sovereignty doesn't break down like a cheap lawn chair. He can still bring His perfect purposes to pass. Remember Joseph? His brothers sold him off like a clearance item, but Joseph ended up second-in-command in Egypt. And when they were finally reunited, Joseph—who could've gone full revenge mode—simply said, "You intended to harm me, but God intended it for good" (Genesis 50:20). That's the dance between permissive and perfect will—what people meant for evil, God wove into salvation.

THE PURPOSE OF GOD'S WILL IN OUR LIVES

Understanding God's two-track will—perfect and permissive—helps believers see the bigger picture. Yes, God has a plan for your life. No, He won't take away your choices. But He will take your choices, even the messiest ones, and use them for something far greater than you imagined.

God's perfect will brings blessings, guidance, and the fulfillment of His promises. His permissive will gives space for growth, challenge, and transformation. Aligning with His perfect will means listening for His voice, leaning into Scripture, and trusting that His direct involvement leads to life—not always easy but always rich.

And when life goes sideways—when we're living through what feels like God's permissive will—we can take comfort knowing He hasn't fallen asleep. He's still in charge. Still good. Still weaving things together in ways we might not see until much later.

God's perfect and permissive wills show us two beautiful truths: He is in control, and He lets us choose. Both reflect His love, His justice, and His sovereignty. And both remind us that even in the ordinary, even in the painful, He is present—and He is at work.

CHAPTER 12

THE BOAT STORY

Sometimes to explain something deep and theological—like God's sovereignty—you need a story. Not a stodgy one with people in togas quoting ancient scrolls but a story that smells like diesel fuel and river water.

So here's mine. I call it *The Boat Story.*

Now before we get too far, let me admit this: The analogy might have a few holes. And yes, that's ironic for a story about a boat. But it works for me. I've always needed simple, visual ways to grasp the greatness of God. Maybe you do too. If not, just humor me. You're already in the boat now.

In this story all of us—every one of us—are aboard a massive ship called *His Great Sovereignty.* It's not a cruise ship with a never-ending buffet. It's bigger. Older. And it doesn't go where *you* want. This ship is sailing on a river longer than a Gordon Lightfoot song—one that winds through a world God Himself created. In fact, He designed the boat, the river, the scenery, and even the passengers—yes, including the one snoring in the corner seat.

And make no mistake, He is the Captain. He's not up in the

control room nervously checking weather apps or waiting for passenger feedback. He already knows the destination. In fact, He determined it long before the journey began—before you bought your ticket, packed your snacks, or asked if this thing has Wi-Fi.

People of all races and nationalities have stepped aboard at different points along the river—some in ancient ports, others just recently at what looked like a glorified canoe dock. The boat is packed with all kinds: introverts reading quietly, extroverts organizing line dancing on the main deck, toddlers throwing Goldfish crackers, and teenagers pretending they're not on the trip at all. And yet somehow everyone's been allowed on. No one is left standing on the shore if the Captain tells them, "You're in."

But here's what's fascinating—every single person on this boat shares one thing: We're all headed to the same destination, one the Captain Himself determined before any of us even had a toothbrush. And not just any destination. It's the best possible outcome for each individual soul on board—designed with divine wisdom and tailor-fit grace.

The daily events of the journey? Also in His hands. He's orchestrating the route and the timing like a maestro conducting a floating symphony. And while it might not always feel like a concert—especially when you're seasick or stuck near the guy who brought a harmonica—it's all being worked out for our good.

Of course, there are storms. Big ones. Some rock the entire ship, making everyone grab a rail and pray like their grandma taught them. Others are smaller, hitting just one section, maybe even just one person. But whether you're in first class or tucked in below the water line next to the ice machine, storms come. Rain pours on the just and the unjust—sometimes in sideways sheets.

And then there are battles. Pirates from the shore. Monsters from the deep. And occasionally, arguments in the cafeteria over whether coffee refills should be free. People on this boat don't always behave. They hurt each other. Sometimes deeply. Emotionally. Physically. Even though we're all headed to the same place, some passengers forget that and throw punches—or worse, silence.

Still, the Captain doesn't abandon ship. Not even close. He sees it all. He steers through it all. And somehow in ways we don't fully understand, He's guiding us exactly where we need to go.

Throughout the long journey the ship gets battered. Sometimes it looks like my old tool shed sneezed. But here's the good news: It's never in danger of sinking. Not once. Not ever.

There are illnesses onboard, of course. You gather enough people in one place, and eventually someone starts coughing. But some days? Some days you wake up, the sun's shining, the coffee's hot, the river's smooth, and it almost feels like everything's right with the world. Those are the days that make you believe the Captain slipped a little bit of heaven onto the deck.

And the provisions? Oh, they're there. Food, drink, joy—all supplied in abundance. But the Captain won't force-feed you. He's stocked the galley with everything needed for joy, but it's up to the passengers how to use it. Some people sit down, give thanks, and truly enjoy the full banquet the Captain's prepared. Others head straight for the dessert table, grab a cupcake, and think they've tasted it all. And then there are the visionaries—busy stacking the dinner rolls like Legos to build their own little empires right in front of the coleslaw.

What's amazing is that none of that changes the ship's course. Whether we act wisely or foolishly, the Captain's steering never wavers. Our buffet etiquette doesn't throw Him off course.

The rules of the ship? They're posted. Clear. Wise. Meant for our good. But the Captain doesn't lock us in cabins if we break them. No, He gives us freedom. Real freedom. You can follow His ways or not. You're not a robot—He made sure of that. But while you get to choose your actions, you don't get to choose the consequences. Those are set by the Captain.

And because we live in close quarters, our choices spill over. We rub shoulders—sometimes literally. We talk. We clash. We laugh. We fight. We get on each other's nerves. And we get to choose—peace or hate, forgiveness or revenge, love or apathy. The Captain hopes we'll choose well. He loves every soul on this boat, and He wants each one to experience peace and joy.

But He won't force it. That's the strange, beautiful risk of freedom. He gave us wills of our own, not because He wants chaos but because He wants real love. And real love, as it turns out, has to be chosen.

One thing is certain: The ship is going to the destination the Captain chose. Passengers can do whatever they want onboard—throw parties, grumble in the corner, even stage a mutiny—but they won't reroute the ship. They can scream at the river or try to paddle backward, but the vessel sails on.

At various ports along the river, passengers disembark. Their journey ends—sometimes peacefully, sometimes painfully. Some made the trip more pleasant for others. Some not so much. But either way their journey with the Captain reaches its conclusion. They step off into the destination chosen by both the Captain and themselves.

During their time aboard, they had the same freedom as the rest—to trust, to ignore, to obey, to reject. When they step off the ship, they face the outcome of those decisions. He honors their choices. Even now they wait at a location set by the Captain with the promise that one day, they'll see Him again on another shore.

Meanwhile, the boat keeps going. The atmosphere shifts with each departure or new boarding. Friendships change. Conversations fade. New ones begin. But none of it alters the course. The Captain hasn't budged an inch from His eternal itinerary.

He's also kept the arrival time to Himself. The final port is set, but He hasn't shared the ETA—not even with the crew. It will come though. The ship will dock.

Until then, the passengers have been given a guidebook—a manual covering everything from how to live well, how to relate, how to talk to the Captain, and even what to expect when stepping off the ship. He tries to describe the final destination, but words fall short. Even so, something deep inside every passenger whispers that the place is real—and better than anything they can imagine.

Not everyone will reach that final port, but everyone has been invited. Once again, the decision belongs to the passengers. Still, somehow all those who got off early will gather near that final docking point too. And when the ship finally pulls in, the brilliance of the Captain's plan will come into full view. There'll be a celebration. A homecoming. A welcome party like no other.

No one knows exactly how it will unfold. We've only been told there will be joy—deep, unshakeable joy—and rest like we've never known. Time as we know it ends there.

And then comes the moment: Every soul who ever rode the ship will stand before the Captain. One by one. Not in line like at the DMV but in a way only He could design. We'll give an account. We had enough light to make our decision. We had enough grace to reach for more. Some will enter into unending joy with the

Captain. Others who chose to go their own way will face an eternity without Him.

It's hard to imagine. It's hard to accept. The sorrow. The regret. Even those who loved the Captain and lived by His guidebook will stand before Him, not for condemnation but for review. Rewards. Crowns. Recognition. And most of all, the chance to hear those words every traveler longs to hear:

"Well done. You were a good and faithful servant. Enter into your rest."

That's the moment. That's the destination. The journey started not when we wanted—but when the Captain said, "Now." He gave us this ride through time. No two journeys were alike, but all were full of the same chance: to know Him.

He never promised perfect clarity. He never promised to explain every wave or detour. But He did promise this: He's working all things for good. And He will never—never—leave us.

CHAPTER 13

IF GOD IS SOVEREIGN WHY BOTHER WITH PRAYER?

Praying for particular things," said I, "always seems to me like advising God how to run the world. Wouldn't it be wiser to assume that He knows best?"

"On the same principle," said he, "I suppose you never ask a man next to you to pass the salt, because God knows best whether you ought to have salt or not. And I suppose you never take an umbrella, because God knows best whether you ought to be wet or dry."

"That's quite different," I protested.

"I don't see why," said he. "The odd thing is that He should let us influence the course of events at all. But since He lets us do it in one way, I don't see why He shouldn't let us do it in the other."

C. S. LEWIS, *God in the Dock*[6]

"If God had granted all the silly prayers I've made in my life, where should I be now?"

C. S. LEWIS, *Letters to Malcolm*[7]

---

6. C.S. Lewis, *God in the Dock: Essays on Theology and Ethics*, ed. Walter Hooper (Grand Rapids: William B. Eerdmans, 1970)

7. C.S. Lewis, *Letters to Malcolm: Chiefly on Prayer* (San Diego: Harcourt Brace Jovanovich, 1964)

I've lost count of how many times I've sat beside someone in a hospital room—or on a saggy couch or at a kitchen table—while they looked at me with eyes full of fear and asked me to pray that God would make things turn out *the way they wanted it to.*

And honestly? That's totally normal. It's very human. We look at our situation—maybe a medical crisis, a financial train wreck, or relationship gone sour—and we imagine how it should go if everything worked out "perfectly." You know, the Hallmark movie version: No one dies, the dog gets better, the bills vanish mysteriously, and there's soup on the stove that smells like childhood.

Then we take that made-for-TV ending, and we pray, "God, please make this exact scenario happen." And sometimes—beautifully—it does. But more often, it doesn't.

And when it doesn't? That's when things get complicated. That's when people start looking at God like He missed the assignment. Or worse, they assume He heard the prayer and just yawned.

And somewhere between unanswered prayer and unmet expectations, we start to stew. We question. We get bitter. We wonder why we prayed at all.

But maybe, just maybe the problem isn't with God's response. Maybe it's with the assumption that we're the ones who know best how this thing should play out.

(And by the way, if God *had* answered every single prayer I ever mumbled, I'd be married to my fourth-grade crush and probably traveling the country on a motorcycle with a bedroll attached to the handlebars.)

So…why pray? Let's walk into that together.

* * *

My father died in 2006 at the age of 77. I loved him dearly and have missed him more and more as the years have passed. His dying process was not an easy one, especially for my mother and sisters. I was in Russia for many of those days, so the burden of care fell on them. They carried it with grace. I'm pretty sure they inherited all the family's available portions of mercy and patience.

My dad had a disease called Lewy Body Dementia, a cruel blend of Alzheimer's-like symptoms and other neurological mayhem. It's one of those conditions that slowly dismantles everything familiar. To care for someone with it requires almost saint-like compassion. And my mother and sisters? They delivered. They showed up. They comforted. They endured. I did what I could to help, but I was not nearly as gifted as they were. We all tried to support each other through the ache of watching a good and hard-working man slowly disappear from the world around him.

He had been the kind of man who earned his dignity through faithful labor and steady presence. He loved his family and worked hard. How his life changed after he came to know Christ personally is a brilliant story of God's grace. Our family changed as my father changed. Everyone would tell you that my father was a good man. But as the disease progressed, his mind and body just began to shut down one slow, frustrating piece at a time. In the final stretch he wasn't really with us anymore.

And I'll be honest here: I quietly prayed that he'd go on to heaven. Not out of impatience but mercy. It was that point in the journey where healing no longer meant recovery—it meant release.

But my mother and sisters? Their hearts were still hoping. Hoping for a turn, for a rally, for a miracle that would bring him back to us. And because they loved him deeply, they'd often ask me to pray for healing, specifically. And not just, "Please pray." No, it came with suggested scripts like, "Pray that God will restore his mind and body completely."

I couldn't do it. I mean, I *did* pray. But I couldn't pray in the exact way they asked. The words wouldn't come. It felt dishonest—like I was writing a check I knew wouldn't cash.

Were they wrong to ask for that? Was I wrong to not pray that way? I'm not sure it's even a right or wrong question. It's more like a *mystery*. A holy, aching kind of mystery that I've wrestled with for years.

And maybe you've been there too. Maybe you're there now. Staring at a situation that seems unchangeable and asking, "Why pray? If God already knows the outcome, what's the point?"

* * *

Let's go ahead and name the elephant in the pew: Most Christians struggle with prayer. Not just occasionally—regularly. It's a weird mix of desire and doubt, faith and frustration. We want to believe it matters, but often we're not sure it's *working*.

Much of that tension ties directly to how we understand God's providence. If God already knows how the story ends—if He's written the final chapter—then what difference do our little sentences make?

But here's the thing: God hasn't just ordained the end of all things; He's also ordained the *means* to that end. He's not just writing the last page. He's using our prayers, our words, our acts of faith to fill in the paragraphs. That's how He's always worked.

Take salvation, for example. Scripture tells us God already desires for all to be saved. But how does that happen? Through the preaching of the Word. Through conversations. Through prayers. Through someone brave enough to say, "I'll go."

So yes—God is sovereign. But He invites us to take part in the process. Not because He *needs* us but because He *wants* us.

Even when our prayers are clumsy. Even when our hopes feel naïve. Even when we aren't sure we're doing it right. He still listens. And somehow He still weaves our trembling requests into the fabric of His perfect plan.

As Paul writes in 1 Corinthians 1:21, "For after that in the wisdom of God the world by wisdom knew not God, it pleased God by the foolishness of preaching to save them that believe."

It's not that God *needs* preaching—He could write the Gospel in the clouds if He wanted—but He *chooses* to use it. He gives the increase, but He often does it through the faithful proclamation of His Word.

So if He's already determined who will be saved, why preach at all? Because that's the path He's chosen to get there. The preaching *is* part of the plan. And the same logic applies to prayer.

Prayer isn't us trying to change God's mind like we're lobbying Congress. Prayer is how He brings about His will through His people. He designed it that way.

So does prayer help God make up His mind? Can we somehow change the direction of the divine? Think about that for more than three seconds, and it gets absurd pretty fast. Like are we really suggesting that the all-knowing, all-wise God of the universe is waiting on *us* to give Him a better idea?

If He's working all things together for our good—and He is—then our plans aren't better than His. They can't be. And frankly, we wouldn't want a God whose best ideas came from *us*.

Prayer isn't informing God of something He missed. You're not coaching Him up with a new strategy from your kitchen table. You're not the divine project manager. He's not up there saying, "Oh wow, great point—hadn't thought of that."

And that's good news.

Because it means that when we pray, we're not twisting God's arm—we're entering into His plan. Not because He needs it but because He delights in it. He delights in us.

Jesus even said it plainly in Matthew 6:8: "Your Father knoweth what things ye have need of, before ye ask him." So there it is—the elephant with the name tag "Why Pray?" strolling through the sanctuary again. If God already knows, then why ask?

* * *

Here's the first reason: **Prayer is for our good, not God's.** God doesn't benefit from our prayers the way we benefit from water or vitamins or Wi-Fi. He doesn't gain new insights from our groaning. He's not learning anything from our late-night pleas. But we are. Every time we pray we are invited into the throne room of the universe—not as spectators but as welcomed sons and daughters. And that's not just poetic language. It's the deep, anchoring truth that should fill our hearts with courage and our bones with peace.

We're not giving Him information; we're being formed by the interaction.

Second, **prayer is not just about asking for things.** Somewhere along the way prayer became shorthand for "heavenly wish list," and that's a shame. The Psalms are full of prayers that don't ask for a single thing—just praise, thanksgiving, confession, and awe. So yes, prayer includes asking, but it also includes worshiping, confessing, thanking, and yes—just enjoying God. You might ask, "But doesn't God already know He's holy and wonderful? Isn't that a little like telling a Nobel Prize winner he's smart?" Sure. But love isn't about surprise; it's about connection.

I've got kids. Over the years, they've written me notes saying things like, "You're the best, Dad!" or "Glad you're my Dad!" I didn't keep those notes because they informed me of anything I didn't know. I kept them because they connected me to their hearts. I still pull them out and read them sometimes—not because I need a confidence boost but because I love hearing from them.

And if I, a very mortal, occasionally cranky father, feel that way—how much more does God our Father?

And while we're at it, **prayer is the gateway to gratitude.** James says every good and perfect gift comes from above. So when we say, "Thank You," we're not just being polite—we're being grounded. Gratitude stops us from becoming the kind of people who think we deserve everything and owe nothing. It humbles us and lifts Him up at the same time.

Prayer also includes confession. It's the place we go when we realize (again) that we've messed up, fallen short, or said something we shouldn't have said in a drive-thru. First John 1:9 says, "If we confess our sins, he is faithful and just to forgive us our sins, and to cleanse us from all unrighteousness." That verse has been a life raft for me more than once. God's not shocked by our sin, but He welcomes our confession. Not to shame us—but to free us.

And what about those **desperate prayers**—the kind that spill out when the wheels come off life's wagon? Those moments teach us something else: Prayer isn't about changing God's mind; it's about learning His heart.

Growing up, my mom had a plaque on the wall that read, "Prayer Changes Things." I didn't think much of it as a kid. But over time

I've come to believe it's more than just a decorative cliché. It's a deep, comforting truth. Prayer doesn't change God—but it can absolutely change **things**.

*   *   *

Look at James 5:13–18. It's a powerhouse passage about what happens when people pray with faith and sincerity:

> Is any among you afflicted? let him pray. Is any merry? let him sing psalms. Is any sick among you? let him call for the elders of the church; and let them pray over him, anointing him with oil in the name of the Lord: And the prayer of faith shall save the sick, and the Lord shall raise him up; and if he has committed sins, they shall be forgiven him. Confess your faults one to another, and pray one for another, that ye may be healed. The effectual fervent prayer of a righteous man availeth much. Elias was a man subject to like passions as we are, and he prayed earnestly that it might not rain: and it rained not on the earth by the space of three years and six months. And he prayed again, and the heaven gave rain, and the earth brought forth her fruit.

James isn't saying prayer guarantees you'll get everything you want, like a divine vending machine. If that were true, verse 16 would've said, "The prayer of a righteous man changes *everything* without fail." But it doesn't. It says it "availeth much"—that it has weight. It moves things. It matters.

And look at Paul's two very different outcomes. In Acts 16, Paul and Silas pray and sing while chained in a prison—and boom! Earthquake. Doors fly open. Chains drop. And the jailer becomes a believer. A heavenly mic drop, right?

But then in 2 Corinthians 12, Paul's dealing with some mysterious thorn in the flesh. He begs—three times—for God to take it away. God says no. But not a cold, hard no. A no with meaning: "My grace is sufficient for you, for. my power is made perfect in weakness" (v. 9).

Sometimes prayer brings earthquakes. Sometimes it brings endurance.

And that's the point: We pray because we trust the One who knows the difference.

Let me offer a frail but helpful analogy. When my kids were little, I pretty much ran the show. I knew when they should go to bed, what snacks would make them bounce off the walls, and which toys would become missiles. They could ask me for anything—but they didn't always get what they asked for. Sometimes I adjusted things to say yes. Sometimes I said no because it wasn't good for them. Sometimes I made mistakes.

But God doesn't make mistakes. Ever.

So when He hears our prayers, He isn't scrambling to recalculate the map. He's weaving those prayers—yours and mine—into His flawless plan. He can change things without ever changing *His* plan. And somehow He does this not just for us but for history, for humanity, and for eternity.

That's why we pray: not to override His will but to align with it.

And that's why we say, "If it be Thy will." Not as a disclaimer. Not as spiritual fine print. But because we trust that He sees the big picture. We don't.

I came across an old hymn recently—written by someone named

Francis L. Hess. I couldn't find much about the writer, but these words are more than enough:

> **The Master's will, for this I pray, Whatever it may be!**
> *I do not want to miss Your best; Reveal it, Lord, to me.*
> *My own desires may lead me wrong, I must consult my God;*
> *His counsel will be justified, When all the way I've trod.*
>
> **O soul of mine, delight in Him! His Word discern, obey!**
> *The plan you seek to know will then unfold from day to day.*
> *We do not live our lives alone: If I am in God's will,*
> *The lives of others will be helped, His purpose to fulfill!*
>
> **My all, O Lord, I give to You, My body, mind and soul;**
> *May all the days that lie ahead be under Your control.*

CHAPTER 14

SURELY THERE'S
A BETTER WAY

One of the most vivid windows into God's sovereignty comes in the final hours of Jesus' earthly life—when He sat with His friends for the Last Supper and then walked into the dark shadows of Gethsemane to pray. It's all there in Matthew 26:17–46: divine control and human agony side by side. And if you look closely, it gives us a rare gift—a glimpse into how both divinity and humanity wrestle with the will of God often in the same sentence.

It's fascinating, isn't it? At the table Jesus feels entirely divine—composed, insightful, prophetically calm. Then in the garden He sweats blood and pleads with His Father like a man on the edge. It's not a contradiction—it's a full picture. One moment He's breaking bread and forecasting eternity, and the next He's asking if there's any other way to redeem the world that doesn't involve Roman nails and public execution.

Now let's not forget who was around that table. These disciples had followed Him for three years—seen the miracles, heard the parables, walked through towns where people literally tried to touch

His cloak just to be healed. And still on this night of nights they're basically operating at "confused but trying." I take great comfort in that. If you've ever felt unclear or uncertain about God's plan, welcome to the club that includes Peter, James, John…and honestly, every human ever.

Jesus on the other hand knew exactly what was coming. And at that table He showed His God-credentials in unmistakable ways. First, He drops the Judas bomb (vv. 20–25)—not in a passive-aggressive way, mind you, but straight-up tells the group that one of them is about to hand Him over. You could hear the forks hit the plates.

Then He takes bread and wine—common elements of every Jewish meal—and turns them into symbols that would echo across history (vv. 26–28). He's not just predicting what's going to happen in a few hours; He's framing it. Giving meaning to the horror before it unfolds. And then in case that wasn't unsettling enough, He lifts the curtain on the future: "We'll do this again someday," He says, "in my Father's kingdom" (v. 29. Translation: This isn't the end.

But He's not done. He stuns the whole group with one more truth grenade: "You're all going to scatter. And Peter, bless your bold little heart, you're going to deny you even know Me—three times—before breakfast, before the rooster finishes waking everyone." (vv. 31–35).

And every single thing He said? It happened. Down to the rooster. Because in His divinity Jesus saw the whole picture. The cross wasn't a detour in God's plan. It *was* the plan. He wasn't surprised by betrayal or denial or soldiers in the night. He walked into it—eyes wide open, heart breaking, and still sovereign.

This story isn't just theology. It's a mirror. We see Jesus at the table and in the garden, and we realize—we often live right between those two places. Half-believing at the table, half-wrestling in the dark. And still He invites us to walk with Him. Because He already knows the ending, and He's not afraid of our confusion along the way.

· · ·

Keeping in mind His divinity, we follow them as they make their way to a place called Gethsemane. According to the Gospels and what we can gather from biblical history, this was the only time they all went there together. A quiet garden at the foot of the Mount of Olives— probably the kind of place where you'd go if you needed some solitude, maybe a few deep breaths, or just a break from people asking if you're the Messiah.

Everyone went with Him—except Judas who had officially clocked out and was off doing…well, Judas things. The kind that involve betrayal contracts and coordinated lantern signals.

Once inside the garden Jesus picked a spot and told most of the disciples to sit and wait. Then He took Peter, James, and John a little further with Him. It's kind of like when you go to the doctor and only a few people are allowed to come back into the exam room. These three, His inner circle, were invited closer. But even they would hit their limit.

As they walked ahead, something shifted. The weight of what was about to unfold began pressing down on Jesus so heavily that He had to stop. He told them, "You wait here. Keep watch." And then He walked alone into the deeper shadows.

What came next wasn't a group prayer with bowed heads and folded hands. This was raw, soul-spilling honesty. It was the kind of moment between a Son and his Father that feels too sacred for an audience. A quiet plea echoing through olive trees.

We don't know exactly how far He walked, but we know this: At some point the burden overwhelmed Him, and He collapsed to the ground. Face down. Grief fully human. And He began to pray.

But here's the surprise. He didn't pray for strength or supernatural reinforcements. He didn't even pray for the disciples, though heaven knows they could have used a "focus and don't fall asleep" miracle.

Instead, He prayed a prayer we've all whispered, one way or another: "Father, if there's any way out of this…if there's another way, I'd take it. But if not—then Your will be done." (Matthew 26:39, paraphrase).

It wasn't weak. It wasn't wavering. It was honest. Human. Holy.

And it reminds us that sometimes the most faithful prayer isn't "fix it," but "Father, I trust You—even in this."

There are many interpretations of what "the cup" represents because it's so rich with eternal weight. But for our purpose here, let's keep it simple: It's the cross. The suffering. The wrath. The full cost of redeeming a broken world.

Matthew tells us that Jesus prayed this exact prayer—not once, not twice, but three times. And with each repetition we glimpse the sacred tension rising: The divine Jesus fully aware of the plan, and the human Jesus fully immersed in the pain. This wasn't just a theological exercise—it was the heaviest moment in human history.

Let that settle in for a second. The One who best understood the Father's sovereignty—better than any theologian or preacher ever could—still asked: "Is there another way?" Not to escape it entirely but to explore if there might be a different route through the same valley.

Jesus wasn't trying to wiggle out of the mission. He was weighing it honestly. Facing it completely. And asking the most human question imaginable: "Is there any other way to accomplish this?"

And we'll never know what He may have imagined in that moment. That's part of the mystery of the incarnation. We don't get a blueprint of alternate redemptive routes. But we do get His question. And it's enough.

Maybe—and I say this reverently—He was asking something like this: "Father, I know sin must be paid for. I know what must be done. But if Your sovereignty makes room for another path, another method—then please...let this cup pass."

But here's the anchor that steadies the whole scene: "Nevertheless, not My will, but Yours be done."

There it is. The hinge of hope. The prayer that changed everything. The reason we can keep praying even when we don't understand. Even when the cup doesn't pass.

In that holy moment Jesus gave us the map. Not to predict the future—but to trust the Father. To pray honest prayers and still walk forward. To believe that sovereignty isn't just some theological wallpaper but the very structure beneath our trembling feet.

We like to excuse ourselves, don't we? "Well, I'm just a regular person. I'm not Jesus." But in Gethsemane Jesus quietly takes that excuse off the table. Because what He gives us here isn't divine muscle—it's divine surrender. And surrender is something even mortals like us can do.

In the greatest collision of heaven and earth the Son trusted the Father. And that trust held the weight of salvation itself. So maybe in our darkest moments it can hold us too.

Yet Jesus also knew something else—something we sometimes forget. Within God's sovereign plan there is still room for movement. Things can be rearranged, timing can shift, details can adjust—*without* altering the final destination. The end—salvation for mankind—was never in question. But the road to that end? That's what Jesus asked about.

So He prayed, essentially, "Is there any other way?" And then in one of the most important moments in all of human history, He added the line that echoes across the ages: "But if not, then Your will be done."

Whatever the Father's response, Jesus was settled. Not necessarily comfortable, not emotionally unburdened—but *resolved*. He knew the decision was good even if the experience would be devastating. And with that He returned to His disciples and said, "Rise! Let us go! Here comes my betrayer!" (v. 46).

It was as if the answer to His prayer had become clear. The Father's will stood firm, and Jesus was now immovably aligned with it. He didn't skip toward it joyfully—but He walked toward it faithfully. Because though it wasn't the way His human side would have chosen, it *was* the only way consistent with God's sovereign love.

And how does it end? Oh, just with the greatest story ever told. His death. His burial. And then—His glorious, stunning, history-shattering resurrection.

So what's the takeaway for us?

Here it is: Just as the Father had Jesus' good, His glory, and the salvation of the world in view in the garden, He also has *our* good, His glory, and the redemptive outcome of *our* stories in mind too. That doesn't mean the worst won't come. Sometimes it must. But if it does, it's not because God has lost control—it's because He's bringing about something even better.

Now for a moment that's both tragic and darkly ironic in Jesus' story: Judas returns. He's brought a crowd—armed, angry, and spiritually tone-deaf. Swords, clubs, lanterns. It's like a poorly organized church picnic but with weapons. And to make sure they arrest the right guy (because apparently "glowing with holiness" wasn't distinctive enough), Judas gives them a prearranged sign: "The one I kiss—that's Him."

In Eastern culture a kiss was a normal form of respectful greeting. So Judas picks that. A sacred gesture turned into a betrayal cue.

As soon as he kisses Jesus, the mob moves in. That's when Peter—God bless him—goes full action hero. He pulls out a sword and lops off a man's ear. Now we don't know if he was aiming for the ear or missed terribly while trying to hit something else, but either way—ears were flying.

Jesus with divine calm tells Peter to put the sword away. "Don't you know," He says, "that I could call on my Father right now and He would send twelve legions of angels?" (v. 53). That's about 72,000 angels. Armed. Glorious. Ready to take care of this bunch of church sponsored thugs.

Then Jesus said something that anchors it all: "But how then would the Scriptures be fulfilled, that say it must happen this way?" (v. 54).

This wasn't just resignation—it was revelation. Jesus wasn't just obeying the Father's will; He was confirming that the fulfillment of God's Word *required* this exact path. The arrest, the betrayal, the brutality—none of it was a detour. It was the main road. Paved in prophecy. And now He walked it with unwavering purpose.

What we see next is Jesus in full alignment—spirit, will, and mission. The same One who had just been face down in the garden is now standing tall before the mob. What changed? Not the circumstances. The cross was still coming. The pain was still guaranteed. But now His inner world was settled.

This is where we learn something priceless. The way Jesus processed the will of God—through honest prayer, through submission, through trust—becomes a model for how we face our own moments of darkness.

. . .

I've lived one of those moments.

I've related to you the story about Wade, my son. My prayer that day, spoken from the deepest well of a father's heart, was simple: "God, don't let my boy die."

It wasn't a theologically nuanced petition. It wasn't written in King James English. It was just raw and real: *There must be a better way. Is there a better way?*

I didn't pray it three times—I prayed it dozens. Hundreds. Desperately. Repeatedly.

And the answer I received was the same one Jesus got in Gethsemane: *No.*

Could God have saved Wade? Of course. That was well within His reach. But in His sovereignty the answer came back firm and final. And so like Jesus I was left not with the outcome I wanted—but with the assurance that it was the outcome He allowed.

Was there not an easier way for Wade to die? I must believe there wasn't.

Couldn't God have rearranged that day? Spared us that grief? Delayed that moment? Allowed that young teenage driver to avoid that tragedy in his own life? Again the answer is no. Because in the great web of His plan that day—painful as it was—became something sacred. For Wade. For me. For my family. Even for the young man who struck him. And for countless others who've since been touched by Wade's story.

It was not possible for Wade to continue living.

Not because God wasn't listening. But because in His mysterious and majestic sovereignty He was doing something deeper than we could comprehend at the time.

And if the garden tells us anything, it tells us this: Sometimes, the answer is no—not because God doesn't love us but because He does. And He sees the whole story.

It still seems to me—sitting here on this side of eternity and in my very human skin—that there must have been a better way. Just as it seemed to Jesus. From my limited, parenthetical view of life, the whole thing feels preventable. My instinct says, "This didn't have to happen."

But I don't have a God-side. I don't see the entire timeline, the ripple effects, the redemption arcs still unfolding across lives I'll never meet. So here like Jesus in the garden I must trust the One who *does* see it all. Who holds it all. And who in the end declares it good. And I must say, "Your will be done."

There must not have been another way. And accepting this was part of my journey to accepting His sovereignty. And it will be yours as well.

CHAPTER 15

FAITH THAT STEPS INTO BELIEF

This is the point of impact, the moment when truth and reality collide and you must choose: Will you believe, or will you walk away? For me, that moment came in a McDonald's parking lot, and it stayed with me for years. I had to decide whether everything I'd ever said I believed—everything I'd built my life and work around—was really true. Your moment might not come with the drama of golden arches and happy meals, but at some point every follower of Jesus hits that wall. Do I really believe?

It's easy to talk about how good God is when the skies are clear and your heart is full. On those days you barely need faith at all. You're more likely to take God for granted than to fall on your knees in desperation. We toss Him a thank you now and then, like tossing peanuts to a monkey at the zoo, while we bask in our own contentment. There's no crisis to navigate, no tears to dry, no bills piling up or diagnoses looming. Of course, God is good when everyone's healthy and the refrigerator is full.

I've seen it often—church members lifting their hands in joy on sunny days, only to unravel the moment a storm cloud rolls in. It's not a new problem. The Israelites sang with tambourines by the Red Sea one day and whined about food the next. The disciples themselves had more emotional dips than a rollercoaster at the state fair. Faith, it turns out, isn't really faith until it's all you've got.

There's a common sermon illustration that gets used more often than a favorite hymn in a Baptist church: the chair analogy. You know the one. Someone says, "Faith is like sitting in a chair. You trust it will hold you." And while that's technically true, I've always thought it was a bit flimsy. I don't think about the chair when I sit down—I just sit. I've probably sat in thousands of chairs in my life and not one of them collapsed. Honestly, I've thrown myself into chairs with zero hesitation, sometimes with the kind of reckless trust usually reserved for toddlers jumping onto bean bags.

But here's the real issue with the analogy: The chair is obvious. You can see it, touch it, hear it creak, maybe even smell it. Every one of your senses confirms it's there. It's not faith when all the evidence is right in front of you. The chair practically begs you to sit. It isn't a leap of trust—it's just gravity and habit.

Faith in God doesn't always come with that kind of sensory support. Sometimes He is quiet. Sometimes the chair is invisible. And sometimes it feels like the room is empty.

This doesn't always line up with what we expect from God. I often quote C. S. Lewis because he was both a fellow traveler through suffering and a guiding voice in my journey toward understanding God's sovereignty. In his book *A Grief Observed*, he wrote honestly about his experience of loss and God's perceived silence:

> Meanwhile, where is God?... Go to Him when your need
> is desperate, when all other help is vain, and what do you

find? A door slammed in your face, and a sound of bolting and double bolting on the inside. After that, silence. You may as well turn away...There are no lights in the windows. It might be an empty house. Was it ever inhabited? It seemed so once.... What can this mean? Why is He so present a commander in our time of prosperity and so very absent a help in time of trouble?

And then he says something that still gives me pause:Not that I am (I think) in much danger of ceasing to believe in God. The real danger is of coming to believe such dreadful things about Him.... The conclusion I dread is not "So there's no God after all," but "So this is what God's really like. Deceive yourself no longer."[8]

It's on days like that—when heaven is silent, when your spirit can't find the frequency to tune in—that faith is either revealed or exposed. Is God still good when He's quiet? Is He still present when He seems hidden? Are we abandoned, or is this what trust looks like when it costs something?

Only faith can answer those questions—and even then, it answers in a whisper. But it's not just faith in God generally; it's faith in His sovereignty specifically.

When we come to Christ, we need faith to believe the Gospel—to accept what He did for us through His death, burial, and resurrection. As we grow, we need faith to believe His Word, to trust His promises, to believe what He says about Himself. But above all else we need faith to believe that He has a plan—for our lives, for this world, for everything.

In other words, we need faith in His sovereignty. The deep-down,

---

8. C.S. Lewis, *A Grief Observed* (New York: HarperOne, 1994)

soul-level trust that no matter what the headlines say or what our hearts feel life is not spinning out of control. There is a divine and eternal plan, and it is unfolding even when it doesn't make sense.

But where does that faith come from—especially when, as Lewis said and as many of us have lived, God seems to go silent right when we need Him most? Where does faith come from when Jesus appears to be asleep in the boat and the storm is flooding your soul?

· · ·

I believe faith is at its core an act of the will. It's not a feeling. It's not a magic surge of spiritual adrenaline. It is a decision—a deliberate choice about where and in whom you will place your trust. And the truth is, everyone puts their faith somewhere. Maybe it's in a higher power. Maybe it's in another person. Often it's in ourselves.

Even those who say they believe in nothing are in a roundabout way placing their trust in that very nothingness. They are banking on the idea that the void will hold. That too is a kind of faith.

At some point we all make a decision: Where will we place our faith? I believe we can choose to trust God based on two foundational truths.

First, we can trust Him because of the truth of His Word. As we grow in our understanding of Scripture, we come to know who He really is—not just in theory but in the thick of life. We begin to grasp those rich, theologically weighty words we've heard in sermons over the years:

He is **omnipotent**—all-powerful. Genesis 18:14: "Is anything too hard for the Lord?" Psalm 115:3: "Our God is in the heavens: he hath done whatsoever he hath pleased."

He is **omniscient**—all-knowing. Psalm 147:5: "Great is our Lord, and of great power: his understanding is infinite."

He is **omnipresent**—present everywhere, always. Psalm 139:7–10:

> Whither shall I go from thy spirit? or whither shall I flee from thy presence? If I ascend up into heaven, thou art there: if I make my bed in hell, behold, thou art there. If I take the wings of the morning, and dwell in the uttermost parts of the sea; Even there shall thy hand lead me, and thy right hand shall hold me.

These are just samples. Scripture is filled from beginning to end with words that reveal a God who is able, aware, and present. A God worthy of our trust.

Second, from experience. Now we could cite again the many stories written about the hand of God in the lives of people in the Bible, but it would be redundant—helpful, yes, but repetitive. So instead we look at God's hand as He has led and sustained us throughout our own lives. If you're unsure of the evidence in your own story, just look around—there are endless accounts in the lives of others left to us in the pages of biographies, journals, and quiet testimonies. People of faith—and even some who wouldn't call themselves followers of Christ—have stories where you can trace the fingerprints of divine sovereignty in matters great and small.

Granted, we can't always connect the dots. God doesn't always show us how each event and circumstance fits into the grand mosaic. But He gives us just enough—enough clarity, enough timing, enough mercy—to keep our faith active and anchored. One of the most striking modern examples of this comes from Pastor Tim Keller, the founder of Redeemer Presbyterian Church in New York City.

Keller wasn't always on a church-planting path. In fact, in his seminary days he had very little interest in evangelism or starting a new church. But everything shifted during his final year when he took a class from a visiting professor. The course changed his outlook entirely. It ignited a passion for church planting and reshaped the direction of his ministry. But here's the part that shows just how precise God's hand can be: That professor almost didn't make it to the seminary at all.

It so happened that the professor was British. And as anyone who's ever filled out government paperwork concerning visiting other countries knows, bureaucracy loves to complicate things. There were real obstacles in getting the visa approved so the professor could travel to the U.S. and teach. Had he not come, Keller might've continued down a very different path—one that didn't involve church planting or New York City or the thousands who would eventually be touched by Redeemer's ministry.

So how did it happen?

One morning during a prayer meeting with staff the dean of the seminary Keller attended was praying about the visa situation. In that moment of honest conversation with God he essentially asked, "Lord, how are we supposed to get this professor here in time to teach?"

Sitting nearby during that prayer meeting was a student—not just any student but the son of the sitting U.S. President at the time: Gerald Ford. After the meeting the young man walked over to the dean and said, "Dean, I might be able to help. I know someone in politics who might be able to move things along."

And move things along he did. The political wheels turned, the snag was smoothed over, and the professor made it to the seminary. Keller took the class. His life changed. And Redeemer Presbyterian Church was born.

But here's where it gets even more fascinating.

Keller reflected on why that student had the influence to open the right doors. It's simple: because his father, Gerald Ford, was President. But Ford only became President because Richard Nixon resigned. And Nixon only resigned because of the Watergate scandal. And the Watergate scandal only erupted because one night a group of men broke into the Democratic National Headquarters and placed wire-taps—and when they left, they failed to close the door properly.

A night watchman noticed that the door was ajar—just two inches. That tiny gap triggered a chain of events that would eventually bring down a presidency.

Keller once said, "If that door had been closed just two inches more, there might never have been a Redeemer Church in New York."[9]

Think about that: no Nixon resignation, no Ford presidency, no well-connected seminary student, no visa solution, no visiting professor, no course that changed Keller's view of ministry, and no church plant in Manhattan.

Two inches. That's the kind of precision we're talking about when we talk about sovereignty. Not luck. Not coincidence. A divine thread stitched through history with intentionality and care.

When we look back at our own lives—our detours, delays, and disruptions—we begin to see those threads too. Sometimes it's only in hindsight that we can trace His hand. But once we do, we realize that faith isn't just rooted in theology or emotion; it's anchored in the quiet testimony of experience. And that too is enough to keep us believing.

---

9. Timothy Keller, *Encounters with Jesus* (Penguin Books, 2013)

. . .

Were these events just coincidence? Another version of the so-called "Butterfly Effect"? You could call it that—but isn't that effect simply a poetic way to describe the sovereignty of God? Call it what you want, but at its core it's divine orchestration. God's sovereign butterfly effect.

Whether you call it providence or just "how things happened to work out," you still have to answer one question: Do you believe this is how God works? That's the question each of us must wrestle with based on what we know—really know—about who He is.

And if you take a good look, you'll likely find similar threads in your own life. Maybe they didn't involve political doors opening or global scandal, but they were real. You'll see moments when the right person said the right thing or when a closed door nudged you down a better path or when timing was just too perfect to be accidental. These threads are everywhere, woven through the stories of our lives. Because this is how God works.

In His magnificence God has ordered the world to interact and intersect in ways far beyond our comprehension. Time, space, nature, people, pain, and progress—all of it moves together toward His glory and our good. When we begin to see life through that lens of faith, even storms begin to make sense. Tragedy may not disappear, but it finds purpose. Heartbreak might still ache, but it no longer feels meaningless.

And as we learn—through Scripture and through life—to see who God is and how He works, we can choose, not with a clenched jaw but with a surrendered heart to believe. Not by sheer willpower but by informed trust. This is what it means to accept His sovereignty. And this is where faith is built.

CHAPTER 16

WHEN GOD'S WAYS DON'T SEEM FAIR

"Jesus Christ did not suffer so that you would not suffer.
He suffered so that when you suffer, you'll become
more like him. The gospel does not promise you better
life circumstances; it promises you a better life."

TIM KELLER

We were in Tampa, Florida, and I was standing in front of a bulletin board in the foyer of the church where the missions conference was being held, doing what I often did in those early days after Wade died—staring at things without really seeing them. In this case it was a printed flyer. It listed the schedule of conference speakers, and I had apparently decided to review it like I was deciphering a classified CIA document. There it was: the name of the missionary currently speaking, and then—ah yes—my name, confirming that I was set to speak later that evening.

I kept staring. I wasn't really absorbing anything. That blank, vacant mental space had become familiar since Wade's death. I could be in a room full of people or Florida sunshine—like the sunlight that was beaming through the glass doors just a few feet away—and yet I'd still feel like I was carrying a thundercloud overhead. And not a poetic thundercloud either. More like the kind that follows cartoon characters who just got hit with an anvil.

My attention was pulled back to the present as the missionary who was now speaking began telling a story from his own life. It was about an automobile accident involving his young daughter. And I froze. The combination of kids, cars, and trauma was now my personal emotional tripwire. So I stayed with the story. Partly because I couldn't move and partly because I wanted to hear how it ended. Maybe—just maybe—he was one of us. One of the broken-hearted. Misery loves company, they say, though that makes us sound like a bunch of emotional pirates sailing on the bad ship Self-Pity. Really, it's just that those who suffer tend to look for others who've been to the same dark places. We want to know we're not alone. We want to know we weren't personally targeted by God for suffering these days.

We want to believe that others hurt too.

I listened as he talked about how the car his daughter was riding in had slid into the path of an oncoming truck. She was pinned in the car for what must have felt like an eternity—until a response crew could cut her free. He described the long, agonizing drive to the hospital and his whispered prayers to God, each one laced with panic and pleading. It was all too familiar. The fog, the fear, the helplessness—it stirred every raw nerve in me.

As he continued, his daughter was rushed into emergency surgery, and he waited for hours to hear the outcome. I knew that kind of waiting. That quiet, suffocating space where every tick of the clock mocks you. When the doctor finally came through the doors to deliver news, it was this: His daughter was going to live, and not only that—she would make a full recovery.

When the congregation heard this, they erupted into applause. There were shouts of "Amen!" and "Hallelujah!" ringing out like fireworks on the Fourth of July. He was smiling, radiant with the joy of answered prayer and the relief of a nightmare dodged.

But somewhere in the middle of all that holy rejoicing, a heavy and uninvited thought muscled its way into my heart. I reached up, tore the flyer off the bulletin board like it had personally offended me, and muttered out loud, "That's not fair." A few heads turned. People stared. I walked out into the Florida sun—which to me felt sarcastic and mocking.

Now don't misunderstand. I wasn't angry that his daughter had lived. Of course I was grateful for him. But underneath the polite congratulations was something darker—bewilderment. Disillusionment. A tangled mess of gratitude and grief that left me asking not, "Why did this happen to me?" but "Why didn't it happen to him?"

Was he more spiritual than I was? Did he pray with the proper theological punctuation? Was his daughter more important to the grand plan than my son? His story got a "happily ever after." Mine got a period and a cold silence.

After wandering around the courtyard of this megachurch-turned-labyrinth, I eventually went back inside. I sat quietly in the back row as the missionary displayed a family photo—his daughter smiling, surrounded by loved ones, healthy and whole. I smiled too, the kind of smile that's mostly for show. The last picture I had taken with Wade was in a cemetery.

I never talked to that missionary. Never told anyone about what was swirling in my soul that day. And truthfully I didn't talk to God about it either. Those thoughts just sat there, like uninvited guests. Heavy and rude, slumped in the corner of my mind, refusing to leave.

They just lived there for a while, and I tried to figure out how to keep living too.

I'm not proud to say it, but in those early days I found it incredibly difficult to rejoice with other parents whose stories turned out better than mine. I didn't want to hear happy endings. Not when mine felt like it had been cut short somewhere around chapter three. When someone's tragedy ends in triumph and yours ends in the kind of silence that fills a child's empty bedroom—it stings. It felt at times like God was playing favorites.

Like C. S. Lewis, I began to wonder if the real fear wasn't that God didn't exist—but that He did and that He was the kind of God who let things like this happen.

What I've found in all my travels is this: In the West people don't usually cry out, "Why?" when something painful happens. They cry, "That's not fair!" It's our go-to phrase. We're trained in it from birth. It comes baked into our democratic, rights-driven, individualistic dough. Fairness is our sacred cow—and every injustice is a reason to moo loudly.

In the East though I hear more of the simple question: "Why?" When life collapses, it's not about fairness—it's about meaning.

Western culture is steeped in the idea that we're all created equal and that we all have the same rights. That sounds noble—and in many ways, it is—but it also leads to a sense of entitlement. Fairness becomes less a virtue and more a demand. It's especially woven deep into the fabric of Gen X and Millennials. "We want fairness for everyone," they say—which often means, "I want life to be as smooth for me as it appears to be for others."

But in the Eastern countries where I've served, people aren't raised with that same script. If you've spent your whole life in a system where the state decides what you're allowed to have, what you're allowed to say, and where you're allowed to go, then fairness isn't an assumption. It's a distant rumor. Life isn't expected to be fair—it's expected to be endured.

Ironically when the idea of fairness does creep into these societies—through media, travel, or stories from the outside world—it often causes deep unrest. It plants seeds of discontent. People begin to notice that other countries have freedoms they can't imagine. They begin to question why they can't speak freely, move freely, or live freely. Fairness, once introduced, is a dangerous idea in totalitarian places.

And me? I'm fully Western. Born and raised on fairness. I wanted it. I expected it. And I definitely didn't feel like I got it.

Where was the fairness in what I had just heard in that auditorium? Why did his child live and mine die? Why do some prayers end in hallelujahs and others end in funerals? It's the question that needles its way into your mind in moments of deep loss. Fairness feels like a basic human virtue—a thing we should all be able to count on. And if God really is sovereign and good and in control, shouldn't fairness be part of the package?

Well, it turns out...it's more complicated than that. But let me offer four thoughts that might help.

1. LIFE, IT TURNS OUT, IS NOT FAIR.

I'm not plowing a new garden here with this fact, and this is not suddenly an "aha" moment for you. Injustice is everywhere in our world. And it's not new to me or this generation. The writer in Psalm 73 talks about how he was envious of the wicked when he saw their prosperity.

Psalm 37 speaks of fretting because of evildoers and being envious of workers of iniquity. Where's the fairness when the bad prosper and the good suffer? This disparity was obvious in King David's day.

Life is unfair because of sin, and we all get caught in situations that reflect the world we live in. We cannot blame God for the injustice of the world; that belongs to all of humankind. In the Garden of Eden before the fall there were no tragedies. No innocent children died, and there were no funerals for blameless victims. Adam and Eve didn't get incurable diseases. They lived in perfect surroundings. But they rebelled against God and exchanged perfection for sin and paradise for a place where awful things can and do happen.

A perfect world became unfair. After sin made it's entrance, the fittest survived, and the weakest succumbed. It began to rain on the just and the unjust at the same time. It became so that the only equality was that there was enough unfairness to go around for everyone on earth.

When my granddaughters Lanie and Vera were still in elementary school, my son, their father, began to teach them this very important lesson. Whenever something happened in their lives that was disparaging or if they saw unequal treatment either to themselves or others, he would have them repeat these words out loud, "Life is not fair."

We were traveling down the road together one day and Lanie, who is the oldest, was talking about an event that took place in a competition in which she was involved. In her story her dad simply asked, "What do we say when things like that happen?" It was obvious that this was not the first time they had been asked this question because they both replied in perfect unison, "Life is not fair!"

I thought immediately about what a good lesson that is to teach young people, and I suggest that for every parent. And if we did not learn it as a child, I suggest we embrace it at whatever age we find ourselves now.

Yes, it is a good thing to fight unfairness in this world. However, no matter how much we fight, we need to be careful to know that it will continue to be unfair until Jesus returns and makes all things right.

To say that life is not fair simply states a very obvious fact. It certainly doesn't make the pain go away; in fact, it causes more because it highlights our weak, fallen state. Like a nagging spouse or an aggravating sibling pointing at our embarrassment and offering no aid. So let's go further.

2. SINCE LIFE IS NOT FAIR, WE SHOULD BE GLAD FOR MERCY.

Fairness assumes we're owed something—and if we don't get it, we've been wronged. That's the engine of entitlement, and it's been roaring through modern society like a leaf blower at 6 a.m. But in truth, God doesn't owe us anything. Not even a refund or store credit. He deals with sinners in only two ways: justice or mercy. If you want justice—if you demand fairness—then be prepared to get exactly what you deserve. And I don't mean that in a warm, fuzzy, grandma-knitting-you-a-scarf kind of way.

In God's economy what we *deserve* is judgment. Which is why mercy is the best news ever printed.

We often hear the question, "Why do bad things happen to good people?" But theologically speaking, we've got that backwards. We're not good people. We're sinners in need of a Savior. The only truly good person to walk this earth was Jesus, the Son of God—and something terrible happened to Him. He became the substitute, the perfect sacrifice, the One who took all the bad so we could receive all the good.

A better question might be, "Why do good things happen to bad people?" And the answer is mercy.

Psalm 103 spells it out: "He does not treat us as our sins deserve or repay us according to our iniquities.... As far as the east is from the west, so far has he removed our transgressions from us."

That's mercy.

When I first began working in rural Russia, I visited tiny villages that looked like they'd missed several decades of progress. Think 1930s. Indoor plumbing was rare, and drawing water from a community well was just how things were done. In one village there was an elderly woman named Alyona who lived with her husband Sergei—a professional scoundrel if there ever was one. Sergei didn't provide, didn't care, and didn't really bother pretending.

At first whenever we came by with aid, Sergei would disappear like we were the KGB. But we always brought food, blankets, medicine—basic humanitarian aid. And no matter how much of a grouch Sergei was, we always left supplies at their house. Not for him, honestly, but for Alyona. We knew she'd share. Over time Sergei warmed up, and we developed somewhat of a relationship. He would come out and meet me with a toothless smile and a calloused handshake when I came to visit.

Eventually I handed off that village outreach to a trusted Russian friend who couldn't deliver aid in quite the same way. Several months later I returned to visit. Sergei was back to hiding again. Word got to me that he was angry—furious, even—that we had stopped bringing him things. He felt abandoned, mistreated, and yes...unfairly treated.

Let's pause here a moment. Before we showed up, Sergei had nothing. No one gave him anything. He didn't earn a living, and he didn't do anything to improve his life. Then we came along—uninvited—and gave freely. He didn't deserve it, ask for it, or earn it. But we gave it anyway.

And once that undeserved stream of mercy dried up, his reaction when I returned was to yell at me from his rickety porch like I was the villain in his story: "Don't come back unless you've got something for me!"

Did Sergei have a right to be upset? Not at all. Was he being treated unfairly? Again, no. He was simply no longer receiving what he never had a claim to in the first place.

That story has stuck with me—because, honestly, it's how we often treat God. We come into the world already in spiritual debt. Because of our inherited sin, we start with nothing and deserve nothing. And yet God gives us life, breath, beauty, and a hundred daily gifts we can't even catalog. He offers salvation, joy, and the promise of eternal life. But if one of those countless blessings gets pulled back— or if we face tragedy—suddenly He's cold. He's distant. He's unfair.

The truth is, pain skews our perspective. We forget that we live in mercy every single day. And when mercy pauses, we cry foul—as if justice would've been better.

But justice would have destroyed us. Mercy saves us.

It's not the Giver who causes the pain. It's the world that's broken and the hearts that have twisted the gifts. God gives anyway.

Job said it best: "The Lord gives, and the Lord takes away. Blessed be the name of the Lord."

3. IT IS IMPOSSIBLE FOR US TO DETERMINE IF SOMETHING IS FAIR OR NOT BECAUSE OUR MEMORIES ARE FAULTY.

When our lives are suddenly changed by events we can't control, we tend to remember those moments with eerie clarity. The sights, the sounds, even the smells—we relive them in slow motion. In the early chapters of this book, I shared the event that shattered my life. I remember it in detail. I'll never forget it.

But memory is a tricky thing. At first we recall the events with raw accuracy. But give it time—and suddenly we're not just remembering the moment, we're editing it. Pain sharpens some parts, blurs others. Emotions take over the script. The story gets retold in our heads but with subtle updates that weren't in the original draft.

It's why fish grow larger the farther you are from the lake. And why some of us were apparently Olympic-caliber athletes in high school—just ask us.

If a moment brought sorrow, the sorrow grows deeper with every passing year. If it brought joy, the joy becomes more magical. And somewhere in all that reprocessing, the line between truth and feeling gets fuzzy.

This is dangerous when we try to assess fairness. Because now we're comparing what we think happened—not just to us, but to others—to a constantly evolving narrative that may not be quite as accurate as we believe. I've met elderly men and women who aged into bitterness, not because the event itself was unbearable but because their memory of it was.

Years ago when I was fresh in ministry, I met a man who would've been a shoo-in for a role in *Grumpy Old Men*. He smiled only when it was absolutely required by law. One day he opened up to me about a hurt he had carried for years—something his wife had said to him that according to him changed how he viewed her forever.

I listened. And based on his telling, I couldn't blame him. It sounded cold, even cruel.

But later—completely unprompted—his wife shared the same story. And her version? It wasn't cruel at all. In fact, it was meant as a joke. A lighthearted comment. Somewhere between her mouth and his ears a miscommunication had transformed into a wound. And over the years he had watered and fed that wound until it grew roots and became part of who he was.

To my knowledge they never resolved it. His memory of that moment was the one he chose to live with. And it darkened the rest of his life.

I've seen this again and again. Friendships broken. Families torn apart. Churches split—because of memory. Because the longer we hold on to a moment, the more room our emotions have to tamper with it.

So when we ask, "Was that fair?" we're often asking it from a flawed premise. From a place where pain has rewritten the facts.

That's why forgiveness, reconciliation, and perspective are so critical. Offenses left unaddressed don't just remain—they grow. And when they grow, so does our sense that life has mistreated us.

Sometimes the thing we're most angry about never happened the way we remember it. And fairness as we see it becomes just another version of that edited story.

It's not that we shouldn't grieve. Or feel. Or even wrestle. But we should do so humbly, knowing that our memories—like our hearts—aren't always trustworthy narrators.

4. FINALLY, IT IS IMPOSSIBLE FOR US TO DETERMINE WHETHER SOMETHING IS FAIR OR NOT BECAUSE WE CAN SEE ONLY THE PAST AND PRESENT.

We can't see even one second into the future. Not even a peek. But God can.

This means we can't see how life *might have* unfolded if that painful event hadn't happened. But God can. That's why He either causes or allows the things that come to pass. He sees what we cannot. And He knows what is ultimately best for us.

God's timeline isn't a line at all—at least not from His perspective. He's outside of time. Above it. Beyond it. He sees it all at once like a finished painting. We, on the other hand, are like ants crawling across a single brushstroke.

We live *in* time. We see only the past—often fuzzily—and the present, which is usually overwhelming. But the future? That's all guesswork. And most of our guesses are about as accurate as weather forecasts made based on someone's bad knee.

In our minds things should always work out for the best. Happy endings. Clear skies. Safe landings. That's what we imagine is good for us. So when tragedy strikes, we assume something has gone terribly wrong. Especially if that tragedy ends in death. Because death, in our limited view, is the worst-case scenario.

Or is it?

In my deepest grief, in my desperate prayers, I imagined only one good outcome—my boy lives. I couldn't picture anything worse than losing him.

But what if God saw something different? Something I couldn't possibly have seen from where I stood? What if Wade's death spared someone from something worse? What if God in His perfect vision was protecting me, my family, or even Wade himself from a sorrow deeper than I can now imagine?

The truth is, I don't know. And I may never know. But God does. And this is where I must fall into His sovereignty, not because I understand it but because I trust the One who does.

In 1932 A. M. Overton was a pastor in Mississippi. He and his wife had three small children and were expecting a fourth. But during delivery complications arose—and both his wife and their unborn child died.

At the funeral as another minister preached, Overton was seen writing something on a piece of paper. After the service the minister asked about it, and Overton quietly handed him what he had written. It was a poem.

He Maketh No Mistake
A. M. Overton

My Father's way may twist and turn,
My heart may throb and ache,
But in my soul I'm glad I know,
He maketh no mistake.

My cherished plans may go astray,
My hopes may fade away,
But still I'll trust my Lord to lead
For He doth know the way.

Though night be dark and it may seem
That day will never break;
I'll pin my faith, my all in Him,
He maketh no mistake.

There's so much now I cannot see,
My eyesight's far too dim;
But come what may, I'll simply trust
And leave it all to Him.

For by and by the mist will lift
And plain it all He'll make,
Through all the way, though dark to me,
He made not one mistake.[10]

---

10. A. M. Overton, He Maketh No Mistake, poem, 1932

CHAPTER 17

THE ACHE OF "NOT ENOUGH"

As I have lived since that day of Wade's passing and even now as I write, I am constantly reminded that no matter what I write—and no matter how truthful it is—there will always be this unfiltered, stubborn, very loud part of me that says: *If I had it to do over, I'd rather have my son alive than dead.*

I know, I know—deep spiritual truths, God's sovereignty, eternal plans, Romans 8:28, all that. And I believe them. I really do. But if you gave me a button that said *Press Here to Have Wade Back,* I wouldn't hesitate to press.

Even though I know that all will work out for good someday, I still want my son back. How can I not say that? Isn't that just the human thing to say? To want the one you love more than the outcome, more than the lessons, more than the silver linings?

I don't know anyone who would argue that—and if they do, I'd be very suspicious of whether they've ever actually lost anything more serious than a TV remote.

I once read the story of a man whose son also died tragically. As he recounted the awful event and its long echo through his life, he said he could see that good things had come from it. Some family members even turned to Christ because of it.

And yet—at the end of telling it all—he paused and said, "But it's not enough. It's not enough."

On my worst days, I echo his sentiment...and on my best days. Take all the good things that might come in the backwash of that day and make them happen some other way; just give me my son back. All those good things are not enough.

When we come up for air as we thrash and splash through our disasters and seek desperately for something to hold onto to stay above water, lifelines are thrown out by well-meaning people, many of whom have never felt the horror of groping and gasping for life. They send out answers to our questions that are correct as far as they go but so desperately unsatisfying. We are thankful, of course, and polite. Yet the ache remains.

There are always ways in which we can, rightly so, see that every situation, even the tragic death of a child, will work for the glory of God. But the parents of that child can be forgiven for crying, "Let God get His glory somewhere else; give us our child back." I know I did. We had other children remaining when Wade died. Someone tried to comfort me by saying, "Thank God, you still have other boys left." However, as precious as they are to me, it was hollow. Nothing could replace the one boy who died. I do not blame the person who said it as there is no way unless he had experienced something similar in his own life that he could have understood my perspective. Your own personal tragedy is the most tragic. No other person's explanation will suit your deepest agony.

* * *

Kierkegaard said, "Life can only be understood backwards; but it must be lived forwards."[11] Regardless of what you think of his theology, that's a truth worth remembering. As I have said and as the old song goes, "We'll understand it better, by and by." Kierkegaard questioned why God's ways often become clear in hindsight only after individuals have already gone through suffering and hardship and in some cases lived an entire lifetime only to find the answers await in eternity. Why not now?

Having said all of that, I fully believe that someday "by and by" when all is revealed, I will be able to put this ache aside and gloriously see that everything that God did was the best way possible. I will be satisfied with the reason, and the ache will be gone. However, that day is not today, and there is still a hole in my heart and questions in my mind and soul.

In fact, I want to make a confession. There are stories I've read in the Bible that when I finish with them, sometimes leave me with more questions than answers. Honestly, I have questioned the outcome of stories and said out loud in my human logic, "I would have done that differently." Also, as long as I'm confessing, I'll tell you that there are times when I wonder why God didn't just give us the story and immediately tell us the reason why, giving an accompanying moral to the story. Even Aesop did that. Seems like God would draw a conclusion for us who are weak-minded sheep. Not so. We are simply left to scratch our spiritual heads for a lifetime. We can throw out lines of conjecture and assumption along with

11. Søren Kierkegaard, *Journals and Papers*, ed. and trans. Howard V. Hong and Edna H. Hong (Bloomington: Indiana University Press, 1967)

really neat conspiracy theories, but in the end we're left with a dull sense of "I don't get it." (The very essence of that scenario causes me to question why.)

Let me give you a couple of examples of my whys from Scripture. Back to the story of Job. Kinda obvious. There are so many lessons that are obvious from his story and a lot that after thousands of years are still not clear. We have to say right away what a great man Job was. It would not be an exaggeration to say that he is among the greatest of all men of all time. If you know the story, then you know how he lived through the nightmare of all nightmares and came out of that lengthy ordeal as an unscathed model for mankind till today. While I'm glad for the example, I've got questions. Partly because he was such a great guy, I've got questions.

The book of Job is all about the very subject of the book you're reading right now: the nature of suffering and God's sovereignty. Yet just like in my own story and yours there are lingering heart-wrenching questions that are not answered in Job's story and in ours. Why did God give the audience to the devil in the first place? Why the extreme? Wouldn't the loss of crops and cattle have sufficed to make the point? Why did all the children have to die? Did the knife need to be plunged so deeply? It's not like Job was insensitive or so stupid to not have been able to be tried by fire instead of hell on earth. While we make our suggestions and theories and while they may all be correct, I'm still left saying, "I would have done that differently." We are never provided with clear answers in this story as to why Job's losses were so drastic.

We do know how his fortune is eventually restored and even a new family is given, but in the end I wonder if Job wasn't left wondering about a lot of things himself? He said in Job 1:21, "The Lord gives and the Lord takes away. Blessed be the name of the Lord" Was it because he didn't have answers, and so he frankly threw up his hands and said, "I don't get it, but so be it. Bless God"? Is that the better way to interpret that verse? It's kinda like reading an email, it's all in how you infer the emotion of the sentence. Hard to tell.

Another confusing story. In Acts 12:1–2, we have the epitaph of one of the twelve disciples, James. It is brief and seems to be insufficient, but that's not the point, even though it appears to be a slight and another "I wonder why" moment. The verses simply say, "Now about that time Herod the king stretched forth his hands to vex certain of the church. And he killed James, the brother of John with the sword." In the context of the book of Acts, James' martyrdom is sudden and comes with no prelude. In fact, it is early in the ministry of the apostles after Jesus' resurrection. It is recorded that James was killed with a sword. End of story. No explanation to a life totally given to Jesus and then not given the opportunity to be a part of the groundwork of the very thing he devoted his life to. Why did James die while others like Peter and John lived longer and continued their ministries? His death raises questions about why his life was cut short in contrast to his peers, particularly since James' ministry is not expanded upon in the text, leaving us to wonder why he was singled out.

We could go through many other stories that make me ask the why question, only to have them left unanswered. I think that just like the man in the story I recounted earlier, if you gave the standard answers that we use for why to the people in the stories, they would also reply to you, "It's not enough. I'd rather have my children back. My time back. My life back." And yet they are left, we are left, only with the ache.

I can genuinely say that in spite of the fog, my faith is not shaken at all. Nevertheless, I need to know what conclusions we can draw from God's lack of explanation.

Through the years I've come to understand that the Bible as well as life is full of unanswered whys. With the passing of time and with a deeper study, they only grow.

By the way, I'm not the only sheep in the worldwide herd who has questioned. C. S. Lewis is among my favorite "questioners" in life. He wrote an entire book, *The Problem of Pain*, that deals with the subject of the goodness and love of God when pain is concerned. Martin Luther wrote, "If God has spoken, why is there not peace, instead of war, tribulation, suffering, and sin?"

So surrounded in a life of question marks, especially concerning deeply important subjects, how DO we reconcile them in order to keep our spiritual balance? I urge you to read about the many good men in the Bible who've run the race before me and learn how they navigated their journeys through this maze. However, for now, I will try to explain what has helped me the most.

Since the fall of man there has been a resulting tension between human understanding and the mystery of God's ways; this tension is highlighted in many Bible stories. In most of these cases, as we said, God's purpose and actions are not fully explained. This lack of explanation gives us the ability then to have the very faith that is necessary to build our trust in Him.

. . .

Let me tell you something that on first read will probably not make sense. But chew on it a bit and see if you can't get some real sustenance. Here it is: The very fact that God's ways are beyond figuring out gives us reason to trust more strongly in His magnificent sovereignty. In His glory God is a mystery. His mind and wisdom are beyond our reach, and He reserves the answers for His own unfathomable desires. God simply calls on us to trust that He will work it out for our good and His glory. Read these verses slowly and allow their power to convince you.

> **Isaiah 55:8–9**—"For my thoughts are not your thoughts, neither are your ways my ways," declares the Lord. "As the heavens are higher than the earth, so are my ways higher than your ways and my thoughts than your thoughts"

> **Romans 11:33–34**—"Oh, the depth of the riches of the wisdom and knowledge of God! How unsearchable his judgments, and his paths beyond tracing out! 'Who has known the mind of the Lord? Or who has been his counselor?'"

> **Job 11:7–9**—"Can you fathom the mysteries of God? Can you probe the limits of the Almighty? They are higher than the heavens above—what can you do? They are deeper than the depths below—what can you know?"

> **Ecclesiastes 3:11**—"He has made everything beautiful in its time. He has also set eternity in the human heart; yet no one can fathom what God has done from beginning to end"

> **Psalm 147:5**—"Great is our Lord and mighty in power; his understanding has no limit"

> **Proverbs 3:5–6**—"Trust in the Lord with all your heart and lean not on your own understanding; in all your ways submit to him, and he will make your paths straight"

Isaiah 40:28—"Do you not know? Have you not heard? The Lord is the everlasting God, the Creator of the ends of the earth. He will not grow tired or weary, and his understanding no one can fathom"

1 Corinthians 2:9—"However, as it is written: 'What no eye has seen, what no ear has heard, and what no human mind has conceived'—the things God has prepared for those who love him"

Deuteronomy 29:29—"The secret things belong to the Lord our God, but the things revealed belong to us and to our children forever, that we may follow all the words of this law"

Psalm 139:6—"Such knowledge is too wonderful for me, too lofty for me to attain"

Jeremiah 10:12—"But God made the earth by his power; he founded the world by his wisdom and stretched out the heavens by his understanding"

1 Corinthians 1:25—"For the foolishness of God is wiser than human wisdom, and the weakness of God is stronger than human strength"

Psalm 18:30—"As for God, his way is perfect: The Lord's word is flawless; he shields all who take refuge in him"

Psalm 92:5—"How great are your works, Lord, how profound your thoughts!"

These verses let us know that though we may wrestle with the mysteries of God's ways, the nature of divine justice, and the meaning of obedience, we will never fully come to the place where we will grasp them. Like it or not, the many, many whys of life in God are beyond human reach. Is that bad? Just the opposite. They serve as reminders of the limitations of human perspective when matched up beside God's wisdom, prompting us to trust God's purposes and sovereignty even when those answers are not immediately apparent.

We live today exactly as the apostle Paul described in 1 Corinthians 13:12: "For now we see through a glass, darkly; but then face to face: now I know in part; but then shall I know even as also I am known."

In other words, right now it's murky. We're squinting through a foggy windshield, trying to read God's handwriting on the wall—and most of us forgot our spiritual glasses. We don't see the answers, and they're not arriving by certified mail. Until the darkness lifts we trust God. For now why will have to sit in the waiting room—and trust will have to carry the weight.

Our pride insists that we deserve an answer. But His holiness says, "Have faith." His wisdom says, "Be still." And the Spirit gently whispers, "You're not God, remember?"

○ ○ ○

Let me tell you how this played out in real life for me. My father was a simple man. Raised on a farm by a hard-working, uneducated father who raised five children on grit, prayer, and probably bacon grease. Their relationship wasn't what you'd call emotionally rich. It was more like a handshake and a head nod at harvest time. But it was what it was, and from that soil grew the father I had.

They called him Rudy at the factory where he worked. His full name was Rudolph, and he passed that name on to me. Neither he nor I used that formal name on a daily basis. He always needed over-time and welcomed it and quietly raised a family he could be proud of. I'm proud to be a Thigpen—and proud of the father God gave me.

Now he wasn't what you'd call an expert in child psychology. He didn't have a bookshelf full of parenting manuals or an app that tracked our feelings. But he had something better: real-life wisdom—the kind you earn when you work hard, love as best you know how, and don't talk just to hear yourself talk.

As kids when we were told something, we'd ask the inevitable question: "But why, Daddy?" And sometimes if we really needed it, he'd explain. But other times—especially when we were just being ornery—he'd respond with something that has lived in my head ever since: **"There ain't got to be no why."**

That was it. That was the whole answer. No charts. No graphs. Just trust me, son. While modern parenting might squirm at that response, I'm here to say—it was holy. There *are* times to explain everything in loving detail to your kids. And there are other times when you say, "Because it's right and I told you to do it."

And I believe our Heavenly Father sometimes says exactly the same thing. Ask Him your questions. Wrestle. Cry. Get honest. But sometimes, in response, He'll quietly say: **"My child…there doesn't get to be a why. Not yet. Just trust Me."**

And in those moments faith means putting your hand over your mouth, and your heart into His. As our knowledge of and fellow-ship with God deepens, the more we will trust Him, and the more we trust Him, the less our need to understand. Once we recognize this, peace of mind and with God lies within our reach.

CHAPTER 18

WHERE GUILT MEETS GRACE AND SOVEREIGNTY

*Digory thought of his Mother, and he thought of the great
hopes he had had, and how they were all dying away, and
a lump came into his throat and tears in his eyes, and he
blurted out: 'But please, please—won't you—can't you give
me something that will cure Mother?' Up till then he had
been looking at the Lion's great feet and the huge claws on
them; now, in his despair, he looked up at its face. What
he saw surprised him as much as anything in his whole
life. For the tawny face was bent down near his own and
(wonder of wonders) great shining tears stood in the Lion's
eyes. They were such big, bright tears compared with
Digory's own that for a moment he felt as if the Lion must
really be sorrier about his Mother than he was himself.*

*'My son, my son,' said Aslan. 'I know. Grief is
great. Only you and I in this land know that
yet. Let us be good to one another.'"*

C. S. LEWIS, *The Magician's Nephew* [12]

---

12. C.S. Lewis, *The Magician's Nephew* (New York: Macmillan, 1955)

*"We are not the playwright, we are not the producer, we
are not even the audience. We are on the stage. To play
well the scenes in which we are in concerns us much
more than to guess about the scenes that follow it."*

C. S. LEWIS, *The World's Last Night* [13]

After Wade died, the first thing I *should* have done was sit my family down and talk about what had just happened. But I didn't.

At the time I couldn't even begin to process what had happened, much less lead anyone else through it. My emotional capacity was like an overloaded circuit breaker—one more jolt and the whole system was going dark.

So instead of dealing with it I dodged it. Not with grace. More like a guy in flip-flops trying to outrun a bear. When the memories surfaced, I swatted them away like annoying pesky flies. And when that didn't work, I just tried to drown them in busyness, still determined to fulfill our mission.

I couldn't even look at a photo of Wade. The thought of him was like accidentally touching a hot stove—you learn quick to yank your hand back. I couldn't bear to hear his voice in home videos or see his name written on anything. Every reminder was a tiny ambush.

We had this little family routine in those years when we were younger—everyone lined up their shoes just inside the garage door. It was like a sacred ritual of suburban life. But after Wade died, I couldn't handle the sight of his little shoes sitting there, looking like

---

13. C.S. Lewis, *The World's Last Night and Other Essays* (New York: Harcourt, Brace & World, 1960)

they were still waiting for him. So before I came home from the hospital, I asked someone to remove them. It felt like betrayal, but at the time it also felt like survival.

So to have gathered everyone together and made that tragic day the focus of our conversation? That was the complete opposite of my defense system. It was like inviting all the pain to come sit down and have coffee. I can offer you some very solid reasons—actually, let's call them what they are: excuses—for why I didn't do it. But none of them are good enough. I should have done it, not for me but for the sake of my family.

It wasn't until twenty-five years later that I finally did what I should've done on day one. I called everyone together, all were now adults, for the long overdue meeting. We gathered in a circle in our home on a weekday evening—just ordinary couches, ordinary people, talking about the most extraordinary pain of our lives. I started first, walking step by step through the events of that day. I tried to reconstruct the moments leading up to the accident, the awful hours that followed, and even the funeral. It wasn't a polished speech—it was a painful, clumsy replay of the hardest day I've ever lived.

When I got to the end, I shared what had weighed on me more than anything else over the years: guilt. That crushing sense that I had failed in my most sacred job—to protect my family. I had carried that invisible backpack full of guilt around for decades. Turns out, I wasn't the only one.

One by one, we went around the circle. And as each family member spoke, something unexpected happened. Everyone—every single one—shared some form of guilt. They all felt like they had contributed to Wade's death. Either they didn't do enough, they did too little, or they simply weren't there in a way they believed they should've been. The details varied, but the burden was the same. I had been carrying my guilt alone, completely unaware that everyone else had quietly packed their own.

After all these years in the school of God's sovereignty—and let me tell you, this is no community college course—I truly believe that what I'm writing in this book is the answer to guilt in the wake of grief. Especially the kind of guilt that attaches itself like a shadow after the death of a loved one.

But guilt is sneaky. It's persistent. And it's often misunderstood. Because it's so common—and so capable of wrecking us—we need to pause here and unpack it a bit. What it is, where it comes from, and what on earth we're supposed to do with it.

WHAT IS GUILT?

Guilt is that uncomfortable emotional backpack we strap on when we realize we've done something wrong—or as it relates to God, when we violate His moral standard. It's often accompanied by remorse, regret, and a gnawing sense that we broke something we were supposed to protect. And no matter how much we tighten the straps, we can still feel its weight.

But here's the thing: Guilt isn't always the enemy. In fact, when it shows up in the right way, it can be a holy nudge from God. It's like the flashing check engine light on the dashboard of your soul—unpleasant, yes, but potentially life-saving.

For those who haven't completely silenced their conscience with distractions, justifications, or busyness, guilt can actually be a helpful guide. It's that internal signal telling us, "Hey, that wasn't right. You need to do something about this." For the believer that signal is often the voice of the Holy Spirit letting us know we've stepped out of alignment with God's will or hurt someone in our path.

So while guilt can crush us when mishandled, it can also correct us when received humbly. The trick is learning to discern when it's from God and when it's just our inner critic going full drama mode again.

TWO TYPES OF GUILT

There are two types of guilt, and knowing the difference can be the difference between spiritual health and emotional exhaustion. If we can sort them out clearly, we can respond the right way—embracing true guilt as a holy invitation to change and rejecting false guilt like a bad email scam.

True or Godly Guilt

This is the kind of guilt that actually helps. It brings a legitimate awareness of sin and a tug in the heart that says, "You need to make this right." It prompts confession, repentance, reconciliation—and spiritual growth. It's the work of the Holy Spirit, not some cosmic guilt trip. For a believer this kind of guilt keeps the compass pointing north. You want this kind of guilt. It's not a wrecking ball; it's a lighthouse.

False or Unhealthy Guilt

This one's sneaky. It doesn't come from actual sin—it grows out of unmet expectations, twisted messages, or manipulative voices that don't know when to stop. This kind of guilt leads to shame, paralysis, and a spiritual fog that won't lift. It weighs you down with things you were never meant to carry. And worse, it often shows up wearing the disguise of "righteous responsibility," making it even harder to recognize. But it's not from God—it's from fear, misunderstanding, or the enemy himself. And it has no business setting up camp in your soul.

ILLUSTRATION OF TRUE GUILT

Bill is a manager at a company. During a particularly stressful meeting, he loses his temper and unleashes a tirade on one of his employees—loud, harsh, and totally unnecessary. The employee is left embarrassed and hurt, and the room gets that awkward, frozen-silence vibe.

Later that day Bill replays the moment in his mind. And instead of justifying it ("Well, stress happens!") or blaming it on stress or pressure, he feels the full weight of what he did. Not just because it could hurt his reputation but because he knows it violated God's call to kindness, respect, and self-control.

That uncomfortable, soul prodding feeling? That's true guilt.

It leads Bill to apologize sincerely to the employee and commit to managing leadership in healthier ways. He doesn't just regret the moment—he learns from it. He grows. He changes.

This kind of guilt doesn't condemn. It convicts. And that's the difference. As Paul writes in 2 Corinthians 7:10, "Godly sorrow brings repentance that leads to salvation and leaves no regret" That's the beauty of true guilt: It doesn't leave us stuck—it leads us somewhere better.

ILLUSTRATION OF FALSE GUILT

John is a young father who like many fathers works long hours to support his family. He feels an enormous amount of pressure—not just from his job but from society, Twitter, parenting blogs, and the imaginary panel of judges that lives in his head. Although he makes intentional time for his children and loves them deeply, he feels guilty every time he can't make it to a school concert or a field trip.

Even when his wife and kids thank him for his sacrifice and say, "It's okay, Dad—we know you're working hard," that little voice still nags: *You're not doing enough.*

But here's the truth: John's guilt isn't anchored in actual wrongdoing. He hasn't abandoned his family. He hasn't acted selfishly. He's just being pulled by internal expectations and external pressures that tell him he should be everywhere, all the time, with boundless energy and marvelous parenting skills.

This kind of guilt doesn't lead to repentance—it leads to exhaustion. It's not constructive; it's corrosive. And most importantly it's not from God.

Unlike true guilt which comes from the Holy Spirit to lead us toward repentance and restoration, false guilt comes from unrealistic standards, misplaced comparisons, and sometimes straight from the enemy himself. It masquerades as moral sensitivity, but it's actually spiritual sabotage.

Romans 8:1 is God's official memo to all the Johns of the world: "There is now no condemnation for those who are in Christ Jesus" In other words—God's not the one sending those guilt notifications. You can block that sender.

False guilt doesn't build—it breaks. And it keeps good people from living in the grace they've already been given. If it's not leading you to freedom, it's not from the Father.

BIBLICAL ILLUSTRATION OF TRUE GUILT
David's Sin with Bathsheba
BIBLICAL REFERENCE: 2 SAMUEL 11–12; PSALM 51

The story of King David's adultery with Bathsheba and the orchestrated death of her husband Uriah stands as one of Scripture's most sobering reminders of human failure—and one of its most powerful testimonies to true guilt and repentance. After the prophet Nathan confronts David, the weight of what he has done crashes down on him. His guilt isn't abstract or theoretical—it's deeply personal and painfully real.

In Psalm 51, we see his broken spirit on full display: "For I know my transgressions, and my sin is always before me. Against you, you only, have I sinned and done what is evil in your sight" (vv. 3–4). That's not damage control. That's confession. And it comes from true guilt.

David's response wasn't to rationalize, deflect, or downplay. He didn't call it a lapse in judgment or blame stress. He owned it, wept over it, and turned back to God with a humbled heart. And what followed was the very fruit of true guilt—repentance, forgiveness, and restoration.

Countless believers across the centuries have clung to David's prayer in Psalm 51. I know I have. It's been a lifeline in my own seasons of brokenness. True guilt, as painful as it may be, has a redemptive purpose: to lead us back to God's mercy.

BIBLICAL ILLUSTRATION OF FALSE GUILT
Elijah's Despair in the Wilderness
BIBLICAL REFERENCE: 1 KINGS 19:1–18

After one of the most dramatic victories in the Old Testament—calling down fire from heaven and proving God's power over Baal—Elijah flees for his life. Jezebel threatens him, and despite everything he's just witnessed, Elijah runs into the wilderness and collapses under a broom tree, praying, "I have had enough, Lord .... Take my life; I am no better than my ancestors" (v. 4).

This isn't just fear—it's exhaustion laced with false guilt. Elijah, overwhelmed and burned out, believes he has failed. His ministry seems pointless. His courage has vanished. And he's convinced he's let God down.

But God doesn't meet Elijah with condemnation. He doesn't say, "Where's your faith?" Instead He lets Elijah sleep. Then He sends an angel—not with a lecture but with a meal. Twice.

Only after Elijah has eaten and rested does God invite him into deeper conversation. And in that gentle whisper on Mount Horeb God reassures Elijah that he is not alone, not forgotten, and not a failure.

Elijah's false guilt came from believing his calling rested solely on his shoulders. That the outcome depended entirely on him. But God reminded him: "You're not the only one. There are still 7,000 in Israel who have not bowed to Baal."

False guilt tells us we're not doing enough—even when we're faithfully doing what God asked. It whispers that our fear, fatigue, or discouragement is failure. But God meets us with rest, nourishment, and reassurance.

Romans 8:1 breaks through even wilderness despair: "There is now no condemnation for those who are in Christ Jesus" Not for prophets under broom trees. Not for exhausted servants. Not for you.

God doesn't shame Elijah for being human. He restores him so he can keep going. False guilt would have left him under the tree. But grace whispered, "Get up and eat...the journey is too much for you without help."

By understanding the nature of true and false guilt believers can respond appropriately: embracing true guilt as a call to repentance and change, while rejecting false guilt as an unhelpful burden that God never intended us to carry. False guilt doesn't just drain your energy—it distorts the character of God. And when we confuse the two, we often find ourselves apologizing for things we never did and ignoring the things we probably should address.

On a Sunday morning twenty years after Wade died, I found myself pulling into the parking lot of a McDonald's in Ellijay, Georgia—the very one where that unforgettable day had begun. I wasn't there for breakfast. This was a pilgrimage, not for pancakes but for peace. I retraced the steps of that day, from that fast-food counter to the hospital just a few miles away, revisiting the scenes that had replayed in my heart for two decades.

I walked them slowly, like a man taking off a heavy coat he didn't realize he'd been wearing all this time. As I walked, I searched my heart, examined my memories, and brought everything into the light. And there in that small mountain town on an otherwise ordinary Sunday I laid it all at the cross. I told Jesus the truth: "I did everything I knew to do. I loved him. I protected him. I wasn't perfect, but I was present."

And in that moment I claimed the promise of Romans 8:1 not just as a verse—but as a verdict: "There is now no condemnation for those who are in Christ Jesus"

I didn't cause Wade's death. I didn't contribute to it. And finally I believed it. Wade's time was up—not because I failed—but because in God's mysterious and sovereign plan that chapter was finished. I still don't understand it. But I can rest in it.

And here's the part that surprised me: The cure for both true guilt and false guilt is exactly the same. Bring it to the cross. Whether it's real or imagined, heavy or subtle, justified or whispered in your ear by your inner critic—bring it to Jesus. Lay it down, and ask Him to carry it. Because He already has.

There's no point in carrying a burden He already paid for.

As I've grown in my understanding of God's sovereignty, the guilt that once haunted me has finally loosened its grip. That August day still matters—but it no longer defines me.

CHAPTER 19

FACING ANXIETY WITHOUT BECOMING A MONK

*"God whispers to us in our pleasures, speaks
in our conscience, but shouts in our pains: it
is His megaphone to rouse a deaf world."*

C. S. LEWIS, *The Problem of Pain* [14]

This chapter is probably going to get me into trouble. I already know it, and ironically enough it's making me anxious. That's supposed to be funny, but I know the anxious people in my life are already tense.

I can already hear the voices of dear friends rising in chorus: "You just don't understand!" Some will offer me grace—sort of a theological participation trophy for effort—while others may offer a less gentle response involving clenched fists and caps lock. And I get it. Really, I do.

---

14. C.S. Lewis, *The Problem of Pain* (New York: HarperOne, 2001)

Anxiety is real. It's serious. And it's everywhere. It's not just the stuff of nerves before a speech or butterflies before a ball game. For many it's a weight they carry from morning until night and then into their dreams. So before I say another word, let me do something up front:

I ask forgiveness.

If you're in that group—those for whom anxiety has planted roots in your soul—I genuinely want to walk gently here. I'm not minimizing. I'm not mocking. I'm not throwing a Scripture verse like a dart and calling it discipleship. I know that anxiety doesn't yield to logic or reason, and it certainly doesn't take kindly to well-meaning people saying, "Just stop worrying."

With all my heart, I try to understand.

The truth is, I'm surrounded by anxious people. And not just casual worriers—I'm talking about close friends and family who wrestle with anxiety and depression to the point of exhaustion. Some fight through foggy days just to function. Some can't even do that. Their courage in simply staying present is evidence enough for me that anxiety is not weakness. It's a battle.

So while I may not have a front-row seat *inside* the storm, I've stood outside holding umbrellas for people in the downpour. I have credentials, in other words—not from suffering in exactly the same way but from loving those who do.

And in the last decade or so this struggle has exploded. It feels like anxiety has become the official mascot of our modern moment. Like it's on the welcome mat of adulthood. If you're reading this, there's a good chance you either suffer from anxiety yourself or love someone who does.

Now here's the risky part: When I try to speak gently about anxiety from the outside, even cautiously suggesting that there may be a *reasonable* response, the anxious folks in my life immediately raise an eyebrow. They remind me that I've wandered into a land where logic doesn't have a passport. And honestly? That... seems reasonable.

Though I don't personally battle anxiety, I have walked through a season of depression. It came a couple of years after Wade's death—a time when grief finally caught up with me, wrapped its hands around my throat, and refused to let go. For about a month it left me feeling helpless and useless to both my family and my ministry. And then just as suddenly as it came, it lifted.

So when I can't fully grasp the experience of anxiety, I return in my mind to that chapter of my life. I remember what it felt like to be overwhelmed—mentally and emotionally—until all strength seemed to drain away. That memory helps me approach this subject with humility and compassion, knowing there are moments in life when we truly are brought to the point of helplessness. That story is another book in itself, but it's from that place of understanding that I write this chapter.

So let's walk through this chapter together with honesty, grace, and a few gentle laughs—not at the struggle but because sometimes laughter is one of the few things anxiety can't predict or control. And that makes it holy.

* * *

In that anxious world all reason seems to vanish at some point. But having asked for forgiveness in advance—and perhaps earned just enough goodwill to proceed—I want to carefully explore this thought: *What if, during the calmer moments between storms, we could find an anchor in the providence of God?*

That's the key: not during the hurricane but in the hush that sometimes follows. In the afterglow. The moment when the panic quiets just long enough for your heart to hear again.

Let's start by asking: How does Scripture actually use the word *anxiety?*

Now let me be crystal clear—I fully recognize that some people suffer from clinical anxiety. That's a real, physiological, and emotional condition. It is complex. There are layers: neurological, environmental, historical, and chemical. There is no shame in therapy. There is no shame in medication. There is no shame in struggle. The church has done great harm when it has implied otherwise.

But that said, anxiety in some of its forms—especially in the day-to-day worry that hijacks our peace—can also be rooted in a spiritual disconnection. It is, in some cases, worry that grows in the absence of trust. Unbelief is not always the *cause* of anxiety, but sometimes it sets up a hammock and gets comfortable there.

I know—I just lost a few readers.

But hear me out. I'm not saying that recognizing this helps you during the actual anxiety attack. I know it doesn't. I hear you clucking your tongue and preparing a lengthy rebuttal. That's fair. But what if after the storm passes, these truths might help you process what just happened? What if they gave you a foothold for the next time?

In his book *Christian Counseling*, Gary Collins writes:

> Worry comes when we turn from God, shift the burdens of
> life on to ourselves, and assume—at least by our attitude
> and actions—that we alone are responsible for handling
> problems. Instead of acknowledging God's sovereignty
> and power, or seeking His kingdom and righteousness

first, many of us…slip into sinful self-reliance and pre-occupation with our own life pressures.[15]

I remember reading that quote during a counseling class I once took—though, to be honest, the course had about the same effect on my counseling skills as watching a cooking show has on my actual cooking. Meaning, I appreciated it…but you don't want me leading your support group just yet.

Still, I think Collins has a point—albeit with some rough edges.

If you're someone who struggles with anxiety, worry, or depression, hear this loud and clear: That does *not* make you a bad Christian. It makes you a human Christian. If anything, your struggle may deepen your need for God—and deepen your ability to see others who are struggling.

I bring up Collins not to shame but to emphasize this: We must look toward God's sovereignty in our deepest valleys. We don't ignore our problems; we just acknowledge that God isn't ignoring them either.

Anxiety is not imaginary. It is not exaggerated. It is not fiction. But neither is God's providence.

Even in the middle of a world that feels like it's unraveling at the seams, Scripture tells us that we are not alone. That we are not left to our own devices. There is enough biblical foundation to believe that God desires to give us peace and stability—not just *eventually*, but *now*. In this moment. In your moment.

We can't ignore Philippians 4:6–7. It doesn't offer a magic cure, but it does offer a map: "Do not be anxious about anything, but in every situation, by prayer and petition, with thanksgiving, present

---

15. Gary R. Collins, Christian Counseling: A Comprehensive Guide, 3rd ed. (Nashville: Thomas Nelson, 2007)

your requests to God. And the peace of God, which transcends all understanding, will guard your hearts and your minds in Christ Jesus"

That verse was written for people like us—people with heavy minds and trembling hands. And if we believe God's Word, then we must also believe that *there is help for the anxious through Him and His principles.*

Divine sovereignty is a vast subject. It stretches across the full biblical picture of God as Lord and King—the One "who works all things according to the counsel of His will" (Ephesians 1:11). Every process. Every outcome. Every moment. His hand is there whether we see it or not.

Truly, if we tried to fully explore that subject here, we'd be opening doors that lead into the deepest halls of theology—predestination, providence, final judgment, eternal mysteries—and unless your coffee is still hot and your chair reclines, that's probably more than either of us signed up for.

So in this chapter we're going to narrow our focus. We're going to look at one slice of sovereignty: God's sovereignty in grace—His almighty action in bringing helpless sinners home through Christ to Himself.

J. I. Packer, in his book *Evangelism and the Sovereignty of God*, put it bluntly and beautifully: God's sovereignty "embraces everything."[16] That's not poetic exaggeration. That's theology with boots on.

To understand this is to realize that nothing is random. God either causes or allows all things—great and small. He signs off on every moment in history, every detail of your life, every surprise, every silence. He is not watching events unfold like we are, nervously checking the news and refreshing the weather app. He is orchestrating it

---

16. J. I. Packer, *Evangelism and the Sovereignty of God* (Downers Grove, IL: InterVarsity Press, 1961)

all. And yes, I know that sounds like something you hear in a seminary classroom. But here's the kicker: It's not just deep theology. It's
daily life.

＊ ＊ ＊

As I write this, I'm sitting in the airport in Iași, Romania. It's January 2024. And looking back over the past five years, I can tell you—
tumultuous doesn't quite cover it. COVID. Global lockdowns. Racial
upheaval. Economic chaos. Wars we never imagined seeing again.
And if that weren't enough, another kind of plague has quietly risen
alongside it all: This thing we're talking about—anxiety.

Yes, I know—it's not new. Anxiety has always been a part of human
life. But not like this. Not with this scale and saturation. Not with
this level of mental anguish. You could argue that other eras of history were more violent or difficult—and you'd be right. But here's
the paradox: Never before have people had this much convenience,
this much access to information, this many tools for managing life.
Especially in the West. And yet we're crumbling.

We have apps for sleep and alerts for hydration. We have virtual
therapists and grocery deliveries and more helpful podcasts than we
have hours in a lifetime. And yet peace seems more elusive than ever.
If anything, our anxiety is more connected to *having too much* than
too little.

And so once again we find ourselves needing something ancient.
Something solid. Something sovereign.

Not long ago I decided to conduct a little experiment in modern convenience. I was in Riga, Latvia, doing missions work, and I
called my son back in Georgia—the state, not the country, home of
my beloved "Dawgs." I asked him to walk outside and stand next

to my truck. As he did, I pulled out my phone, opened an app, and pressed a button. From 5,000 miles away, I cranked my truck.

He smiled. I smiled. Then I turned it off—because, well, I could.

Now I know that kind of tech is already old news to most people, but that's exactly the point. We've never had more convenience at our fingertips. You can talk to your lights, and they obey. You can clap your hands, and with the right setup things happen—though usually just confusion unless you've programmed it right. You can sit in your recliner in your movie room, surrounded by surround sound, and never get up to change the channel because, shockingly, the remote is now in your voice.

That is quite a contrast to the ancient world of my childhood.

Back in those days our television was only slightly smarter than a brick. It had three channels—on a good weather day. At our house we'd worn the channel-changing knob completely off the TV, so when it came time to switch between one of our *three* viewing options, we had to find a special pair of pliers. These pliers lived on top of the television, and their sole purpose was to twist what remained of the little metal stub where the knob used to be. That was after someone adjusted the "rabbit ears" antenna, often with one arm raised like they were doing an interpretive dance to appease the TV gods. Relatively speaking, that was not that many years ago. This scene simply highlights the mad dash to convenience we've lived through in the last fifty years.

Fast food wasn't fast enough, so now we have people delivering tacos by bicycle, sushi by scooter, and frozen yogurt by drone. We don't even need to walk to the door—just ping them to leave it on the porch and pretend we're not home.

Now if you're sensing a little generational tone creeping in here, you're right. And unapologetically so. It's not that the "good ole days" were perfect—they weren't—but it does seem that despite all our modern upgrades, anxiety has become a national pastime.

I don't remember hearing the word *anxiety* much growing up. Maybe it existed and just had a different name—like "nerves" or "being keyed up"—but it didn't seem to take up this much space.

I've looked into it, and the majority of the research and writing on anxiety has come in the past thirty years. That alone says something. Maybe the old days were less safe, less comfortable, and less informed—but they also seemed to be a bit more grounded.

And speaking of safety, we've turned that into both a virtue and a vice. Safety now drives everything. It's the ruling value of our time. We fear so many things that we've built our entire society around avoiding risk, insulating ourselves from pain, and preventing every bump and bruise imaginable.

And let's be clear—some of this is good. I'm genuinely thankful that we no longer let toddlers roll around in the back window of a speeding car like they were loose produce. By the way, my oldest son sat on my lap in the front seat while I *drove* when he was two. Not my best parenting moment. These days kids are basically strapped into NASCAR-grade cocoons, and that's a good thing. Though I despise putting them in and taking them out of any vehicle.

Workplaces are different. Games are different. The way we eat, dress, sleep—it's all different now and mostly for safety's sake.

But somehow with all of our safety improvements we've become the most frightened society in history.

We live with more safeguards than ever, yet we tremble more than ever. We have more control, and somehow we feel less secure. It's as if the more we try to bubble wrap the world, the more we discover just how fragile we really are.

And maybe that's the real lesson in all of this: That all the modern marvels and padded corners in the world can't protect us from what really threatens us. Because anxiety doesn't live outside of us—it lives *inside* us. And no amount of convenience can fix what only trust was meant to carry.

Author Jonathan Haidt in his book *The Coddling of the American Mind* coined a term that fits this moment like a seatbelt: "Safetyism." He writes, "Safetyism is the cult of safety—an obsession with eliminating threats (both real and imagined) to the point at which people become unwilling to make reasonable trade-offs demanded by other practical and moral concerns."[17]

In other words, we've gotten so good at making the world soft, quiet, and carefully temperature-controlled that we've forgotten how to live in it. We're not brave because we're secure; we're scared *because* we're secure. We fear for the sake of fear.

I remember standing in a train station in a foreign country years ago. I was with a seasoned traveler—a guy who spoke the language, knew the customs, and looked like he could fold his map without wrinkling it. I was the rookie. And being a rookie meant I didn't even know which foot went first.

We had a train to catch, and I was scanning the signs (in a language I couldn't read), watching the clock (which I didn't trust), and anxiously trying to make sense of it all. Meanwhile, my friend calmly wandered off to look for food. Yes, food. I'm sweating bullets over departure times, and he's craving a sandwich.

I finally turned to him, baffled, and started to tell him my worries

---

17. Greg Lukianoff and Jonathan Haidt, The Coddling of the American Mind: How Good Intentions and Bad Ideas Are Setting Up a Generation for Failure (New York: Penguin Press, 2018)

about missing the train. He gently smiled and said, "Buddy, are you just looking for something to worry about?" Ouch. But fair.

I've used that line many times since—with other rookies and occasionally in the mirror.

The truth is, that's where many of us live today. Even when everything is going fine, we search for something to worry about. Like anxiety is some kind of hobby we're trying to perfect.

And that's what's so puzzling: We have more than any generation before us. We have tools, medicine, information, access, and luxuries that would've made our great-grandparents faint with disbelief. We have smart homes, smart devices, and smart cars—but we can't seem to outsmart our own unease.

We should be the calmest, most serene, most at peace generation in history. But we're not. Not even close.

Today depression and anxiety are very real parts of life. Once again, I'm not here to minimize them. If you suffer with them, you know how real they are. And if you don't suffer but love someone who does, then you know the helpless feeling of wanting to offer help and not knowing how.

In fact, I'll admit it: The anxious people I'm surrounded by sometimes make me nervous. Yes, irony intended. As I intimated earlier, I'm even a little anxious about how anxious people will feel after reading this.

I'm simply trying to make a point.

Maybe it's not more technology we need. Maybe convenience isn't the cure. Maybe what anxious and depressed hearts need most isn't a better app or a quicker answer—but a deeper confidence in the sovereignty of God.

And here's the kicker: Shouldn't it be *easier* for the believer to find rest than for anyone else?

Shouldn't we be the ones who exhale first? Who sleep better? Who live looser and freer with the peace that surpasses understanding?

It would seem that way. But sadly, that's not always the case.

There's a significant percentage within the Christian community who quietly suffer with stress, anxiety, and depression. They love Jesus. They read Scripture. They serve and give and pray. But they still struggle.

This is not a failure of faith—it's a reality of living in a broken world with fragile hearts. And it's why the conversation about God's sovereignty matters so much.

According to a *Forbes* article from October 2023,

1. Anxiety disorders are the most common mental illnesses in the U.S., affecting more than 40 million adults—or 19.1% of the population.

2. Generalized Anxiety Disorder (GAD) is the most common form, impacting 6.8 million adults.

3. Nearly 50% of those aged 18 to 24 report symptoms of anxiety or depressive disorders.

4. Women are more than twice as likely as men to experience an anxiety disorder.

5. Anxiety disorders are highly treatable, yet more than 60% of those suffering do not seek treatment.[18]

Those numbers aren't just national—they're also congregational. They don't stop at the church doors or get turned away by the greeter

---

18. National Institute of Mental Health, "Any Anxiety Disorder Among Adults," *NIMH: Health Statistics*

with the bulletin. These statistics are just as true *inside* the body of Christ as outside it. Which means if the church is meant to be a body of support, then we've got a limp. And I count myself among the limping.

I've often said to Christian friends with as much pastoral concern as I can muster, "Never forget—He's sovereign." I say it like it's a magic phrase. Like they'll hear those words and immediately toss their anxiety aside like last winter's coat on a sunny spring day. But usually they just look at me with the same expression you'd give someone who offers you a mint when you've just lost your job. It's a nice gesture but not quite enough.

This, of course, speaks volumes about my own counseling skills—which are about as sharp as a spoon. I graduated from the Bob Newhart School of Psychological Therapy, which isn't actually accredited, in case you were wondering.

For those unfamiliar with Bob Newhart, he was a brilliantly dry comedian from the last generation. On his TV show he once performed a skit that—unfortunately—resembles some of my less effective attempts at helping others. He played a therapist listening to a patient describe her neuroses in exhausting detail. She poured out her soul, her trauma, and her bizarre compulsion that was ruining her life. After a long silence, Dr. Bob leaned forward and delivered his life-altering counsel:

"Stop it."

That was it. Just "Stop it."

If only it were that easy, right?

I've tried that approach in real life. It rarely works. In fact, it never works. Because anxiety doesn't go away with a snap of the fingers or a punchline. It's stubborn, persistent, and deeply personal.

What we need isn't a quick fix. We need something stronger. Something deeper.

We need truth that anchors us—not advice that bounces off. We need hope that holds—not just slogans that sound good on mugs.

We need to know that our fears are seen. That we are not alone. And that God in His sovereignty hasn't left us to flail around in a world that feels constantly out of control.

*   *   *

Of all the people in the history of the universe who *should not* have been anxious, it was the disciples. But they certainly were. It seems to me that they were anxiously anxious. So anxious people, take heart—you're in elite company. Olympic level. Platinum club.

Seriously, you're doing better than that crew most days—and they were literally in the presence of God. For heaven's sake, they *rode in boats with Him.* If anyone had a reason to be calm, it was them. But have you ever heard of a more panicky bunch? You'd think they were filming a spiritual reality show called *Who Can Worry the Loudest?*

Let me give you just one example (but trust me, there are many). The story shows up in Matthew 8, Mark 4, and Luke 8—when Jesus says to His disciples, "Let's go over to the other side of the lake." That's it. A simple plan. A clear promise. You'd think they'd take Him at His word.

But then as so often happens when you're boating…a storm hits.

And not a mild drizzle either. We're talking about the kind of storm where you start checking the shoreline and wondering whether sharks really can sense panic. The Bible says the boat was "being swamped"— which is the ancient translation for "we're all gonna die."

Now here's the detail that makes this so relatable: Jesus is *asleep*.

The God of the universe, the One who calms the wind and walks on water…is downstairs in the boat taking a nap. That's not even a metaphor. That's the actual story.

And this is the moment when anxious people everywhere say, "Yup. That's how it feels."

You believe in God. You trust that He's good. But sometimes it really feels like He's asleep at the wheel—or at least snoozing in the hull while your life takes on water.

The disciples understandably panic. They wake Him up in a flurry of fear and frustration. "Don't you care that we're drowning?" they ask, which is kind of gutsy when you're talking to the Creator of the sea.

But the most fascinating part of this story isn't the storm—it's that Jesus *already told them* how the trip would end. "We're going to the other side," He said. Not, "We're going to die halfway across." Not, "We'll see how it goes." It was a statement of divine certainty.

And they missed it.

They had the promise, and still they panicked.

Did they think Jesus was going to let them drown? Did they think *He* was going to drown? That the Messiah would go down with the ship?

They had seen miracles. They had watched Him heal, feed, and command the elements. But they hadn't yet *rested* in the knowledge of who He really was—the sovereign God who never slumbers or sleeps. The One whose plan is not subject to storms. But they would learn. Eventually they would.

On the other hand, there's the remarkable story of Esther. Now here's a narrative so saturated with God's providence, it practically glows—and yet not once does it mention His name. Not once. God is invisible in the entire text of the book of Esther, but He's unmistakable in the outcome.

If anyone had a reason to feel anxious, it was this young Jewish woman, thrown into a role and a world where women rarely held influence, let alone saved nations. And yet she stood up, straightened her crown, and uttered those iconic, courageous words: "If I perish, I perish" (Esther 4:16). That wasn't dramatic flair. That was a death sentence she was willing to walk into.

But when you look back at the story—at the intricate dance of decisions, the perfectly-timed conversations, the overheard plots and sleepless nights—it's impossible to miss the real Author behind it all. God was in every detail, even though He never signed His name.

Now don't misunderstand—this wasn't some reckless leap into the unknown. Esther didn't just throw up her hands and hope for the best. She had a *plan.* She fasted. She strategized. She took deliberate steps to confront the evil of Haman while working within the greater story God was orchestrating.

She couldn't see the full picture at the time—but she believed there *was* one. She stepped forward anyway.

Sometimes faith looks like sleeping through the storm. Sometimes it looks like standing before a king. Either way it rests in the sovereignty of a God who is always present—even when He seems hidden.

Do you remember the *Where's Waldo?* books?

When they first came out, I was fascinated. Probably because I was primed for this sort of visual scavenger hunt thanks to *Highlights Magazine*—a staple of every pediatrician's waiting room in my youth. We couldn't afford a subscription growing up, but Dr. Hamm's office had a stack that could've passed for fine literature in a child's world. Inside there were pages filled with drawings of playgrounds, forests, and birthday parties—each with hidden objects tucked away like Easter eggs for your eyes. I sat for hours trying to find them all.

Where's Waldo? took that same idea and cranked it up to 11.

Every page featured a wildly busy cartoon scene—think marching bands, amusement parks, or birthday parties. And somewhere in all that glorious chaos was Waldo: thin, striped, bespectacled, and harder to spot than your car keys when you're already late. He was always there...just expertly camouflaged, hiding in the scene.

That's the point of the book, of course. You're supposed to find Waldo. And sometimes you did, proudly pointing him out like you'd just solved a national security crisis. Other times you stared until your eyes crossed, convinced the artist had cheated.

But here's what I came to learn over time: Waldo was *always* there. Every single time.

I might close the book in frustration. I might walk away convinced it was a hoax. But if I returned with fresh eyes—or a little more patience—there he was. Just where he was supposed to be.

Here's the point" That whole experience reminds me of what it's like searching for God in our own story.

Life gets crowded. The picture gets messy. People, pressures, distractions—they all pile in like a cartoon city crammed onto one double-page spread. And somewhere in it all we pause and ask, "Where's God?"

We wonder if He's missing. Or worse, if maybe He didn't make it into *this* chapter.

But eventually if we keep searching and stay still long enough to let the picture settle, there He is. Right where He said He'd be.

And in that moment there's this quiet voice inside that says, "How could you ever doubt He was here?"

Because the whole story—the *entire book*—is about Him.

I'll be honest, there were times I closed those Waldo books without finding him. But I never questioned his presence. I just needed more time.

And if Waldo was that good at being ever-present without being obvious…imagine what God can do.

Sometimes like with the disciples, God feels very near. You think you know where He is. You can almost hear Him snoring below deck. (Did Jesus snore? I mean, He was fully human—it's at least possible.)

You know at least He's only a call away. The storm is raging, but at least you know He's in the boat.

Then there are other times—times when He doesn't even seem to sign in. The silence is thick. The plan is unclear. The map is missing. And we start asking the age-old question: "God, where are You?" This triggers spiritual anxiety, for sure.

Well, here's the thing—His visible presence is never a prerequisite for His active hand. Just because you can't *see* Him doesn't mean He's not working. Just because you can't *feel* Him doesn't mean He's not moving. God's sovereignty is not dependent on our perception.

His plan is unfolding whether or not we understand it. Our clarity doesn't make His will more effective. Our confusion doesn't make it less certain. And the comfort we crave—of knowing exactly what He's up to—is often not given.

> Our role? To trust. Even in the silence. Especially in the silence.

There are storms and bad guys written into every person's story—enough to keep every "Doctor Bob" therapist busy and booked until the next century.

But for those of us who've walked with Christ for any length of time, the key is not to panic at the plot twist. It's to remember who the Author is.

Imagine the perfect novel—each chapter crafted by the Master Storyteller. Every character, every conflict, every twist of fate written with purpose. Some chapters burst with joy and triumph. Others are filled with shadow and struggle. But no page is wasted. And every line is moving toward something beautiful.

God's sovereignty is like divine authorship of a novel titled *Life*. His omniscient thought and foreknowledge allow Him to understand exactly how each character, each event, and each seemingly insignificant detail contributes to the grand narrative. He's not just writing history—He's writing *your* story.

Just like any good novel our lives are filled with tension, uncertainty, and the occasional plot twist that makes you want to skip ahead to the last page. But the sovereignty of God assures us that no matter how chaotic or confusing our individual chapter may feel the Author knows exactly where the story is going.

He knows the beginning. He knows the middle. He knows the end.

And in the grand finale everything will come together. Every twist, every heartache, every delay will be seen for what it really was—a necessary turn in a much bigger, more beautiful story.

I was recently reading about one of my favorite authors, John Grisham. I've read a lot of his books and always appreciated the way he builds a story. In an interview he said that he never begins writing a novel until he knows what's in the first chapter—and the last.

He creates the characters with the ending already in mind. He knows where they're going even when the reader doesn't. So as I turn the pages, I get baffled, amused, angry, even a little heartbroken. But

I keep reading because I trust the author to take the story somewhere meaningful.

And that's how it is with God.

He created us. He knows where He's taking us. Every sentence of our lives is written with the ending in mind. And yes, we live those sentences in real time—tripping over commas, stuck in parenthetical detours, and staring at punctuation marks that look more like question marks than periods.

Some of those sentences end in "What?" Others in "Why???" And a few, let's be honest, in all caps.

The analogy breaks down a bit, of course. Grisham doesn't necessarily write his endings with the good of his characters in mind. Sometimes it's just an entertaining story.

But God? His ending is always written for *our* good and *His* glory.

That's not fiction. That's theology.

And maybe, just maybe, that's the kind of truth that can help push back the fog of anxiety.

We spend billions treating anxiety these days. And understandably so—because we don't know the ending.

But what if we reminded ourselves—every day if needed—that the Author of our lives *does*?

You may have lived through years of pain. You may still be in a chapter titled "Heartache" or "Loneliness" or "This Doesn't Make Any Sense."

But keep turning the page.

Because the last chapter is already written.

And it ends with good.

It may take some time to believe that. It may take days—or years—of wandering through anxiety before you truly begin to feel secure. That's okay. That's part of the journey too.

When you feel lost, remember the disciples. Their faith wobbled too. And they were on the boat *with* Jesus. If they stumbled, it's okay if you do too.

Or look at Paul. The apostle of strength and theology who also admitted to being downcast and in need of comfort. He had his days. You will too.

But over time they all came to see God's hand more clearly.

And you will too.

Sometimes the best we can do is let the truth run alongside us— like a faithful companion on the road—ready to remind us where to return when we drift.

So don't be too hard on yourself.

Just keep walking.

And try to leave anxiety behind.

CHAPTER 20

THE MASTER BUILDER AND THE FIXER-UPPER SOUL

We've talked about sovereignty, now let's talk about something called sanctification. And when we're done let's tie them both together.

Sanctification: It's one of those churchy words that tends to stop us in our tracks. The moment the pastor utters it something strange happens—our eyes fog up, our brains take a coffee break, and before you know it, we're sneaking glances at our phone screens at a game of solitaire while pretending to be deeply engaged with that sanctification verse on our Bible app. At the risk of losing any lingering theologians who've made it this far in the book (God bless you, by the way), I'll admit it: I'm not a fan of the word either. It's right up there with soteriology and dispensationalism. (You've got your list of theological tongue twisters, and I've got mine.)

Don't get me wrong—the truths behind these words are beautiful, vital, even glorious. But the words themselves? They sound like they belong in a dusty textbook that hasn't been opened since the Nixon administration. So instead of throwing the truth out with the vocabulary, I've decided to do what works best for me: break it down to picture-book level. Because, to be honest, I do much better with picture books than with technical manuals. (If you ever want to teach me something, just add stick figures and arrows. Works every time.)

Let's get to the meat of it. There are actually two parts to this thing called sanctification. Think of it like a two-for-one deal, except both parts are priceless. The first is *positional sanctification,* and the second is *progressive sanctification.* And before you panic, don't worry—there won't be a quiz at the end.

Positional sanctification in Christian theology (the kind my Bible college professors tried valiantly to pound into my eighteen-year-old, sleep-deprived brain) refers to the state of being set apart for God. It happens the moment you accept Christ's offer of salvation. You are moved, just like that, into a new category: holy, chosen, set apart. First Corinthians 1:30 says it like this: "But of him are ye in Christ Jesus, who of God is made unto us wisdom, and righteousness, and sanctification, and redemption." That sanctification mentioned here is the once-and-for-all kind. God does the work. It's part of the salvation bundle. Hebrews 10:10 adds, "We are sanctified through the offering of the body of Jesus Christ once for all." That's positional sanctification. You believe in Christ, and—BOOM—you're set apart for God permanently. No receipt needed, no returns accepted.

Now let's turn to the second part where most of us live every day: *progressive sanctification.* This is the part that feels a little more familiar—and honestly, a bit messier. Progressive sanctification is a big term that simply means we are becoming more like Christ over time. It's the slow, sometimes plodding, occasionally inspiring effect of obeying God's Word as we grow in faith. It's the spiritual version of watching paint dry—except the paint is your character and the drying time takes a lifetime.

Second Peter 3:18 puts it this way: "But grow in grace, and in the knowledge of our Lord and Saviour Jesus Christ. To him be glory both now and for ever. Amen." And Paul chimes in from Philippians 1:6 with this encouragement: "Being confident of this very thing, that he which hath begun a good work in you will perform it until the day of Jesus Christ." In other words, God started the remodeling job in your soul, and He's not walking off the construction site until it's done—even if there are days you catch your reflection and think, "This fixer-upper still needs a lot of work."

So yes, sanctification may be a theological word with some extra syllables and a tendency to cause eyelid droop, but don't let that scare you off. It's the heart of how God transforms us—first by setting us apart and then by patiently making us into whom we were meant to be. One divine brushstroke at a time.

Here's where a little story helps. Think of positional sanctification like planting a seed in the ground. That seed isn't confused about what it's supposed to become. It's not lying there thinking, "Am I a tomato? Am I a bonsai?" No, from the very start it's been set apart to grow into a tree. That's its identity—even if it currently looks like something you'd flick off your shoe.

Now let's bring in the idea of progressive sanctification. Over time that seed begins to change. It puts down roots, sprouts a little stem, and maybe—if it doesn't get stomped on by a squirrel—starts to look like an actual tree. Eventually there's fruit. Growth. Maturity. All of it slow. All of it invisible at times. But none of it accidental.

That's sanctification in bottom-shelf language.

It means being set aside for God's purpose. Romans 8:29 says that

God predestined us (yes, another word that causes people to shift uncomfortably in their seats) to be conformed to the image of His Son. That's the whole point. He didn't save us just so we could sit around in pews like redeemed mannequins. He saved us to grow—to mature—to bear fruit. To be like Jesus.

James 1:18 says God gave us life through the word of truth, and Philippians 2:13 tells us that "it is God who works in you to will and to act in order to fulfill his good purpose." So who does the sanctifying? God does. He's the gardener. He's the one working in the soil of your soul, pulling weeds, pruning branches, and occasionally saying, "Well, that's new," when we surprise even Him. If I could paraphrase the thoughts of those verses using the kind of language that doesn't require a theological degree and a pot of coffee, I'd say this: God saw us coming, chose to set us aside, and started a work in us so that the rest of the world could see what His love and leadership can produce in a person's life.

God does not want any person to perish. He has chosen all of us to be redeemed. That's what He determined, yet we have the free will to reject that salvation if we want to. He'll never force heaven on anyone. However, when any person chooses to accept this predetermined plan for redemption, God's next goal is for that individual to work within His (that is God's) framework for life and for humankind to grow to be like Jesus. This growth is also a free will decision. If we accept it, then we should accept the fact that He will work all of life for our good.

And let's be clear: This growth isn't automatic. It's not like spiritual puberty where one day you wake up and suddenly you're holy. It takes intention. You have to choose it.

Which is why I say it this way: Make a conscious decision. Not a passive one. Because spiritual growth doesn't come baked into the salvation package like a free toaster with a bank account. You don't drift into maturity. You decide.

For some of us (and I raise my hand here) that decision has to be made over and over. It's less like a one-time pledge and more like a daily wrestling match between your will and your calendar.

Romans 12:1 says it straight: "Present your bodies a living sacrifice, holy, acceptable unto God, which is your reasonable service." In other words, slide yourself onto the altar and stay there—even when everything in you wants to roll off. We must willingly sacrifice our lives for His will.

So why spend an entire chapter on this church word that's usually avoided like the green Jell-O˙ salad at the family reunion?

Because sanctification is hard. It's uphill. You don't choose it unless you understand that God is wiser than you are and that what He's doing—even when it hurts—is actually better than what you would've picked.

Here's something you've heard before from hundreds of preachers, teachers, and evangelists down through the years (and from me just a couple of paragraphs ago). I can hear them in their ministerial splendor as they point a finger at us and tell us that "God has a plan for you." Maybe it has lost its impact on us, but it's true. It's not a "maybe," or a "hope so": It's a divine certainty, it's eternal, and it's been crafted by His sovereign hand. This plan is not just about where you'll spend eternity—though that's part of it. It's about who you're becoming right now and in this life. God's goal is to shape you into the likeness of His Son, Jesus Christ. That essentially is what sanctification is all about. It is at the heart of God's purpose for your life.

THE MASTER BUILDER

Let's try thinking about sanctification like a construction project. And not one of those slap-up-in-a-weekend projects either. This is full-on, long-term, home-improvement-meets-eternity level building. In this story God is the Master Builder—and your life is one of His construction sites.

Now before you panic: You're not His first project. And thankfully not His practice run either. God's not winging it with a half-used toolbox and a YouTube tutorial pulled up on His phone. From the very moment you gave your heart to Jesus, He pulled out the blueprint for your life—a blueprint He drafted long before you were even born. He predestined you. He set His sights on you. And no, not just to keep you out of hell but to build you into the masterpiece He envisioned from the beginning—a reflection of His Son.

But here's the thing about this Master Builder: He doesn't use a cookie cutter. Every house is custom-built. Some have big changes right up front—others need slow, behind-the-walls rewiring. Yours won't look like mine, and mine won't look like yours. Why? Because God knows every crack in our foundations, every hidden corner of our hearts, and every beam that needs reinforcing. He knows which habits need displaying, which wounds need mending, and which doors still squeak with fear or pride.

And because He's sovereign—and wise beyond measure—He uses *everything* in the construction process. And I do mean *everything*. Blessings? Sure. Loss? Yes. Traffic jams, grief, laughter, setbacks, career detours, that one neighbor who always mows at 7 a.m.—all of it can be poured into the foundation He's laying in you.

For me the loss of my son Wade was not just a chapter in my life—it was part of the blueprint. I don't say that lightly. But in God's hands even pain becomes a sacred tool. You've got your own stories—moments that didn't make sense at the time and maybe still don't. But I'm telling you: If God is the builder, nothing is wasted.

He uses blessings like paint and sunshine—they brighten; they encourage; they show us His goodness.

He uses hard times like hammers and chisels—painful tools, yes, but necessary to shape what's misshapen, to break off what doesn't belong.

And even the boring, in-between Tuesday afternoons of life? Those are the sandpaper days. The repetitive, unnoticed moments that smooth out impatience, develop endurance, and build character in the quiet.

He's building something beautiful in you. It may not feel like it yet. In fact, some days you might walk through your own spiritual hallways and think, "We're still at the drywall stage?" But make no mistake—He's not done. And the final design? It's supposed to look like Jesus.

SANCTIFICATION AND GOD'S SOVEREIGNTY

We already know that God's sovereignty means He is in complete control; there are no exceptions when it comes to our sanctification. You're not being transformed by accident or coincidence. Philippians 1:6 assures us, "He which hath begun a good work in you will perform it until the day of Jesus Christ." Sanctification isn't about you striving to be more like Jesus all by yourself. It's about God working in you, shaping you by His Spirit.

Paul makes this clear in Philippians 2:13: "For it is God which worketh in you both to will and to do of his good pleasure." You're not alone in this journey. God's Spirit is actively at work, enabling you to desire what pleases Him and empowering you to live it out. For me this is sometimes vague, and I don't even realize it is happening at the moment of instruction. It is not until the good, the bad, or years of the usual have passed that I understand He indeed was there teaching and building me from inside.

Something super important to remember is that God's sovereignty doesn't negate your responsibility. You're not just throwing up your hands and becoming possessed to the point that you are possessed but with no will of your own. Sanctification is a divine partnership. God provides the power, but you must cooperate with Him.

It's like sailing. God provides the wind for us, but we have to raise the sails. He's not asking you to steer the ship in your strength alone, but He is asking you to man the sails and keep them facing in a wind-catching direction.

PRACTICAL STEPS IN SANCTIFICATION

Sanctification might sound like a "front-row" theological concept, but it is actually very practical, touching every aspect of your daily life. There are some ways to cooperate with God in this divine process.

1. Spend Time in God's Word

The Bible is your sanctification playbook. Through its pages God reveals who He is, who you are, and whom He wants you to become. As Paul writes in 2 Timothy 3:16–17, "All scripture is given by inspiration of God, and is profitable for doctrine, for reproof, for correction, for instruction in righteousness, that the man of God may be perfect, thoroughly furnished unto all good works."

If we make time to read, study, and meditate on God's Word, it will shape our thoughts, transform our attitudes, and guide our decisions. It works like a mirror, showing us what needs attention. It's also a lamp to our feet, lighting the next step we should take.

In our day reading the Bible seems to have lost its appeal. Not because it's lost power but because our lives are saturated with distractions—notifications, scrolling, headlines, and endless noise. Just glance around the next time you're in a café or waiting room. Heads are bowed but not in reverence. We're a society of neck-bent screen scrollers. And yes, I include myself in this.

But here's the quiet truth: The Word of God doesn't compete with flashing lights or vibrating alerts. It doesn't shout over the noise. It waits. But without it there is no sanctification. Period.

Let's be honest: You probably won't feel the earth move every time you read it. Growth is often invisible. Just like planting a seed doesn't give you a flower overnight, neither does a single reading produce instant fruit. It's a process. One that takes root deep in the soul before anything appears above ground.

Every year thousands of believers start Bible reading plans. And every year around the second Friday of January—aptly nicknamed "Quitter's Day"—many quietly fold. Why? Because they didn't see results fast enough. We're addicted to instant gratification, but the Word grows slow and deep.

Keep reading. Let it work. Your roots are growing even when you don't see them. One day there will be fruit.

2. Pray

Romans 12:12 states: "Rejoicing in hope; patient in tribulation; continuing instant in prayer."

Prayer is another vital step in the sanctification process. This is where you confess your sins, seek God's guidance, and align your heart with His will. It may not always feel powerful—but it is always forming you.

Let's face it: Prayer isn't easy. Not for me. Not for most. We say grace before meals, toss up flares in crisis, and promise ourselves we'll do better next week. Prayer can feel like talking to the ceiling. But it's not.

Think of prayer less like a religious duty and more like a conversation with Someone who knows your soul better than you do—and still wants to hear your voice. It's dialogue with a present, loving Father—not a disconnected cosmic landlord.

I'm not a "prayer warrior," but I've met a few. One dear lady I know, mostly homebound, has turned her tiny room into a war room of prayer. She prays with fierce love and specific passion, almost begging for requests so she can take them to God. Her life speaks with quiet spiritual thunder. But that didn't happen overnight. It came from years of isolation, time with God, and sacred conversation.

That's how it works. The more time you spend with someone you trust and love, the more you begin to think and act like them. So it is with God. The more you talk with Him—and listen—the more you grow.

3. Obey

James 1:22 says, "But be ye doers of the word, and not hearers only, deceiving your own selves."

Obedience isn't just rigid compliance. It's not gritting your teeth and forcing yourself to play by the rules. It's a relational act of trust.

We obey God because we believe He knows best. And as we obey, He shapes us.

Obedience grows us—just like rules help kids grow into adults. Forgiveness is a great example. Ephesians 4:32 tells us to forgive just as Christ forgave us. When I refuse to forgive, I cling to a right I surrendered at the cross. But when I obey and forgive, something shifts. I let go of bitterness and gain grace. Obedience doesn't just bless others—it transforms us.

Right now as I write this, I'm walking through a season that requires patience. And let me tell you—I am not gifted in that department. My worst mistakes have been made when I acted in anger, so now I'm trying to obey and wait. Waiting feels unproductive, but God uses it to deepen trust, build endurance, and smooth out impatience (a project still very much in progress). I often say I'm impatiently waiting for patience. That's sanctification.

4. Embrace Trials as Tools

The hard stuff is part of the process. Trials aren't signs that God's forgotten you—they're often signs that He's working deeply in you.

James 1:2–4 tells us to "count it all joy when ye fall into divers temptations; knowing this, that the trying of your faith worketh patience. But let patience have her perfect work, that ye may be perfect and entire, wanting nothing."

Trials reveal what's buried inside. They scrape off layers of self-dependence and expose where we really need Him. When we ask, "Why is this happening to me?"—maybe the better question is, "What is God teaching me through this?"

Sanctification isn't comfortable. It's character forming. And God uses every joy, every sorrow, every ordinary weekday to build us into the image of His Son.

5. Alone Time and People Time

Sanctification is both a solo endeavor and a group venture. There seem to be two basic groups of people in the world: those who need to be with people all the time and those who never want to associate with people at any time. There must be a third group within this basic set—those who find the balance between alone time and people time.

For me I lean toward the lone wolf camp—that second group. Which might seem a bit ironic given that I've spent my life working with people in churches and all kinds of group settings. But it's true. I've had to learn to be with people. It hasn't come naturally. As a kid I was painfully shy—like, "too scared to ask the teacher for a bathroom pass" shy. I've never met a child more bashful than I was.

So even now I don't mind being alone. I actually like it. But I've also come to understand how deeply I need other people—and how much God uses them to sanctify me. Proverbs 27:17 says, "Iron sharpeneth iron; so a man sharpeneth the countenance of his friend." In community we are refined. We learn to love, to forgive, to wait, to listen.

God teaches us through people—friends, church members, small group companions, coffee shop conversations. They speak truth into our lives, pray for us, and (when they're being honest and brave) hold us accountable.

But let's not discount the value of solitude. There's a depth that comes from time alone with God—a kind of soul searching that's hard to access when we're constantly surrounded by noise, even well-meaning people-noise. For those who love being around others, solitude must also be cultivated. Without it sanctification can stay shallow. Roots grow in quiet places.

And just a quick disclaimer: working with people—even beloved church people—can be rough. I've joked more than once that ministry would be perfect if it weren't for the people. But people are the point. People are what we're called to. And all people, like us, are broken. So yes, sometimes we get wounded in community. But those wounds teach us how to heal—and how to help others heal too. These are lessons we simply can't learn on our own.

6. Keep Your Eyes on Jesus

No doubt, this is the most important step in our sanctification journey. Hebrews 12:2 urges us to continue, "Looking unto Jesus the author and finisher of our faith; who for the joy that was set before him endured the cross, despising the shame, and is set down at the right hand of the throne of God." He is both your model and your source of strength. When you stumble, look to His grace. When you grow weary, remember His endurance.

Jesus is not only the goal of sanctification but also the means. As you abide in Him, He transforms you from the inside out. "I am the vine, ye are the branches: He that abideth in me, and I in him, the same bringeth forth much fruit: for without me ye can do nothing" (John 15:5).

THE EVIDENCE OF SANCTIFICATION

How do you know sanctification is happening? Look for fruit. Paul describes the fruit of the Spirit in Galatians 5:22–23: "But the fruit of the Spirit is love, joy, peace, longsuffering, gentleness, goodness, faith, meekness, temperance: against such there is no law."

Love, joy, peace, forbearance, kindness, goodness, faithfulness, gentleness, and self-control—these qualities don't just appear out of nowhere. They're evidence that the Spirit of God is actively at work in you, gradually shaping your character to look more like Jesus.

But remember—fruit takes time. Apple trees don't panic in winter, and neither should we. Be patient with yourself. Celebrate the little wins, the quiet shifts, and the slow-growing roots. God is faithful. He's not rushing the process, but He's not abandoning it either. He will complete the good work He started in you.

SOVEREIGNTY AND SANCTIFICATION COMBINED

Sanctification and sovereignty are not separate tracks; they are woven together in the very fabric of our lives. God's sovereignty assures us that nothing happens outside His rule, and sanctification shows us how He uses those very events—the ordinary and the unbearable—to shape us into the likeness of His Son. The hammer blows we feel are not random strikes of fate but the careful hammering of a Master builder who sees what we cannot. Because He is sovereign, our sanctification is not left to chance. Every unanswered question, every sleepless night, every loss becomes raw material in His hands to refine our faith and deepen our trust.

For me, this truth became painfully real in Wade's death. That loss was not something I would ever have chosen, and from my perspective it shattered the story I thought I was living. Yet even in the valley of grief, God was at work in my sanctification. Through Wade's death, I was confronted with the frailty of my control, the depth of my dependence, and the sheer necessity of clinging to Christ when nothing else made sense. That sorrow is a wound I carry, but it is also a place where God has carved His likeness more deeply into me. In His sovereignty, He did not waste Wade's life, nor my grief—He has been sanctifying me through it, teaching me to trust His heart when I cannot trace His hand.

THE END GOAL OF SANCTIFICATION

The ultimate goal of sanctification isn't just self-improvement. God's not trying to make a shinier version of you—He's revealing Christ in you. Your transformation glorifies Him and points others toward the source of that change.

He predestined us to be conformed to the image of His Son. That's the blueprint. That's the plan. And one day the renovation will be finished. First John 3:2 says, "Beloved, now are we the sons of God, and it doth not yet appear what we shall be: but we know that, when he shall appear, we shall be like him; for we shall see him as he is."

Until that day rest in this: God is sovereign. He's in control. He's working everything together for your good and His glory—and He won't stop until the work is done.

> Judge not the Lord by feeble sense
> But trust Him for His grace.
> Behind a frowning providence
> He hides a smiling face.

> His purposes will ripen fast
> Unfolding every hour.
> The bud may have a bitter taste
> But sweet will be the flower.

Blind unbelief is sure to err
And scan His work in vain.
For God is His own interpreter
And He will make it plain.

WILLIAM COWPER,
God Moves in a Mysterious Way[19]

---

19. William Cowper, "God Moves in a Mysterious Way," in *Olney Hymns* (London: W. Oliver, 1779)

CHAPTER 21

WHAT HAPPENS ISN'T KING—RESPONSE IS

*"Be not deceived, Wormwood, our cause is never more
in jeopardy than when a human, no longer desiring but
still intending to do our Enemy's will, looks round upon a
universe in which every trace of Him seems to have vanished,
and asks why he has been forsaken and still obeys."*

C. S. LEWIS, *The Screwtape Letters*[20]

O n Monday of the week I wrote this, a Russian bomb struck
a children's hospital in Kyiv, Ukraine. Someone sitting safely
behind a screen in a command center somewhere inside Russia pushed
a button. And with that one decision forty-nine innocent lives were
taken. It was mass murder hiding on a battlefield. The kind of atroc-
ity that gets labeled "war" on government briefings and international
news programs, but in any other context, would have the world hunt-
ing Vladimir Putin down for crimes against humanity.

---

20. C.S. Lewis, *The Screwtape Letters* (New York: Macmillan, 1943)

One of the victims was thirty-year-old Svetlana Lukianchyk, a pediatric doctor. She had been working in the cancer ward and was helping evacuate children when the missile hit. She didn't make it out.

Two days later on Wednesday mourners gathered in the western city of Lviv to bury her. A reporter at the funeral spoke to her grand-mother, Alla Zherebetska. Her words were like a punch to the soul: "She was a golden child. I don't understand how this could have happened. How the Lord could have taken her away. I have no idea why. I don't have the strength for this. She was supposed to live a long life. She just got married."

And there it is—that word again: why. Probably the most repeated word on earth in times of suffering. Why? Why her? Why now? Why would God let this happen? When life stops making sense, the human heart reflexively reaches for that question. Because we are sense-making creatures living in a world that often refuses to make sense.

And if we can't find the reason, we start looking for someone to blame. When the cause isn't clear, that blame often lands on God.

This reflex to assign blame isn't new. In fact, it's ancient. Straight from the opening chapters of our history. Remember Adam's answer to God in Genesis 3 when God asked, "Have you eaten from the tree I commanded you not to eat from?" Adam didn't just fess up. He went full courtroom defense mode. In one sentence he managed to blame both Eve *and* God: "The woman (blame) You gave me (double blame) made me do it."

And there it was. The birth of the blame game. Humanity's original knee-jerk reaction to crisis. If something's broken, someone must be held responsible. Preferably someone else.

The instinct is old, and it's strong.

I saw it firsthand not long ago, courtesy of a middle-aged woman whose travel day had been thrown off course when she was inconvenienced by an airline company. She stood at the gate, red in the face, temples pulsing, voice escalating. "I am not moving until you find me a seat!" she barked. The gate manager, already worn thin, gently responded, "Ma'am, your plane has already taken off."

Undeterred, she doubled down. "Then I demand to know who is responsible! And I want to speak to someone who can help me!"

Trying not to roll his eyes out of his head, the agent offered her a seat on the next flight, a dinner voucher, and even some free miles. "You've got forty minutes to the next gate. You'll be there in no time," he said.

But it wasn't about the miles. Or the next flight. Or even dinner. It was about someone paying for the injustice she felt. "No," she snapped. "I want to know who is responsible. My husband and I are medallion members. We've flown this airline forever. We will not be treated like this."

She wanted satisfaction, which in this case looked like finding someone to blame and wringing an apology out of them like water from a sponge. I watched the whole episode like we do when we witness a meltdown in public—part horror, part entertainment. It was painful to see but also impossible to look away. I'm not sure if she ever found closure, but people like that rarely do.

I fly a lot. Once upon a time it felt like an adventure. These days it feels more like being stuffed into a pneumatic tube like a bank envelope and shot through the sky until I'm delivered at my final destination. It's not glamorous. But it is enlightening.

Because airports for some reason have a way of revealing the unedited version of people. When flights get delayed or gates get switched, you start to see what's been hiding under the surface. Just watch the pre-boarding lineup. It's not a race, but you'd never know that by the way people lunge forward when their flight is called as if they're auditioning for the Olympic 100-meter dash. Their seats are assigned. The plane isn't going to leave without them. And yet—full-blown tension.

Why? Because pressure reveals priorities. And when people feel squeezed, they squeal.

And when things don't go as planned, we do what we've always done—we look for who to blame. Instead of asking, "How do I move forward from here?" we reach for the easier question: "Who made this happen to me?"

We've come to the point in society where we believe we are so entitled that we deserve full access to every intricate detail in every situation—ours and everyone else's. We want to know what went wrong, who said what, and whose fingerprints are on the mess. Politicians, celebrities, coworkers, pastors, lawn guys—nobody's exempt. If you're a public figure of any kind at all, your personal life is considered public property. If you mess up? We want the details—preferably in high definition with multiple camera angles.

Especially if the mistake somehow disrupts our routine or offends our sensibilities. The moment we're inconvenienced, the blame radar kicks in. Who did this to me? Where's the guilty party? Who's going to pay?

And we don't mind spending hours to find out. Fueled by irritation and the thrill of righteous anger, we scroll, dig, and research until we've built a nice, tidy narrative with a villain we can yell at.

Have you noticed how many ads there are now for attorneys who will get you "maximum compensation" for just about anything that wasn't your fault? I'm a sports fan, and I root for any team that even remotely smells like Georgia. But lately every game I watch or listen to is interrupted by lawyers shouting at me, offering to avenge any stubbed toe and make the other guy pay millions. One guy's motto is that he'll "strong arm" your enemies until you can retire early. It's like justice has been replaced with jackpot.

Now don't get me wrong. Sometimes people need to be held accountable. There is a time and a place for justice. But when blame becomes our default setting—our go-to mindset—we lose something crucial: responsibility. We stop looking inward and forward, and instead we obsess over what's behind us and who to pin it on.

And that backward-looking habit? It almost always comes wrapped in anger. Just like our friend at the airport. That kind of response might give us five minutes of emotional ventilation, but it leaves behind relational wreckage and regret that's a lot harder to clean up.

There is a better way.

It's always refreshing to see people respond to pain with grace and clarity. There are people in my life I've lost respect for—not because they failed but because they followed their failure with bad behavior. Sometimes the event isn't what burdens us most—it's the ugly reaction afterward that weighs down the memory.

God gives us space to respond differently. And in that space something holy can happen.

For example, I love the game of golf, though I'll be the first to tell you that the PGA Tour has not called asking me for tips. Still in recent years one of my favorite pros to follow has become Scottie Scheffler. I wasn't instantly drawn to him, but my admiration has grown over time—not just because of his skill with a golf club but because of his calm, collected character under pressure.

A while back Scheffler found himself in a bizarre and troubling situation at the PGA Championship in Louisville, Kentucky. On a rainy Friday morning during a tragic and chaotic scene outside the course where a man had been fatally struck by a vehicle, Scheffler was mistakenly arrested by tournament security in the confusion. To say it shocked the golf world would be an understatement. ESPN practically stopped breathing.

But here's what stood out: Scheffler's response. While many people might have erupted, argued, or pulled the "Do you know who I am?" card, he didn't. He stayed composed, followed instructions, and cooperated fully—even though he later admitted to shaking uncontrollably from the stress of the moment.

When he finally addressed the incident publicly, he didn't lash out or demand justice for himself. He expressed sorrow for the tragic loss of life, showed respect for those involved, and calmly moved forward. No vengeance, no theatrics, no public scolding of security. Just humility and perspective. It was a masterclass in how to behave when the pressure dial is turned to ten.

His attitude said, in essence, "Yes, it happened. Yes, it was hard. But there are bigger things than my discomfort. Let's honor what matters and keep going."

That's what sanctification looks like on a golf course—and on a stage. Crisis managed.

Many of us want to believe we'd respond that way. We picture ourselves as the calm, grounded person when adversity hits. But wanting and hoping aren't strategies. Without formation and intentional growth most of us will respond with panic, not peace. Reflex, not resolve.

What I've learned over time is this: The truths we're talking about—this divine authority of God, this call to maturity—don't eliminate the human feelings that rise up when life hits hard. But they *do* form us to live through those moments differently. Not perfectly. But more faithfully. More graciously. And more like Christ.

As I have slowly accepted His providence in my own life, especially for Wade's passing, I have told my children that the way you react to a situation is often more important than the situation itself. The death of my son was as great a nightmare as any parent can suffer. However, it has not been the only valley I've gone through in life. I, like you, live in a fallen world—and as we walk through it, we find there are as many deep valleys and inclines as there are leisurely downhill strolls.

It would be an added disaster to walk through them all and not come away with lessons learned. Let me share with you a few that God has graciously shown me concerning how we respond to our tribulations in life.

ASSESS WHAT HAS HAPPENED REALISTICALLY.

When my wife came to me and said, "Wade has been run over," on that fateful Sunday, my first thought was denial. That sort of thing happens to other people, not to us. But it did happen. And the shock of it was paralyzing.

As I've listened to others tell their stories, I've learned that disbelief is often the first reflex. Maybe it's a built-in mercy mechanism—our minds buffering the blow so we don't fall apart instantly. But denial doesn't last. It didn't for me. The parking lot scene made it real. The unimaginable had entered my life. And now came the harder question: What do I do with this reality?

Even wise people who spend a lifetime walking with God are

stunned when suffering becomes personal. The disciples had Jesus Himself tell them more than once that He was going away, that He would suffer, and that He would die. But when it happened, they scattered. In fear. In disbelief. In heartbreak.

And thank God the Bible shows us their failures. It helps me. Because I've failed too. And I can relate.

I believe it wasn't until the disciples got some distance, both in time and space, that things began to make sense. When it was happening, it was a fog. Later in hindsight the pieces started to fall into place. So it is for us. Sometimes the fog is thick. But when it lifts, clarity comes. And when it does, we must assess—not with denial or despair—but with honesty. What just happened? What are the consequences? What are the next steps?

Only then can healing and direction begin.

I was in Estonia several years ago when I finally picked up Viktor Frankl's *Man's Search for Meaning*. I'd heard about it all my life but never read it. It's short—but it hit me deep. Frankl, an Austrian psychiatrist and Holocaust survivor, endured horrors in the Nazi concentration camps, losing nearly everything and everyone.

But somewhere in the middle of the suffering, surrounded by bunkmates either asleep or silently unraveling, Frankl pulled out a small notebook and began to write. Not because he understood the pain. Not because he made peace with it. But because he *accepted* it. He couldn't change what had happened—but he could decide how he would respond.

That decision gave birth to a book that has helped millions.

And it reminded me again: We live in a broken world. No one gets a pass. And when the shrapnel of that brokenness slices into our lives, the first step isn't to fix it. It's to accept that it happened. That this is *your* day. That you are *in* this story now. Not because you're worse. Not because you're better. But because you're human.

Which brings me to Chernobyl.

On April 26, 1986, during a late-night safety test, the Chernobyl Nuclear Power Plant in Ukraine (USSR) experienced a catastrophic explosion. Reactor 4 went critical, igniting a nuclear firestorm that would poison the land, the sky, and thousands of lives. It remains one of the worst nuclear disasters in human history.

At the center of it was Anatoly Dyatlov, the deputy chief engineer who oversaw the fateful test. Despite repeated warnings, he insisted on pushing forward, disabling safety systems and dismissing danger signs.

When the explosion happened, eyewitnesses said Dyatlov froze. Reality had finally overtaken denial, and he was unable to process or respond. Like many in power, he couldn't accept what had just occurred—and that inability only made things worse.

Then in steps Boris Shcherbina, chairman of the USSR's Chernobyl commission. With all the classic traits of a Soviet official—pride, denial, and an aversion to bad news—he refused to believe the scale of the disaster. He ignored scientific counsel. Refused protective gear. Scoffed at evacuation requests. Even as radioactive winds carried death into the city of Pripyat, he held the buses at bay. Not until a full day and a half later when the radiation was off the charts, were citizens allowed to flee.

But by then it was too late for many.

Shcherbina's failure to accept and assess the crisis in time cost lives. His pride blinded him. His denial prolonged suffering. And his legacy is a cautionary tale of what happens when we refuse to face hard realities.

These are extreme examples, yes. But they mirror the smaller, quieter failures we're all prone to when crisis hits. If we won't accept what's happened—if we insist on denial or delay—we risk compounding the damage.

As painful as it may be, truth must come before healing. Acceptance is not surrender. It is clarity. And with clarity we can finally begin to move forward.

AFTER ACCEPTANCE, WHAT DO I DO NOW?

"Don't dwell on what went wrong. Instead, focus on what to do next. Spend your energy moving forward together towards an answer."

DENIS WAITLEY

"If you can't fly then run, if you can't run then walk, if you can't walk then crawl, but whatever you do you have to keep moving forward."

MARTIN LUTHER KING JR.

"Life is like riding a bicycle, to keep your balance, you must keep moving."

ALBERT EINSTEIN

Let's just say it out loud: Finality is brutal.

They're gone. The relationship has unraveled. The job disappeared faster than cookies at a second-grade snack break. The diagnosis didn't get better after a second opinion. And no matter how many times you refresh the screen or rewind the moment in your mind, you can't undo what has already taken place. Final is...final. Heavy. The kind of word that makes the room feel smaller.

If you've ever read a book or watched a movie that ends with "The End," you know how it works: You close it, stretch, and move on. But when the casket closes or someone you love backs out of the driveway for the last time, moving on isn't so simple. It doesn't come with popcorn or credits. And how we respond to that moment—to that heavy finality—will shape not just the rest of our lives but also the lives of those who walk beside us.

I've met people who got stuck there. Ten years later, they're still saying things like, "I can't believe this happened to me," or the timeless classic, "Why me?" These are the emotional equivalents of calling tech support after the device is covered in orange juice. It's not that the emotion is wrong—grief is human. But if you live in the question forever, you never get to the answer.

The better question? "What do I do now?"

C. S. Lewis said it perfectly: "Getting over a painful experience is much like crossing monkey bars. You have to let go at some point in order to move forward."

Which is both wise and slightly terrifying if you've ever tried monkey bars as an adult.

In his nostalgic, haunting novel *Great Expectations*, Charles Dickens tragically illustrates this danger in the life of an old spinster known in the book as Miss Havisham. She was jilted at the altar on her wedding day and as a result shut herself off from the rest of the world to become a bitter recluse. Stuck in the tragedy, she never leaves her house and stops all the clocks so that she will not be reminded of the passing of time. She wears her wedding dress every day and keeps the spoiled wedding dinner on the table for the mice to devour. She grows to hate humanity, especially men, and in her misery she devises a bitter plan.

She adopts a young girl, Estella, and she attempts to train her to be cold and cruel so that she will learn to break men's hearts the way one of them broke hers. Miss Havisham invites a young man named Pip to the house so that Estella can practice on him and so that her teacher can watch as she does so. Pip mistakenly believes that Miss Havisham wants them to be together, and he also thinks that she has become his mystery benefactor. In the end, she realizes the mistakes that she has made, and she wants to change, but it's too late. Her story ends in a tragic accident where she is burned when her wedding dress catches fire, and she dies as the result of the tragedy.

I've met Miss Havisham from time to time in life, people who are paralyzed by a broken heart and unable to move forward. They just grotesquely writhe away in the singular spot in life where the dreadful day left them. They can often be heard muttering, "I can't believe this happened," or "Why me?"

If there is to be fulfillment in life, there must come a day in which every survivor of heartache and sorrow takes a step forward and leaves that scorched earth behind them. That first step begins with asking yourself, "What do I do now?" Life is not over, and you still have life to live. Failure to live purposefully means that whatever caused the pain you are suffering has double victory. It has devastated you and is further destroying your ability to retain a meaningful existence.

It seems that the emphasis in the Bible is not to look backward and find out if God is responsible in order to accuse Him…the emphasis is rather on looking ahead to what God can make of seeming tragedy.

Let me give a real-world example. President Donald Trump has repeated more times than a kid who just discovered the echo in a canyon: "If I had been President, the war in Ukraine never would have happened."

We get it. You think things would have gone differently. But repeating it like a political version of a broken record (ask your grandfather what that means) doesn't do a thing to stop bombs from falling or families from fleeing. It's just noise at this point—and an irritating one.

"If I had been president, the war in Ukraine never would have happened." (There it is again!!!)

Maybe. Maybe not. But here's what we know: It *did* happen. He wasn't President. And the war is real. Right now. Bombs are falling. Cities are crumbling. Mothers are fleeing. Soldiers are bleeding. And no number of hypotheticals is going to un-bomb a building.

Speculating about alternate timelines might feel empowering—like you're one wise decision away from being a Marvel superhero—but in the end, it doesn't help the people who need help now. Healing doesn't come from rewinding.

God doesn't dwell in the "what if." He lives in the "what do we do now."

For me the "what do I do now" looked like this: I was one week into our calling to Russia when we lost our son Wade. The grief hadn't even had time to settle before I was standing in a church the next Sunday after his death, still raw, still bleeding, still trying to be faithful. My kids needed a dad. My wife needed a husband. And somewhere inside I needed to believe I could be one of those people I had read about—the ones who walked forward through the tears.

Let me just say it: I should have waited. I thought I could outrun grief. Turns out, it laces up sneakers faster than you. A few years later the mourning I tried to sidestep caught up to me and beat me up really badly. I wrestled that angel, and I still have the internal limp to prove it.

But the important part isn't that I rushed. It's that I didn't stop.

The grief didn't leave me. It didn't pack a suitcase and wave good-bye. But over time it became…bearable. Not gone. Just…not crushing.

Even now I still tear up remembering. But I'm still moving.

I've traveled into some of the places in the world where many years ago the apostle Paul also traveled. Even today some of those places are difficult, and I wouldn't want to live there. I sometimes pause and think about how incredibly hard it must have been for Paul and the crew he was responsible for to go forward in those rather primitive days. There was daily news that brought heartache and tears. Daily, not once in a lifetime, but daily. Paul himself had his own self-confessed burden that he desperately asked God to take away yet it was never removed. By his own confession at times he became incredibly weary, both by physical suffering and the exhausting demands of ministering to difficult people. In 2 Corinthians, he writes, "We were under great pressure, far beyond our ability to endure, so that we despaired of life itself. Indeed, we felt we had received the sentence of death. But this happened that we might not rely on ourselves but on God, who raises the dead" (1:8-9).

To suffer as he did and to consider the surroundings and isolation in which he lived is remarkable and deserving of sainthood. Yet even Paul despaired, even to the point of feeling like he was going to die. Don't miss the fact that in those conditions, he moved on. Had he stopped to spend time in much deserved pity parties, we may still be waiting for the church to flourish. He moved forward. He did the next thing.

Which brings us to you.

Only you can answer the question, "What do I do now?" And no, you don't need to have the full GPS route mapped. You just need to take the next faithful step. Not build a shrine to the pain. Not organize your whole calendar around your heartache. And please, don't start wearing your emotional wedding dress every day.

Jesus gave us the Lord's Supper to remember His death—yes. But He also told His followers to go into the world and live. To move. To witness. To make disciples. Not to hold funerals for the rest of their lives.

Teddy Roosevelt said it well: "In a moment of decision, the best thing you can do is the right thing. The next best thing is the wrong thing. And the worst thing you can do is nothing."

So take time to grieve. Carve out space to remember. But don't let your calendar become Miss Havisham's time capsule.

You're still here.

You've still got breath.

So ask it:

What do I do now?

EVERYTHING IS GOING TO BE ALL RIGHT BY AND BY

I had the blessing as a young man of sitting under the philosophical greatness of one of the most underrated minds of our time. I never met him, but I heard his voice nearly every day while bouncing down the highways and backroads of North Georgia. His name was Ludlow Porch. Well, his *real* name was Bobby Hansen, but if your name is Bobby Hansen and you get a chance to rebrand as Ludlow Porch, you take that deal every time.

Ludlow was a radio host for over thirty years, mostly around Atlanta, but his voice spread across eight Southern states like molasses on a warm biscuit. He had that slow, comfortable drawl that made you feel like the world wasn't quite as crazy as the news was trying to make it sound. And every show without fail he ended with the same gentle benediction: "Whatever else you do today, you find somebody to be nice to!"

That should be etched in granite and placed somewhere that is internationally important.

But there was another phrase he said that stuck with me—one I now find myself repeating when I'm sitting across from someone in pain, not sure what to say but desperate to say something true. Whenever a caller rang Ludlow's show with a problem too tangled for easy answers, Ludlow would listen, maybe offer a little counsel, and then wrap it all up with this: *Everything's gonna be all right by and by.*

Y'all, that's not just homespun wisdom. That's straight-up theology with a Southern accent. Seriously, you could spend a semester unpacking Romans 8:28 in seminary—or you could just translate it into Ludlow Porch's paraphrase: *Everything's gonna be all right by and by.* Same message. Fewer tuition payments.

It doesn't mean the pain disappears on cue. This isn't spiritual ibuprofen. Even Jesus wept. Even Jesus got heartbroken looking out over Jerusalem. Pain is part of the package when your mailing address says "Earth" and you are a part of the human species.

But Romans 8:28 reminds us that God's not done. He's not ignoring the chaos. He's weaving it. And there is a day—out there in the mysterious timeline of the kingdom—when the wrong will be made right. When tears will be wiped. When the aching will finally give way to peace. When everything really will be all right.

When Wade died, I didn't hear Ludlow's voice echoing Romans 8:28 in my head. I didn't hear anything, honestly. Grief doesn't come with a soundtrack. But in time with the slow healing that only grace and calendar pages can provide, I began to see it. To trust it. And eventually to believe it. That phrase—that simple, slow, deeply Southern phrase—was no longer just a sign-off from a radio show. It became a whisper from heaven.

Everything's gonna be all right. By and by.

BY AND BY TIME RIGHT NOW

"By and by time" isn't always a distant someday on a church calendar. For me it started showing up in the here and now.

In those raw, blurry first hours after Wade died, I sat on the front porch of the home he'd never come back to and wondered if I'd ever smile again. Really smile. Not the kind you fake for family photos or strangers in the cereal aisle. The kind that starts in your soul.

And now I do. Somehow I do. I marvel at what God has allowed me to experience since that unspeakably hard day. It's not a résumé I would've chosen—but it is a testimony I wouldn't trade. I count it a strange and holy honor to serve Him, even from the scarred places.

Now if you asked me, "Would you go back and change it? Would you bring Wade back if you could?" The answer is easy and aching: Of course I would. No question. I would give anything to hold him again.

But God in His mysterious sovereignty has made it clear that somehow—somehow—it had to be this way. I don't camp out there or try to untangle the logic. I accept it by faith. And from that place I can say—with no bitterness in my voice—that I have no complaints about life, not even on the darkest day I've ever lived.

God is good. But let's not kid ourselves into thinking He's only good when the story goes the way we wanted. He wouldn't be a better

Father if He had allowed Wade to live. He's not less good because He didn't.

As I write this part of the book, it's been just a couple of weeks since the attempted assassination of President Donald Trump. His life was spared. But a man named Corey Comperatore—a fifty-year-old fireman, a husband and father—was killed.

In the aftermath I heard people say, "What a miracle! God saved Trump! Isn't God good?"

And yes. Yes, He is. But what about the Comperatore family as they stood over a casket? What are they supposed to say? "Isn't God awful?" "Isn't He unjust?"

Of course not. But this is where our theology often gets stuck in the mud. We like God's goodness when it aligns with our version of victory. But real sovereignty means God was just as good, just as wise, and just as present at the graveside as He was at victory rally.

That's hard to say out loud. Harder still to believe. But it's true.

He is a miraculous God in both moments. And if He chooses to heal or chooses not to, He is still God. Still good. Still writing a story that is bigger than what we can see.

And it's in trusting that truth—sitting in it, even when it stings—that the "by and by" isn't just a future hope. It becomes a present peace.

BY AND BY TIME OF THE FUTURE

By and by time also awaits in the future. That might sound like the kind of line you stitch on a pillow, but it holds a weight of eternal promise. A simple, unshakeable understanding of what the "by and by" actually means—of what heaven truly is—is absolutely essential if we are to live in peace about where we're going and those we've loved and lost.

We'll talk more about this in the final chapter, but for now, just hear this: According to Scripture, there is a day marked on God's calendar when Wade will be reunited with us. A real day. Not a metaphor. Not a wistful hope. A literal, appointed day.

On August 24, 1994, we laid Wade's body to rest in Alta Vista Cemetery in Gainesville, Georgia. We said goodbye with broken hearts and buried him in hope. And one day—on a date known only to the Father—that ground will open, and his body will rise. Not because of our longing but because Jesus already walked out of His own grave three days after His death. That's not just a miracle—it's a prototype.

That day will come for all who have trusted in Christ's death and resurrection. The journey we're on doesn't end in dirt and silence. It ends in resurrection and reunion. The ship we're sailing on will dock in a heavenly port. And when it does, the gangway will be lined with saints and songs.

Jesus said it plainly in John 14: "Don't let your hearts be troubled. You believe in God; believe also in me. I'm going to prepare a place for you. And if I go, I *will* come again and take you to be with me" (paraphrased, emphasis added).

He didn't say "might." He didn't say "if the schedule works out." He said *will.*

Paul doubled down on this in 1 Thessalonians 4:16–17: "The Lord himself will descend from heaven with a shout, with the voice of the archangel and with the trumpet of God" That's not a subtle return. That's a cosmic arrival.

And then Paul gives us the rest of the story: "The dead in Christ will rise first." That's Wade. That's millions of others. But he doesn't stop there: "Then we who are still alive will be caught up together with them in the clouds to meet the Lord in the air"

Together. Forever. With the Lord.

That's the by and by. And yes—it's worth singing about.

Sanford Bennett isn't a household name. But on June 21, 1836, he entered the world in New York, and by the time he left it in 1898, he'd gifted us with something enduring. During the Civil War, Bennett moved to Elkhorn, Wisconsin, served as a Second Lieutenant with the Wisconsin Volunteers, and later opened a drugstore—even before having a proper medical degree. (It was the 1800s. Apparently you just needed a store and some jars.) Eventually he earned his credentials from Rush Medical College in Chicago in 1874.

But Sanford's legacy wasn't forged in medicine. It came from a friendship—with a man named Joseph Webster.

Webster was a musician, and like many artistic souls he had a melancholy streak. He battled periods of intense depression—what they called "fits" in those days—and it often left him feeling like life was all clouds and no silver linings.

One day two concerned women walked into Sanford's store and let him know that Webster was deep in one of those episodes. Sanford with a touch of humor and a whole lot of compassion said, "Well, you know how temperamental musicians can be, but I know just what to do when I see him."

He wasn't bluffing. Sanford had discovered that music could lift Joseph out of the fog. Years before music therapy was a clinical thing, Sanford Bennett was prescribing lyrics instead of pills.

Here's how he tells the story himself:

He came into my place of business [in Elkhorn, Wisconsin], walked down to the stove, and turned his back on me without speaking. I was at my desk. Turning to him, I said, "Webster, what is the matter now?"

"It's no matter," he replied, "it will be alright, by and by."

The idea of the hymn came to me like a flash of sunlight, and I replied, "The Sweet By and By! Why would that not make a good hymn?"

"Maybe it would," he said indifferently.

Turning to my desk, I penned the words of the hymn as fast as I could write. I handed the words to Webster. As he read the words, his eyes kindled. I stepped back to my desk and he began writing the notes seated at the stove. Taking his violin, he played the melody and then jotted down the notes of the chorus. It was not over thirty minutes from the time I took my pen to write the words before two friends with Webster and myself were singing the hymn.

As we were singing the new hymn, R. R. Crosby, my uncle, came into the store. "I never heard that song before," exclaimed Mr. Crosby. "I heard it across the street and couldn't resist coming in to hear it better. That hymn is immortal." It was used in public shortly after, for within two weeks children on the streets were singing it.[21]

---

21. Sanford Fillmore Bennett, "Hymn History: 'Sweet By and By'," *Enjoying The Journey*, September 7, 2022.

The hymn caught fire. The hymn became a gospel standard and has been included in hymnals ever since.

I remember singing it in the pews of Riverside Baptist Church in Savannah, sitting with my mother. It got sung so often it started to feel like church wallpaper. I even found myself wondering if "the beautiful shore" was more poetic license than proper doctrine.

But now? In this season of life? It doesn't sound corny. It sounds comforting. I don't even need to sing it. I just need to read it—and let it work its way into my bones.

> There's a land that is fairer than day,
> And by faith we can see it afar,
> For the Father waits over the way
> To prepare us a dwelling place there.
>
> In the sweet by and by,
> We shall meet on that beautiful shore;
> In the sweet by and by,
> We shall meet on that beautiful shore.
>
> We shall sing on that beautiful shore
> The melodious songs of the blest;
> And our spirits shall sorrow no more—
> Not a sigh for the blessing of rest.
>
> To our bountiful Father above
> We will offer our tribute of praise
> For the glorious gift of His love
> And the blessings that hallow our days.

In the sweet by and by,

We shall meet on that beautiful shore;

In the sweet by and by,

We shall meet on that beautiful shore.[22]

Call it heaven. Call it the sweet by and by. Call it whatever name gives your soul a breath of peace.

But believe this: It's coming. And it will be sweeter than we dare imagine.

And we will be together. Forever. With the Lord.

22. Sanford Fillmore Bennett (lyrics) and Joseph Philbrick Webster (music), *In the Sweet By and By*, 1868. First published in *The Signet Ring*.

CHAPTER 22

THE LONG WAIT
FOR GOD'S REPLY

*"Clearly, unless the Lord chooses to explain Himself
to us—which, let's be honest, He often does not—His
motivations and purposes are beyond the reach of mortal
man. What this means in practical terms is that many of
our questions, especially the ones that start with the word
'why,' will have to remain unanswered for the time being."*

JAMES DOBSON[23]

S ince Wade's death, I've been surrounded by kind people who've reached out with words of comfort. Some do it with Scripture, some with personal stories, and some give me books like this one. Most of these kind-hearted souls carry a deep gift of encouragement and feel a strong nudge to use it when they hear my story. I truly am grateful for them all. Every warm word has been like a soft patch on a very torn heart.

---

23. James C. Dobson, *When God Doesn't Make Sense* (Wheaton, IL: Tyndale House, 1993)

One of the most common lines of comfort I've received goes something like this: "One day, everything will become clear, and you'll understand why this happened." Sometimes it's followed by a Hallmark-worthy tale of someone who went through deep pain only to discover a miraculous silver lining—usually something involving a baby, big bills paid off, or a ministry that now spans six continents.

But here's the thing: That doesn't always happen.

It's been thirty years since that dark August day in 1994, and I still don't have a great, miraculous, or satisfying explanation for Wade's death. No ribbon neatly tied on the pain. No heaven-sent PowerPoint explaining the purpose. Just a gaping space where the answer should be—and a God who while silent still somehow stays.

One of the tougher realities of the Christian life is this: Not every question gets answered. Some of them don't even get a decent shrug. We ache for explanations, for meaning, for dots to connect. But Scripture never promised a tidy Q&A session before we leave Earth.

There is a scene from the television series *The Old Man* that comes to mind. Jeff Bridges plays Dan Chase, an aging former CIA operative whose past catches up with him in the worst way. After decades off the grid, he's back in Afghanistan, staring down a final mission that might just cost him his life—offering himself up to save his daughter.

As they make their way toward this ominous showdown, his old boss (now high-up in the CIA) starts drilling him with questions—deep, unresolved, psychological stuff. Chase tries to dodge but eventually snaps. He says: "I understand there are things that you would like to know, battles that we could reenact, wounds that we could pull apart. It's just not how I choose to spend my last few moments of sunlight. *So, sometimes there are things that you don't get to know before the curtain comes down.*"

That line stopped me. Because it feels like it was written not just for ex-CIA agents but for people like us—people with real loss, real faith, and real unanswered questions.

Sometimes we don't get to know. Not before the curtain drops. Not even with years of prayer, counseling, fasting, journaling, and sitting in awkward small groups where someone inevitably says, "Well, maybe this happened so you'd write a book about it." (Please don't.)

We carry these unresolved questions quietly—like emotional carryons we didn't mean to pack but now have to lug around the terminal of life. They sneak up on us at 3:30 a.m., usually when the house is dark and quiet and the only voice left to echo through the room is your own.

What is the answer to this pain?

That's not a rebellious question. It's whispered by honest souls who believe enough to ask. It's an intelligent, aching inquiry that longs for clarity, for some hint of divine logic.

But more often than not, what we get is silence. Not cold, dismissive silence—but a kind that somehow feels more like a sacred pause. A space where God is present but not explaining. Close but not giving up anything.

And that's not satisfying—but it is an invitation. An invitation to trust anyway. To sit in the tension with faith. To believe that perhaps the curtain may fall without the answers we hoped for—but with the God we've learned to trust.

For many these unanswered questions aren't just theological speed bumps—they're the reason they veer off the road entirely. Christianity's long and winding history is scattered with people lying along its shoulder, spiritual castaways clutching questions that broke them. Good people. Smart people. People who really tried. They didn't leave the faith because they wanted to. They left because they couldn't square what they were told with what they lived.

Even the best of us—the ones who know better, who've read the footnotes, who've taught the Bible study—have had our own mental mutinies. Little rebellions of the heart. Quiet uprisings where we wonder, just for a second, if maybe we've missed something…or been missed ourselves.

The Bible isn't shy about this tension. It doesn't sweep life's hard questions under the ecclesiastical rug. Instead, it meets us there. It acknowledges the ache, nods at the mystery, and then gently points us forward. It reminds us that faith isn't built on answers but on trust. This is the cadence of a believer's walk: trusting in what we cannot see, holding on through what we cannot explain.

While we may not get the clarity we crave this side of heaven, Scripture whispers that the silence isn't wasted. God has a reason for it. And because His nature is good, His reasons are too—even when they leave us hanging. Even when all we have is the pause, the ache, and the promise that one day it will make sense. And even if it doesn't, He will still be worth trusting.

LIFE'S PAINFUL MYSTERIES

We've all witnessed moments in life that are, for lack of a more theological term, just plain baffling. A child dies unexpectedly. A faithful and much-needed servant of God is sidelined by a devastating illness. A promising opportunity vanishes faster than the last donut at a men's meeting. It doesn't make sense—and that's exactly what makes it so painful.

Like David we watch as the wicked seem to waltz through life with a smile, while the righteous limp through hardship. We echo the cry of the prophet Habakkuk: "O Lord, how long shall I cry, and thou wilt not hear! even cry out unto thee of violence, and thou wilt not save! Why dost thou shew me iniquity, and cause me to behold grievance? for spoiling and violence are before me: and there are that raise up strife and contention" (Habakkuk 1:2–3).

If we're honest (and why not be, God already knows), we've had those moments too. Moments where we stare at the sky and ask, "God, are You even paying attention?" And if He is, the follow-up: "Then why aren't You doing something about this?"

These aren't signs of unbelief. They're signs that we're still in the fight—still engaged in a faith that dares to wrestle with the hard things. These questions rise not from rebellion but from the wounds of living in a world where things break and often don't get fixed.

Which brings us back to Job. Good ol' Job, the poster child for "Things Can Always Get Worse." Here's a man who feared God, lived with integrity, and probably flossed after every meal—and still lost everything in a single day. His wealth, his children, even his health. And as if that wasn't enough, his friends came over, sat with him in silence for a bit (which was great), and then opened their mouths (which ruined it).

They tried to explain the mystery, but their explanations only deepened Job's pain. Job didn't want clichés. He wanted answers. And when God finally did speak, it wasn't to clarify but to question: "Where wast thou when I laid the foundations of the earth? declare, if thou hast understanding" (Job 38:4).

Translation: *Were you there when I spun galaxies into place and stitched DNA molecules together? No? Then maybe—just maybe—you're not in the best position to evaluate My decisions.*

God never explained Himself to Job. He didn't hand over a divine spreadsheet labeled "Why This Happened." What He did offer was Himself—and somehow that was enough.

Isaiah says it best: "For my thoughts are not your thoughts, neither are your ways my ways, saith the Lord. For as the heavens are higher than the earth, so are my ways higher than your ways, and my thoughts than your thoughts" (Isaiah 55:8–9).

We don't get to see the full story right now. But the Author does. And even in the mystery, even in the silence, we are still held by the One who sees the end from the beginning.

FAITH IN THE FACE OF MYSTERY

Faith, if it's going to be faith at all, must involve some level of mystery. If everything made perfect sense, it wouldn't be called faith—it'd be called sight. Hebrews 11:1 defines faith as "the substance of things hoped for, the evidence of things not seen."

Faith doesn't wait for everything to line up in bullet points. It doesn't demand a syllabus or a detailed itinerary. Faith walks forward when the lights are still off. It survives in the space where answers don't. In fact, it only *exists* because there are no answers. If all our questions were resolved, we wouldn't need faith—we'd need a spreadsheet.

Abraham gives us one of the clearest examples. God tells him, "Leave everything you've ever known, and I'll show you where we're going." Abraham's GPS destination reads: "Unknown." And yet he obeys. Hebrews 11:8 puts it this way: "By faith Abraham, when he was called to go out into a place which he should after receive for an inheritance, obeyed; and he went out, not knowing whither he went."

That's faith. He trusted God's promise even when the path ahead looked like a foggy country road with no street signs. He walked forward with nothing but a promise and a God who cannot lie.

But faith isn't passive. It's not just waiting around, humming hymns in a holy recliner. Faith is active. It's a stubborn, day-by-day, foot-in-front-of-the-other choice to believe that God is who He says He is—even when life screams otherwise. Faith whispers, "I don't need to know *why*—because I know *Who*."

Faith shifts our focus away from the mystery and onto the Master. It refuses to let the why define us and instead anchors us in the unchanging character of God. He is faithful; He is good; He is just—even when life feels wildly unjust.

THE NECESSITY OF PATIENCE

Here's the part we'd rather skip: Faith and patience go hand in hand. Hebrews 6:12 says: "Be not slothful, but followers of them who through faith and patience inherit the promises."

Patience isn't just waiting—it's how you wait. It's the ability to keep trusting, even when nothing's changing. It means sitting in traffic on God's timeline without honking the horn.

Patience is what holds you steady when your prayers haven't been answered, your miracle hasn't come, and the only thing growing is your frustration. It's trusting God's *when* just as much as His *what*.

Joseph is a model of this. Unlike so many other Bible heroes, his story doesn't include a moral breakdown or a dramatic moment of doubt. He didn't lash out or lose it (though who would've blamed him?). His brothers betrayed him. He was sold as a slave. Falsely accused. Left to rot in prison. If anyone had cause to throw in the towel and mutter, "Well this is a fine reward for obedience," it was Joseph.

And yet—he didn't. He waited. Not with gritted teeth but with grace. He served faithfully in every unjust place he landed. And in time God revealed the masterpiece behind the mess. Joseph rose to power and helped save not just Egypt but also his own family. When the moment came to confront his brothers, he didn't say, " You monsters ruined my life." Instead he said: "But as for you, ye thought evil against me; but God meant it unto good, to bring to pass, as it is this day, to save much people alive" (Genesis 50:20).

Patience allows us to wait for the bigger picture. It reminds us that God is always up to something—even when we can't see it, even when we wouldn't have voted for it. He is the Great Weaver, and we are living inside the knots and tangles. Someday we'll see the tapestry. But for now we trust the hands that hold the thread.

HEAVEN: THE PLACE OF FULL REVELATION

And so we look ahead—to the hope that heaven brings. While faith and patience are our trusted companions now, we hold fast to the promise that there will come a day when every why will be eclipsed by glory. Paul captures it beautifully in 1 Corinthians 13:12: "For now we see through a glass, darkly; but then face to face: now I know in part; but then shall I know even as also I am known."

In heaven the scattered puzzle pieces of our lives will come together into a mosaic of divine wisdom and beauty. The things that seemed so random, so unjust, so utterly senseless—will suddenly make sense. They'll click into place like the final piece of a 10,000-piece puzzle that you were sure had been eaten by the dog.

And yet even in heaven we must remember: God is not obligated to explain Himself—not now, and not then. If He chooses to reveal

His purposes, it will be pure grace, not duty. But I truly believe that once we stand in the light of His glory, we won't care about the questions anymore. His majesty, His holiness, His love—they will wash over us like a tide, and every earthly ache will vanish in the presence of the One who makes all things new.

LIVING IN THE TENSION

Until that day comes, we live in the now—not quite seeing, not fully understanding. This requires humility. It means acknowledging that we are, in fact, not God. (A hard pill to swallow, especially for those of us who like to manage everything.)

Deuteronomy 29:29 puts it clearly: "The secret things belong unto the Lord our God: but those things which are revealed belong unto us and to our children for ever."

In other words, there are some files marked "classified" in heaven's cabinet—and we're not getting clearance. But God has revealed enough for us to trust Him. And that's the tension we live in: walking in what He has shown while trusting Him with what He hasn't.

So what do we do with our unanswered questions?

We bring them to God. Not in polished prayers but in honest ones. The Bible is full of people who asked hard questions—who vented, wept, wrestled, and groaned. And in doing so they found a God who could handle their cries.

David asked: "Why art thou cast down, O my soul? and why art thou disquieted within me? hope thou in God" (Psalm 42:11).

Job asked: "Why died I not from the womb?" (Job 3:11). And later confessed: "I know that thou canst do everything" (Job 42:2).

Habakkuk cried: "O Lord, how long shall I cry, and thou wilt not hear!" (Habakkuk 1:2). Yet later affirmed: "Yet I will rejoice in the Lord" (Habakkuk 3:18).

Gideon asked: "Oh my Lord, if the Lord be with us, why then is all this befallen us?" (Judges 6:13). But then built an altar and called it peace.

Thomas doubted: "Except I shall see... I will not believe" (John 20:25). But later declared: "My Lord and my God" (John 20:28).

These are not stories of perfect faith. They're stories of raw faith. Struggling faith. The kind of faith that shows up anyway, even with skinned knees and unanswered questions.

THE CROSS: GOD'S ANSWER
TO ALL OUR QUESTIONS

At the center of every question is a cross. It doesn't explain everything, but it proves something: that God is not distant from our pain.

The cross tells us He stepped into our suffering. He bore the weight of injustice, cruelty, betrayal, and abandonment. He entered the very pit we cry from.

Jesus Himself, hanging on that cross, gave voice to the greatest question ever asked: "My God, my God, why hast thou forsaken me?" (Matthew 27:46).

And though no thunderous answer followed, His death gave way to resurrection. The silence turned to salvation.

In the cross, we see justice and mercy embrace. We see suffering transformed into glory. And even when we don't understand God's ways, we can trust His heart—because He has shown it to us in the shape of a cross.

CONCLUSION:
FAITHFUL IN THE MYSTERY

Unanswered questions don't destroy faith—they refine it. They push us to stop anchoring our hope in answers and instead root ourselves in God.

We want clarity. But God wants character.

We want a reason. But God offers a relationship.

So what do we do in the mystery? We live by faith. We walk in patience. We trust that God knows what He's doing—even when He doesn't tell us what He's doing.

Job, who lost everything and got no explanation, still gave us the anthem of the faithful: "Though he slay me, yet will I trust in him" (Job 13:15).

This is our call. Trusting that the God who holds the universe also holds our story. Trusting that one day when we see Him face to face, every question will be drowned out by the light of His glory.

And somehow in that moment we will know: He was worth it all.

CHAPTER 23

THE DAY EVERYTHING MAKES SENSE

When Christ's glory swallows sorrow and reveals meaning

"People have a secret history with God and we can never read the pages of a person's secret history. We see them on the mountaintop, but we do not know of the climb to the top or of the descent into the valley."

RON DUNN[24]

"If I find in myself desires which nothing in this world can satisfy, the only logical explanation is that I was made for another world."

C. S. LEWIS[25]

Clarence Larkin didn't exactly burst onto the historical stage with a parade and confetti. Born in 1850 in Delaware County, Pennsylvania, his early years are largely a mystery—which is probably just how

---

24. Ron Dunn, *When Heaven Is Silent* (Nashville: Thomas Nelson, 1994

25. C.S. Lewis, *Mere Christianity* (New York: Macmillan, 1952)

Clarence liked it. There are no dramatic childhood stories of divine visitations or miraculous escapes from runaway wagons. He simply appears on the post–Civil War scene at the age of eighteen, quietly working at a bank and somewhere along the way falling in love with Jesus.

Now switching from banking to engineering isn't your average career pivot. But at twenty-one Clarence packed up his abacus—or whatever bankers used back then—and went to college to study mechanical engineering. After graduating he became a professional draftsman. It was where precision met imagination. And it turns out, Clarence had both in spades.

Here's where the story gets interesting. Somewhere along the way, Larkin began working with the blind. And in teaching them how to navigate life without sight, they taught him something far more profound: how to *see* with imagination. Not the whimsical "imagine you're a dolphin" kind of imagination—but the deep, inner capacity to perceive what isn't visible.

That shift changed everything. Clarence began combining his technical skill with this new visionary insight to create teaching tools—visual guides that made the invisible truths of Scripture somehow graspable. (Is that a word?) Magnificent graphs and charts and creative drawings. It was like someone took a theological encyclopedia and gave it a visual translator.

In the 1880s Larkin became a Baptist pastor in Pennsylvania. And true to form he didn't just preach sermons—he *drew* them. As he studied biblical prophecy, he began to sketch increasingly elaborate charts and graphs to illustrate what he believed Scripture revealed about the end times. If you've ever thought Revelation was confusing, Clarence had your back—with a pencil, some drafting tools, and what was probably an unhealthy amount of spare time.

Now remember, this was long before digital tools or Photoshop. Everything he created was by hand—old-school pencil and compass work, the kind that would make your hand cramp just looking at it. These weren't doodles in the margins of his Bible; they were detailed, wall-sized prophetic schematics. And churches across the country—regardless of denomination—began using them. Because apparently when it comes to understanding the tribulation, everyone loves a good diagram.

His magnum opus was a book titled *Dispensational Truth*. Think of it as the ultimate visual commentary on prophecy. It tackled everything from the rapture and tribulation to the millennial kingdom and the second coming of Christ. But what set it apart wasn't just the theology—it was the *charts*. Massive, intricate, and astonishingly clear, they mapped out concepts like the timeline of dispensations, the symbolism of the tabernacle, and apocalyptic imagery in Revelation.

Larkin didn't just teach theology—he *drafted* it. He helped people visualize the invisible, chart the unchartable, and maybe, just maybe, see a little more of God's glory through the pencil strokes of a man who once worked with the blind.

And isn't that just like God? Using a draftsman with a mechanical mind and an awakened heart to show His people what lies beyond the veil. Larkin saw what others couldn't—and then helped the rest of us take a peek.

His was a secret history, slowly revealed—not through loud declarations or viral sermons but through charts, lines, and a quiet imagination that had learned how to see.

Unless I miss my guess, about now you're wondering why I'm giving you a capsule bio of a little-known nineteenth-century theologian. Fair question. It's because his story is part of *my* story—part of how

God worked behind the scenes in my own life, years in advance, laying the groundwork for what I'd need in days of sorrow and searching. Clarence Larkin was without knowing it helping prepare me for what was to come.

I first saw his book, *Dispensational Truth*, as a young theology student. And right then and there, I knew I had to have it. Not just for the content—but because it looked great on a bookshelf. For anyone born after 1990, you should know there once was a time when grown men collected hardcover books like trophies. We'd curate shelves like they were museum exhibits. Larkin's book had the kind of title and binding that could singlehandedly raise your IQ just by sitting next to it.

At the time I was particularly drawn to the prophecy sections. World events yet to come have always fascinated me, and I wanted to know what the experts thought. Larkin seemed like the kind of guy who could draw you a chart of the end of the world and hand you a compass just in case.

Now let me say this clearly: This book you're reading is *not* about prophecy. It's not a deep dive into eschatology. But I've learned that without even a basic grasp of how the story ends, our belief in God's control of *our* stories starts to feel shaky. It's like reading a novel with no final chapter. You can't judge a story until you know how it ends.

That brings me to a personal lesson, courtesy of a very different book series. I won't name the author—some of you might be fans, and I'd hate to start a literary turf war. It wasn't a theology book, so it lived on the lower shelves of my library. Several floors below Larkin—in both literal and literary terms.

I read the first few books in the series and enjoyed them. But then I looked up how many books were in the series and realized it was approximately the length of the Old Testament. By book three,

I was lost in an avalanche of characters and side plots. I kept flipping back to earlier volumes just to remember who married whom and why everyone was suddenly fighting.

Eventually I gave up. I never finished the series. To this day I don't know how the story ends. I lost confidence in the author and decided not to follow him anymore.

You see where this is going, don't you?

If we don't know where the Author of our lives is taking the story—if we're unaware that there *is* a final chapter, and a good one—we, too, will grow weary. We'll get frustrated, confused, and maybe even give up on the whole thing. But unlike that mystery novelist, the Author of our faith doesn't get characters confused. He doesn't lose the plot. And He certainly doesn't forget to wrap things up.

We are strangely and wonderfully both the heroes and the complicated side characters of our own stories. And God already has the final chapter in His mind. Not just written but written *perfectly*—with a plot line that keeps us engaged, intrigued, and hopeful until the last page.

I won't go too far down this rabbit trail, but I'll go far enough to say this: God really does work all things perfectly—in His time and for His glory. Even through the pages of forgotten theologians, dusty books, and young students who just wanted an impressive library shelf.

It really shouldn't surprise us that events still to come will tie God's divine sovereignty together in ways we couldn't have imagined. The destination port has always been set—before we even packed our bags. Every storm, every detour, every awkward layover has been part of the route. Let me show you how this truth became personal to me—and how it can become personal for you too.

Back in chapter 2, I told you about the first ray of light that cracked through the darkness after Wade's death. The first fresh breath I took that didn't taste like sorrow. That moment came not from some inspirational meme or counseling session, but from God's Word—specifically 1 Peter 4:12–13: "Beloved, think it not strange concerning the fiery trial which is to try you, as though some strange thing happened unto you: but rejoice, inasmuch as ye are partakers of Christ's sufferings; that, when his glory shall be revealed, ye may be glad also with exceeding joy."

That passage was like a life jacket tossed to a man who couldn't swim. I wasn't yet on dry ground, but at least I wasn't going under anymore. I clung to those words with the grip of someone who knows they can't hold on much longer.

We've already walked through those verses, but now I want to circle back to one line that takes us to the heart of this story. In verse 13: "When his glory shall be revealed."

Let's pause there. What does that mean? And when will it happen?

It means there's coming a moment—a real, breathtaking moment in eternity—when the full worth and majesty of Jesus will be unveiled. Like the final act of a long-awaited play, every doubter, every critic, every casual scroller who skipped past the gospel will see and know: This is who He is. No more debate. No more hiding behind philosophical objections or bad church experiences. When His glory is revealed, it will silence every other voice.

And in that moment—this is the part that still gives me goosebumps—we, because we are in Him, will be seen as meaningful, too. Not because we nailed the spiritual life. Not because we aced theology or managed to read Leviticus without skimming. But because we shared in His suffering, we will share in His glory.

Romans 8:16–17 says: "The Spirit Himself bears witness with our spirit that we are children of God, and if children, then heirs—heirs of God and joint heirs with Christ, if indeed we suffer with Him, that we may also be glorified together"

That "glorified together" part is the best. It's like Jesus saying, "You're with Me," and heaven echoing back, "Yep, they're with Him."

So when does this magnificent reveal take place? Paul gives us a glimpse in Romans 8:18: "For I consider that the sufferings of this present time are not worth comparing with the glory that is to be revealed to us"

Peter chimes in too in 1 Peter 5:1: "To the elders among you, I appeal as a fellow elder and a witness of Christ's sufferings who also will share in the glory to be revealed"

In other words, there's coming a day—yes, an actual day on the eternal calendar—when every ounce of suffering will be swallowed whole by glory.

So let me ask you: What's the worst thing that's ever happened to you? Go ahead, think about it. Your most gut-wrenching loss, your most unjust wound, your deepest regret. The kind of pain that makes you wince even now.

Now stack it next to the most horrifying events in all of human history—the betrayals, the wars, the genocides, the unspeakable evil that slithers through the cracks of our broken world.

Now imagine that all of it—your pain and the world's pain—is swallowed up in that moment when Christ returns and reveals His glory. The magnitude of His presence will be so great that every horror will be rendered obsolete. Obliterated. And not just erased—but replaced.

And what will replace it? Rejoicing. Eternal, uncontainable, over-the-top joy. The kind that makes laughter ring louder than weeping ever did.

For me the Lord's Word, His promises, and yes even the painful education of learning to trust His sovereignty have helped me navigate the years since that awful day in 1994. I've tried to live a life that's at least somewhat productive for Him. But the truth is, there's still a hole in my heart. I still miss Wade. I still ache.

Yet I remember a moment—just weeks after Wade's death—when God gently lifted my eyes forward. He showed me that one day even that ache would be gone. And in its place? Not just healing. Not just closure. But joy. Exceeding joy.

That's what He promises. Joy that exceeds anything I've ever experienced. And I've had some joyful moments—like the time I found an extra french fry at the bottom of the bag after I thought they were all gone. But this? This joy will outdo every kind of joy we've ever known.

It will rise as high as our sorrow sank deep. It will be what the Bible calls "joy unspeakable." Which is a little frustrating for someone trying to describe it in a book. I mean, I'm literally trying to put into words something the Bible says can't be put into words. That's like trying to explain Wi-Fi to a dog.

But even in the mystery, there's no fear. Just longing. A longing that tugs at the soul and whispers, "Hold on. It's coming."

And then add to that joy—reunion. I want to adamantly proclaim that I am certain I will see Wade again. No doubt. No hesitation. And if you're a believer, you can proclaim with just as much confidence that you will be reunited with your loved ones who died in Christ. Maybe you've lost a child, a spouse, a parent, a friend. If we're old enough to read a book like this, chances are we're well acquainted with grief. Every year more of our people leave this world. But for the believer death isn't the end of the story—it's just a change in the setting.

WHERE ARE OUR LOVED ONES NOW?

Over the years people have asked me, "Where is Wade right now?" Or they'll say, "I know we'll see them again, but where are they right now? What happened after they took their last breath?"

That's a big question. A tender one. And an important one—because how we answer it shapes whether we believe God really is working all things together for good or if we're just hoping He might.

The Bible teaches that Christ's resurrection is the cornerstone of our hope. Paul makes that crystal clear in 1 Corinthians 15:13–14: "If there is no resurrection of the dead, then not even Christ has been raised. And if Christ has not been raised, our preaching is useless and so is your faith." In other words, if Easter didn't happen, we should all go home.

Now our culture has some…let's say…imaginative ideas about the afterlife. When my dad passed away, a well-meaning, kind-hearted man came up to me and said, "Your dad is sitting in his recliner right now, just waiting for your mom to bring him his supper." It was sweet, and I appreciated it. But…really? I mean, is he still checking his watch in eternity, wondering if supper is ready?

And then there's the classic eulogy: "Bobby loved NASCAR, and I believe right now he's up there in heaven, rounding turn three in a heavenly Chevrolet while the angels cheer him on." Cue the sniffles, the nods, and the polite, tearful "Amen."

Look, I get it. People are trying to comfort each other with what they know. And maybe—just maybe—there are recliners and racetracks in glory. (Though if you ask some folks, NASCAR in heaven would feel more like divine punishment.)

But what does Scripture say? Where are our loved ones who died in Christ? Where is Wade who passed before he could fully understand salvation? What do we know for sure?

The short answer to where he is? Paradise.

Here's where it gets fun. Is paradise the same as heaven? Or are they different places? Some theologians—especially the front-row, pen-in-pocket types—will tell you they're the same. And God bless them. They probably did their homework.

But I'm more of a back row guy myself. So let me offer a view that's brought me peace: I believe paradise and heaven are two distinct places—but one presence. We go to be with Jesus. That's the point. That's the hope.

John Wesley once wrote in his commentary on Luke 23:43: "Paradise is only the porch of heaven; and, as it were, the beginning of it.[26]" I'm not Methodist, but I'll stand with Brother Wesley on that porch.

Here's how I understand it in plain English: When a believer dies, the soul goes immediately to paradise. There in the presence of Christ we wait. Not bored. Not in limbo. But in peace, in joy, in Him. Then at the final resurrection (Philippians 3:20–21) that soul will be reunited with a glorified body—and together they'll enter into the eternal reality we call heaven. New heaven. New earth. New everything.

So if you've lost someone in Christ—and I'm guessing you have—take heart. They are not lost. They are with Him.

THE MOST FORTUNATE MAN ON EARTH...MINUTES BEFORE HE DIED

Luke 23:35–43 paints one of the most astonishing pictures in Scripture:

---

26. John Wesley, Explanatory Notes upon the New Testament (London: Epworth Press, 1755)

And the people stood beholding. And the rulers also with them derided him, saying, He saved others; let him save himself, if he be Christ, the chosen of God. And the soldiers also mocked him, coming to him, and offering him vinegar, and saying, If thou be the king of the Jews, save thyself. And a superscription also was written over him in letters of Greek, and Latin, and Hebrew, This Is The King Of The Jews. And one of the malefactors which were hanged railed on him, saying, If thou be Christ, save thyself and us. But the other answering rebuked him, saying, Dost not thou fear God, seeing thou art in the same condemnation? And we indeed justly; for we receive the due reward of our deeds: but this man hath done nothing amiss. And he said unto Jesus, Lord, remember me when thou comest into thy kingdom. And Jesus said unto him, Verily I say unto thee, today shalt thou be with me in paradise.

On the day Jesus died, no one would have looked at either of the men being crucified beside Him and thought, "Well now, there's a blessed guy." But that's exactly what one of them was—the most fortunate man on earth…just minutes before he died.

In a moment of furious agony yet spiritual clarity, this condemned man somehow, some way, pieced together a final prayer: "Lord, remember me when You come into Your kingdom." A dying man hanging on a cross used his last breath not to curse the injustice of Rome, not to beg for another chance but to cry out in mustard-seed-sized faith. And Jesus responded—not with silence, not with pity but with a promise: "Today you will be with Me in paradise."

Charles Spurgeon captured the wonder of this moment: "This man was our Lord's last companion on earth and His first companion at the gates of paradise."[27]

What a moment. What an exchange. What a Savior.

And because Jesus is both God and Savior, every word He speaks carries weight—eternal weight. When He says "paradise," He isn't being poetic. He isn't picking words at random. He is using a specific word with a specific meaning. In the original Greek of the New Testament the word is *paradeisos*—meaning "a garden" or "a park." This is the same word used in the Septuagint (the Greek translation of the Old Testament) to describe the Garden of Eden.

So when Jesus used *paradeisos*, people listening in that time would have thought of Eden—a real place, lush and sacred, where humanity once walked with God. Some theologians believe that paradise may, in fact, be that very garden—the one that was never destroyed, only sealed off. Genesis 3:24 says, "He drove out the man; and he placed at the east of the garden of Eden Cherubims, and a flaming sword which turned every way, to keep the way of the tree of life."

Could it be that Eden has become the future paradise? Is this the place where Jesus told the thief, "Meet Me there"? Maybe. I certainly wouldn't argue with anyone who believed that. I kinda like the idea myself.

But let's not miss the point. Paradise is a real place—and it appears to be distinct from heaven.

This brings us to an important clarification. In Greek the word used for *heaven* is not *paradeisos*. It's *ouranos*. These are two different

---

27. Charles Haddon Spurgeon, *The Believing Thief*, sermon on Luke 23:42–43, preached at the Metropolitan Tabernacle, Newington, September 23, 1888, in *The Metropolitan Tabernacle Pulpit*, vol. 34 (London: Passmore & Alabaster, 1888)

words, used for two different realities. *Ouranos* refers to the heavens, the sky, the cosmos—and the spiritual realm where God dwells in His fullness. For example, when Jesus taught His disciples to pray in Matthew 6:9, He said, "Our Father which art in heaven." The Greek word there—*ouranos*. A different word describing a different place.

So when Jesus said to the thief, "Today you'll be with Me in *paradise*," He wasn't referring to the same destination He meant when He spoke of *heaven*. He was referring to a place of beauty, peace, and the immediate presence of God—but it's not yet the final destination. Not yet the new heaven and new earth. It's the porch. The waiting room. But not like the DMV—it's a waiting room where you actually want to stay awhile.

To be clear, Jesus wasn't offering the thief a shortcut out of suffering or a delay in dying. Both of them were going to die that day. But what Jesus *was* promising was both a place and a presence. He wasn't saying, "See you later." He was saying, "You'll be *with Me*—today."

And that's the heart of it, isn't it? It's not just about where we go when we die. It's about *who* we're with. That's why Paul would later write that to be absent from the body is to be present with the Lord.

This is the principle the church has lived on for centuries. When someone dies in Christ, they go immediately into His presence. Not floating on a cloud. Not stuck in limbo. Not bored. But *with Him*. And apparently that first stop is paradise.

So what happened to that thief? He closed his eyes in pain—and opened them in paradise, standing beside the very Savior who'd just promised him grace. And what happens to our loved ones who trusted in Christ? The same thing.

Paradise. Presence. Peace.

That's the hope. That's the promise. And that's why even in grief we don't grieve as those who have no hope.

We know who holds the keys. We know what He said. And we know where He is.

And where He is—that's where we'll be too.

ABRAHAM'S BOSOM

There was a certain rich man who was clothed in purple and fine linen and fared sumptuously every day. But there was a certain beggar named Lazarus, full of sores, who was laid at his gate, desiring to be fed with the crumbs which fell from the rich man's table. Moreover the dogs came and licked his sores. So it was that the beggar died, and was carried by the angels to Abraham's bosom. The rich man also died and was buried. And being in torments in Hades, he lifted up his eyes and saw Abraham afar off, and Lazarus in his bosom. Then he cried and said, "Father Abraham, have mercy on me, and send Lazarus that he may dip the tip of his finger in water and cool my tongue; for I am tormented in this flame." But Abraham said, "Son, remember that in your lifetime you received your good things, and likewise Lazarus evil things; but now he is comforted and you are tormented. And besides all this, between us and you there is a great gulf fixed, so that those who want to pass from here to you cannot, nor can those from there pass to us." Then he said, "I beg you therefore, father, that you would send him to my father's house, for I have five brothers, that he may

testify to them, lest they also come to this place of torment." Abraham said to him, "They have Moses and the
prophets; let them hear them." And he said, "No, father
Abraham; but if one goes to them from the dead, they will
repent." But he said to him, "If they do not hear Moses
and the prophets, neither will they be persuaded though
one rise from the dead." (Luke 16:19–31)

The story of the rich man and Lazarus is one Jesus told, recorded
in Luke 16:19–31. It isn't a parable in the abstract sense—it's grounded
in names, specific imagery, and deeply theological meaning. Jesus
draws a contrast between two men: a wealthy man (not named) who
lived in luxury and a poor beggar named Lazarus who suffered terribly during his life on earth.

The rich man wore purple and fine linen, which in that day was
like driving a Tesla while wearing a tailored Armani suit—every day.
He ate lavish meals, lived in comfort, and didn't have a worry in the
world. And just outside his gate was Lazarus whose body was a billboard of suffering, covered in sores. He was so hungry he longed just
for the crumbs that fell from the man's table. Even the dogs—more
sympathetic than the people—came to lick his wounds.

I've seen this kind of contrast in real life. When I travel through
Romania, I've walked through open markets and seen people from
gypsy clans—mothers with children in hand—begging for help. I've
also seen others shout at them, scold them, wave them off with frustration. That's what I imagine the rich man's attitude was: indifference with a splash of annoyance.

Then suddenly they both die. Jesus doesn't give us details. There's
no explanation, no dramatics—just a change in scene. I've always

imagined they died the same day or close to it. It reads that way. But what happens next is where the real contrast begins.

Lazarus is carried—not dragged, not shoved but carried—by angels to Abraham's bosom. Just that image alone is enough to make your heart swell. After a life of pain, rejection, and misery, he is cradled in peace, surrounded by the righteous, welcomed into comfort.

Meanwhile, the rich man is buried. That's it. Just buried. And then he wakes up—in torment. There's no one there to comfort him. No attendants. No friends. Just pain. And what's worse? He can see across the divide. He sees Lazarus—yes, *that* Lazarus—the one he passed daily without care—now resting with Abraham. That contrast must have hit like a lightning bolt of regret.

In a strange reversal the rich man begins to beg. But not to Lazarus. He can't bring himself to address him directly. Instead, he calls out to Abraham, asking him to send Lazarus like some kind of celestial servant: "Send Lazarus to dip his finger in water and cool my tongue." Even in torment he sees Lazarus as beneath him.

But Abraham calmly and truthfully replies: "Son, remember." And then comes the truth bomb—"You received your good things in life, and Lazarus his evil things. But now he is comforted, and you are tormented."

Then Abraham adds the final blow: "There's a great gulf fixed between us. No one can cross."

That's when the rich man shifts to intercession. "Send Lazarus to my father's house—to warn my five brothers!" Again using Lazarus as the messenger. But Abraham tells him they already have Moses and the prophets. And when the man insists that someone rising from the dead would surely convince them, Abraham delivers one of the most prophetic lines in Scripture: "If they do not hear Moses and the prophets, neither will they be persuaded though one rise from the dead."

Throughout this exchange Lazarus says nothing. Not a word. No anger. No gloating. Just rest. That silence speaks volumes. In the agony of regret and the noise of torment Lazarus' peace is deafening.

The rich man's agony is full-sensory—he sees, hears, feels, remembers. He's haunted by his past and terrified of the future. Lazarus, on the other hand, rests in a place of deep, personal comfort—the bosom of Abraham.

Now let's talk about that place.

"Abraham's bosom" appears to be a holding place—a kind of intermediate paradise for the righteous who died before Christ's resurrection. It's not described as heaven, per se. That's where the distinction becomes vital. In heaven (*ouranos*) our complete comfort and eternal solace will be in God's presence alone. But here Lazarus is seen in the comfort of Abraham—a picture of covenant faithfulness and righteous fellowship.

When we read Revelation's description of heaven—the New Jerusalem descending, the river of life, the tree bearing fruit year-round, no more pain or death—it's clear that this final destination is far grander. As Wesley put it, paradise is the porch; heaven is the home.

And Jesus uses specific Greek words that underscore this: The word for paradise is *paradeisos*, often used for garden or park—a term tied to Eden itself. The word for heaven is *ouranos*, meaning the sky, the cosmos, the dwelling of God. They're different words. Different realities.

So while Abraham's bosom may be a place of rest, heaven is a place of radiant, unveiled glory. In heaven:

- The city shines with God's brilliance (Revelation 21:11).
- There's no need for sun or moon (21:23).
- The streets are made of gold (21:21).
- The river of life flows from the throne (22:1).
- The tree of life heals the nations (22:2).
- There is no more death or mourning or pain (21:4).
- And best of all, "They shall see His face" (22:4).

Paradise is a temporary and holy place of rest, a blessed haven where the righteous are comforted after death. It is peaceful and joy filled, marked by the nearness of God—but it is not the end of the journey. That place—glorious, eternal, and utterly complete—is heaven. There every longing is fulfilled, every tear wiped away, and every sorrow finally and forever undone.

You see the difference? Let me attempt to explain the nearly unexplainable with one of my more embarrassingly human stories. It won't be perfect—it never is when we try to describe the infinite with the vocabulary of carburetors and cassette decks—but maybe it will offer a glimmer.

The first car I ever owned was in 1973, and the car was a 1964 Chevrolet Chevy 2. It had some miles, some rust, and a radio that bravely played only AM stations. I traded a Honda 175 motorcycle for it. (That trade may sound like a downgrade, but keep in mind that at seventeen, I had never had a car that wasn't technically my dad's.) No air conditioning. No seatbelt laws. But it had a bench seat—which meant that if a girl sat next to you, she'd be practically in your lap. We thought of it as dating proximity, not a traffic hazard.

I loved that car. I drove it around Savannah like I was the mayor of the city and the Chevy 2 was my chariot. In my adolescent heart life had peaked.

However, later in life came the game changer: In 1979 I got a two-year-old 1977 Ford Thunderbird. Black, red pinstripe, and roughly the length of a cargo ship. The thing was so smooth it practically floated. AM *and* FM radio. And—brace yourself—a cassette player. When someone showed me the cruise control button, I thought it was sorcery. "Wait, I don't *have* to press the gas pedal?" Next thing you know, I expected the car to start making me coffee.

I bought it. How could I not? That Thunderbird was the best car I ever owned. And suddenly my beloved Chevy 2 felt like it had been made during the Industrial Revolution.

That's the difference between paradise and heaven. Not that heaven is a Ford product—but rather, the comparison lies in the upgrade. Paradise is good. Really good. But heaven? It's the glorious upgrade you didn't know existed.

Paradise still hums within time and space. It's familiar. Connected. It's that old Chevy 2—it gets you where you're going, and it's got charm. But it has limits. It's not the final destination. It's the rest area on the eternal highway.

Heaven is like opening the door to that Thunderbird. The scent of newness. The flawless design. The feel of gliding over pavement as if you were weightless. It's the realm of perfection. The eternal showroom of God's glory. Paradise may hold you in comfort. But heaven embraces you in completion.

In Scripture Abraham's Bosom is paradise. A place of blessed waiting. But it is not the grand finale. Heaven is that finale—the place of unveiled glory where the redeemed live face-to-face with God.

I don't know if Clarence Larkin agreed with my view on this. I suspect we'll have time to talk about it over celestial coffee someday. And one of us will nod and say, "Ah, that's how it was," and we'll laugh—not because it was a competition but because finally everything will make sense.

Now you see why this matters so deeply to the sovereignty of God. Without heaven, without that eternal, perfect destination, the whole journey crumbles. Suffering is just pain. Loss is just absence. Death is just final. If there's no heaven, then nothing redemptive ever happens. But with it? Everything—every tear, every dark valley, every unanswered prayer—becomes part of a grand mosaic of glory. With heaven the pain gets swallowed up in a glory so complete we'll forget the questions we swore we'd ask God.

THE BEST DAY WE'VE EVER KNOWN

Let's bring it home. Because, yes, our loved ones who died in Christ are gone from our sight. That's a weighty sadness. If that were the end of the story, we'd all be wandering around in a fog of grief with no reason to ever hope again.

But here's where God's sovereign plan does what only God's plans can do. He scheduled a reunion. And not just any reunion—this will be the final reunion.

It's called the second coming of Jesus or the rapture. And it's not subtle. According to 1 Thessalonians 4:16–17, Jesus will descend with a shout, an archangel will yell something that I imagine sounds both terrifying and comforting at once, and a trumpet will blast loud enough to wake the dead. Literally.

First, those who've died in Christ will rise. Their glorified bodies will be like heaven's version of "body 2.0"—fully upgraded and completely redeemed. And then if we're still alive at that moment, we get caught up too. (No need to pack a bag. Heaven doesn't charge for checked luggage.)

Then it happens. We're all gathered together with the Lord. The curtain falls on the old world. A new one begins.

Matthew 25 describes it as the moment Jesus sits on His throne and welcomes His people into the kingdom prepared for them from the foundation of the world. That's what all the waiting, all the praying, and all the enduring was for.

All of it—every sorrow and joy—will finally make sense.

Dr. R. G. Lee was the legendary and much-loved pastor of the Bellevue Baptist church in Memphis from 1927 to 1960. One day when he was a little boy, he asked his mother what had been the best day of her life. Dr. Lee's mother's name was Elizabeth. Dr. Lee said that he looked at his mother and could tell that her thoughts were taking her back to a time from many years ago, back to when she herself was just a little girl and just after the Civil War. She answered, "Son, you've asked a good question, but it's easy for me to answer." And she told the story. Elizabeth's dad had fought for the South, and like many wives with children during that day, her mom had to work the fields to support the family while he was away.

One day a letter came saying that her father had been killed in battle. Elizabeth's mother didn't cry much during the day, but she could hear her sobbing in the night in their small house. There were mouths to be fed, and life had to continue, so Elizabeth's mother had to be strong. The months passed, and one day in the summer Elizabeth and her mother were sitting on the porch shelling peas when her mother looked up and saw a man in uniform coming down the road. It wasn't unusual to see soldiers walking the roads on their way home during those days. Elizabeth's mother watched this soldier for a while with some curiosity and then went back to her bowl of peas. A few minutes later she looked up again to check on the soldier's progress, and this time, she said, "Elizabeth honey, that man coming yonder walks a little bit like your father." Elizabeth looked up and felt sad at her mother's longings. They both kept shelling, and her mother looked again and noticed an empty sleeve where an arm once hung, and she said, "Elizabeth, honey, I swear that man looks like your father." Elizabeth, trying to comfort her, said, "Mama, it's ok, I understand, but you know Daddy is never coming home."

By now, the man was nearing the break in the fence that turned to the house, and Elizabeth's mother waited to see if he'd turn in. He did, and about that time Elizabeth said peas and shells went one way and her mother went the other as she screamed, "Elizabeth, it is your father!!!" She said they both ran the length of the road to where he was, and she flew into the arms of the man that she thought was dead but had now come back to her life. Elizabeth said that her father reached down with his only arm and brought her close to his heart, and she reached over and felt the empty sleeve where the arm that he gave to keep her safe had been. Elizabeth said to Dr. Lee, "It was the best day I ever knew."[28]

One day Jesus will come back. And when He does, it'll be the day we've been aching for since Eden. The day when we run down the road, see the One we thought we'd lost, and feel His embrace again. And all of this, all of it, will be swallowed in the joy of the best day we've ever known.

---

28. Robert Greene Lee, *Memoirs of R. G. Lee* (Nashville: Broadman Press, 1963)

CHAPTER 24

WADE'S STORY—
FINAL CHAPTER

*"But between them and the foot of the sky there was
something so white on the green grass that even
with their eagles' eyes they could hardly look at
it. They came on and saw that it was a Lamb.*

*'Come and have breakfast,' said the
Lamb in its sweet milky voice.*

*"Then they noticed for the first time that there was a fire
lit on the grass and fish roasting on it. They sat down and
ate the fish, hungry now for the first time for many days.
And it was the most delicious food they had ever tasted.*

'Please, Lamb,' said Lucy, 'is this the way to Aslan's country?'

*'Not for you,' said the Lamb. 'For you the door
into Aslan's country is from your own world.'*

*'What!' said Edmund. 'Is there a way into
Aslan's country from our world too?'*

*'There is a way into my country from all the worlds,' said
the Lamb; but as he spoke, his snowy white flushed into*

tawny gold and his size changed and he was Aslan himself,
towering above them and scattering light from his mane.

Oh Aslan,' said Lucy. 'Will you tell us how to
get into your country from our world?'

'I shall be telling you all the time,' said Aslan. 'But I will
not tell you how long or short the way will be; only that
it lies across a river. But do not fear that, for I am the
great Bridge Builder. And now come; I will open the
door in the sky and send you to your own land.'"

C. S. LEWIS, *The Voyage of the Dawn Treader* [29]

As believers our thoughts about death are not left to memes, vague hopes, or random speculation—thank God. The Bible doesn't treat death like an unsolvable riddle or the plot twist of a poorly written book. It speaks clearly, even if not exhaustively, about what comes after. Still mystery lingers. Not confusion but reverent mystery.

I've read stories through the years from people who claim to have died, taken a stroll into the afterlife, and then returned to tell the tale—usually involving bright lights, stunning landscapes, and occasionally, a conversation with someone who looked suspiciously like Morgan Freeman. Entire books have been written about these experiences. Some people see pearly gates; others see waterfalls. One saw her long passed Pomeranian.

I'm not here to discredit anyone's story. I don't know what they saw or what they believe they saw. But the variety in detail does make you wonder if the afterlife operates like a spiritual Amazon where you can order what you want or if we might be dealing more with

---

29. C.S. Lewis, The Voyage of the Dawn Treader (London: Geoffrey Bles, 1952)

how our minds process trauma, fear, or hope in the most intense moments of life.

What we *do* know is this: We all came into this world the same way. No one teleported in or parachuted from a celestial shuttle. We were born red-faced and wrinkled, crying like we'd just been handed a bad report card. We know how we arrived.

But leaving? That's still a mystery. We don't know the time, the place, or the manner. There's no countdown clock on our dashboard. There's just one certainty: It will happen.

And for those who trust in Jesus, there's another certainty: It will not be the end.

The Bible offers us glimpses—snapshots, really—of heaven and paradise. Not a floor plan but a promise. Not a travel brochure but a guarantee signed in blood and sealed in resurrection. It tells us enough to give us hope and then invites us to trust God with the details. And that trust includes the most unnerving moment of all: **the transition.**

What will it be like, that moment of crossing over? That's the part no one can fully describe. The Bible doesn't offer a play-by-play. There's no YouTube preview. What we're left with are the words God *has* chosen to give us and a holy imagination shaped by those words. For centuries believers have pondered it—sometimes with theological depth, other times with the creative flair of a Hallmark special.

Yet this much is undeniable: Every person, regardless of belief, contemplates life after death. And rightly so. For beyond death there is infinitely more life than we've ever known on this side of eternity. And if that doesn't make your brain feel like it's trying to drink out of a fire hose, you're probably not paying attention.

How do you imagine eternity? The greatest minds, the holiest of saints, and all the front-row guys have wrestled with that question—and none of them has fully grasped its enormity.

Neither have I. But like you—and all who came before us—I've pondered it. Not just my own eternity but the eternity of those I love. Not in a gloomy, Edgar Allen Poe kind of way but with joyful anticipation—like when the flight attendant says, "We're beginning our descent," and you're headed home.

In doing so, I've taken what I've read in God's Word, considered the character of God, and allowed my imagination to fill in the gaps. What follows is a glimpse into that vision—my personal imagining—of what might have taken place in the moments after Wade's death. It may not be entirely factual, but it is entirely possible. And more importantly, it is shaped by the truth of who God is and what He has promised.

THE MOMENTS AFTER
What We Know and What We Imagine
As Wade Enters Paradise–in His Own Words

I now understand what happened, though at the time it unfolded so quickly that my three-year-old brain had no chance of keeping up. Honestly, I was barely old enough to string together a decent sentence, much less have a dramatic final monologue. I didn't panic—mostly because I didn't have the cognitive capacity to. And strangely that was its own mercy. I was too young to have last words or to watch my life flash before my eyes. If it had, it would have been a very short clip.

One moment I was just a toddler waddling outside a McDonald's. The next, I was…somewhere else. It was as if all the lights dimmed at once, not just in the world but inside me too. Physically, mentally, spiritually—I shut down. And in that quiet instant my earthly life ended.

But death wasn't the end. It was the transition.

Something enveloped me—swift, full, and strangely peaceful. It didn't feel like being pulled away. It felt like being gathered in. I wasn't walking into eternity as much as I was being carried. I arrived at a place I couldn't name, a place between what had been and what was to come. That threshold where the world grows quiet and eternity begins to hum.

And then…I met him. My first encounter with the eternal: an angel.

He didn't have wings flapping dramatically in slow motion or a harp or a booming voice. But his presence—it was unlike anything I'd ever known. He wrapped me in a gentleness so real it felt like being hugged by peace itself. He said something—not just to me but somehow to my dad too. Words that didn't echo in the air but in the soul. Words that calmed us both.

He lifted me—not like a weight but like a child who finally knows they're safe. We moved together—not through streets or skies but through something that can only be described as *more*. More than time, more than space. Neither seemed to matter anymore.

There was no darkness, but it wasn't fully light either. It was like standing in a room where the shades are drawn and you know the sun is there—it just hasn't broken through quite yet.

Was it a long journey? I don't know. Was it far? I couldn't tell you. But I do know this: I never felt afraid.

What I experienced in those moments can't be charted or timed. It wasn't a trip—it was a transformation. A once-in-a-forever moment that every person will one day walk through. And when they do, they'll understand what I do now:

There is no fear.

. . .

When the transition concluded, I did not wake up, for I had never truly been asleep. Instead, I found myself standing bathed in light as if that shade had been drawn aside to reveal a world permeated with a divine radiance. This light was not the harsh glow of a bulb but a living presence and a voice of clarity amid all that was new. I could not discern what lay beneath my feet or above my head; all was enveloped in this sacred light. Somehow I realized I was no longer the three-year-old child I once was; my mind had blossomed with mature thoughts and emotions. All around me every inch of reality took on profound meaning—I had stepped into the very essence of it.

The angel remained by my side, his presence growing more familiar and comforting. He became a dear and trusted companion—more than a man yet less than a god. Up to that point he had cradled me like a helpless child; now he stood as a strong, caring friend, someone I trusted instinctively and without reservation. Noticing that we had not yet formally introduced ourselves, I asked, "Could you please tell me your name?"

He turned his kind gaze upon me, as if recalling all the moments we had shared, and replied, "My name is Agapaidon. I was given this name by the Grand Master when He created me many centuries ago. It means 'lover of children' and bears with it the honor of caring for them both on earth and through this transition journey we are on now. I have had many charges in my care and like with them all, I have been with you since your conception as a helper to Him who also created you."

At last I took the opportunity to fully observe him. He was the very embodiment of humble strength. His controlled power radiated a calm that filled the entire space around us. He was not at all like the angels depicted in children's books or the pictures that once hung on classroom walls in the life I had left behind. There were no grand wings, halo, or resplendent golden glows surrounding him, and he was not dressed in an ancient, flowing robe paired with sandals. He was a figure unlike any I had ever seen—a specimen perfectly fashioned for the tasks for which he was created. His height would not have been considered too tall, but neither was it average. It seemed his was the perfect height for who he was and what he was made for. His muscles, though defined, were not for display but served as a testament to the strength necessary for protection. His movements were fluid and graceful as he glided effortlessly. His garments, impeccably woven and tailored, enhanced every motion rather than restricting it. They were designed not for modern fashion but for enduring beauty and practicality, reflecting the exquisite craftsmanship of its maker. His bearing was more akin to a steadfast guardian than any worldly conqueror.

Without a moment's hesitation, I asked, "If you were entrusted with my care, why did you allow such a tragic end to my life?"

With a face full of compassion he answered, "Oh, my dear one, the decision was not mine to make. The eternal mysteries are woven by the One who holds every life in His hands. My role was to carry out His perfect will. There were moments in your brief earthly journey when you did not even know it, yet He called upon me to shield you from harm—and I did so gladly. There were also times when He guided me to step back, and I obeyed with an aching heart, like as His. In both moments of protection and in times when you were vulnerable, His wisdom and love were ever-present. Soon you will understand how all these pieces fit together, but for now there is still need for patience."

Then gently he turned toward the light and said, "Welcome," his voice more clear and real than any voice I had ever heard. "You are here."

I blinked—or at least I think I did—and asked, "Where is…here?"

"Paradise," he replied simply.

· · ·

And though the word was brief, it landed with all the weight of home. My mind understood. It felt like we had arrived at a destination that had long been planned and even longer awaited.

"Come, there is much to see," the angel said.

It would have been rude to decline, though I still had questions—questions that were heavy and dear to me. But something in his tone reassured me: The answers would come. And so I followed.

The angel led me along a well-worn path—a path clearly trodden by many before me. Yet even that familiarity held wonder. For this path was not dirt or stone. The act of moving itself had been transformed. It was no longer walking as I had once known it but a gliding motion—a levitation that felt natural, graceful, and entirely effortless.

As we traveled, the light unfolded around us. It was as if every step forward revealed more of the radiance ahead. A new horizon emerged—one not defined by mountains or rivers or trees but by glory. It wasn't a place made of matter but of meaning.

Colors shimmered into being—colors more pure and vivid than I had ever known. They pulsed with life and significance, never fading. It was as though every hue was a language of praise, and every breath was filled with awe.

And all of it whispered the same truth: You are safe. You are loved. You are home.

All around me I saw objects and vessels—some familiar, others entirely new. Nature, alongside beings whose names were unknown to me, flourished in its celestial habitat with innate beauty.

Whether the symphony of sound had always been audible or had just begun, I cannot say, but in an instant I was enveloped by quiet music that resonated through my very being. Every note was perfect, and it seemed to be made up of all the greatest songs that had ever been written for as long as time existed. These songs were all combined together to make one monumental sound that was so beautiful it became a vehicle to carry my joy. It was accompanied by the relaxing sounds that this form of nature conjured. There were familiar sounds like birds, wind, and a gently running river. But there were new sounds—like no other sounds on earth—that calmed my spirit and brought what I think was a smile to my face.

"Where are we going?" I asked.

"To Him," the angel said.

And those words—simple as they were—sent a tremor through me. Through what I could now only describe as the essence of my spine. For I realized then that I indeed had a body. But it was not the small, fragile frame I once knew on earth. It was whole. Grown. Uninjured. And somehow I knew without being told: It was perfect.

In this new form we moved closer to the place where He stood.

The moment I beheld Him, I understood why Moses had hidden his face, why Isaiah had cried out, "Woe is me," and why the apostle John had fallen down at His feet like a dead man.

However, for me there was no woe here. Only awe.

Awe so profound it felt as though it would undo me—even in this perfect state. And yet I was not undone. Quite the opposite—I was more whole than I had ever been. There was proper fear. Not terror. Not dread. But fear that had found its rightful place. Fear that beheld glory and brilliance and bowed in reverence.

The fear of God.

It seemed that we were in the very heart of paradise. A magnificent throne stood, glowing with that same brilliance that engulfed all of paradise but more vivid. The One seated upon it radiated the light, and it flowed from Him, shimmering with fiery reds and cool, clear hues. While it was radiant, there was no heat, only a perfect warmth that conveyed security rather than fear. Encircling the throne were the luminous colors that marked this whole country. They made a rainbow effect, soft and almost pastel-like but just a shade brighter. These colors mingled with flashes of lightning and deep rumbles of thunder that echoed through the space. Before the throne seven blazing lamps burned brightly, and it seemed like a vast sea of glass, smooth and clear as crystal, stretched out, covered by a mist that emanated from the throne. Surrounding the throne were twenty-four beings, clothed in white robes with golden crowns upon their heads. They sat in reverence, ready to rise and cast their crowns at the feet of the One they worshiped. Closest to the throne were four living creatures, each unique in form—a lion, an ox, a man, and an eagle. Their bodies were covered in eyes, seeing all things, and their six wings fluttered as they in the undertone of the aura softly sang without ceasing, "Holy, holy, holy is the Lord God Almighty, who was, and is, and is to come." Above and around, countless angels raised their voices in unison, their songs blending with the others in perfect harmony. At the center of it all stood a Lamb, bearing the marks of sacrifice, and as He stepped forward, every creature in heaven and on earth joined in a chorus of praise, declaring His worthiness to receive all glory, honor, and power. It was a scene of unending worship, a place where the beauty of holiness and majesty met in perfect, eternal harmony.

* * *

In a slow procession all others made their way to other places in paradise, and I was left alone before the One with whom we all have to do. In His presence I stood. It was not exactly like standing before a king on a throne as I would have expected, though He was certainly kingly. It was like being in the eye of a great and powerful storm with all its magnificence and yet finding it to be warm, safe, and as kind as it is powerful. A feeling of total security in the presence of unconquerable might. "Welcome, my dear, dear, son. Come closer," He said. His voice struck a chord both within and beyond me, and I obeyed. Just then I found myself not staring at but into the very presence of God. Time itself seemed to pause, becoming utterly irrelevant. I was surrounded by a majesty that transcended any earthly realm—a universe of grandeur, yet I felt a deep comfort like being in my mother's arms. In my short life I had scarcely known turmoil, but now I was immersed in a peace that exceeded all understanding. I believed I had known peace before, yet here in this sacred space I recognized that this was the only place in all of creation where absolute peace resided.

In His presence I, Wade Thigpen, became the sole focus of His divine attention—as though nothing existed in eternity except Him and me. "Look here," He said. And at His word everything around me transformed in an instant, and within that space He graciously began to let me see my former life. I saw both the unfolding of those events on earth and the timeless perspective by which He viewed them, all the while He answered questions I had never had the chance to ask. "All is new to you, My child, and all is becoming more clear as you journey forward," He said, reading my soul as a book.

Some things I knew instinctively, but there were questions that He wanted to verbalize for me and for the whole universe to hear. I asked, "Is this the fulfillment of the Bible stories I heard from my mom and dad and my Sunday school teachers on earth? I was too young to understand it completely then. Can You tell me now?"

In an act of divine humility God came off the throne and to my level, His eyes filled with a warmth that made the light of heaven feel even brighter. His presence was overwhelming in its gentleness, and His smile felt like home—familiar, safe, and full of love. God's smile deepened, and when He spoke, His voice was both strong and tender—the voice of a Father and a Friend, full of love beyond words. "Yes, My precious one, this is the fulfillment of all those stories your mom and dad told you, the ones your teachers shared with you. Every story was pointing to Me and to this very moment when you and I are together."

My words seemed a tinkling cymbal compared to His when I said, "But...I didn't understand everything they said. I was too little. I didn't know what to believe."

God gently cupped my face in His hands, His touch warm and comforting. "That's true; you were still growing, still learning. You didn't fully understand because your heart was still innocent, untouched by the dark and heavy things of the world. You hadn't yet reached the age where you could truly choose between right and wrong. But you see, My love doesn't wait for you to be old enough to understand everything. My love was always with you, even when you were too young to see it clearly."

I was filled with joy somehow, and my heart felt lighter, but I was still curious. "But how did I get here then?" I whispered.

God's eyes softened, and His voice grew even gentler. "Because My Son, Jesus, made a way for you. Long before you were born, He went to earth, lived a perfect life, and took all the sins of the world upon Himself—even for those too young to know what sin is. He died on the cross, and when He rose again, He opened these gates wide for everyone who would believe—and for little ones like you whose hearts were still innocent. My grace covered you from the very beginning."

My eyes were wide, and a smile tugged at the corners of His mouth. "So Jesus brought me here?" I asked, wonder filling my voice.

God nodded, His heart also full of joy. "Yes, My beloved. Jesus brought you here because His love is bigger than anything you could ever imagine. You didn't have to earn it, and you didn't have to understand it fully. My love for you is a gift, and I've been waiting to welcome you home."

With the most exceeding full emotion I sincerely said, "I'm glad I'm here."

He responded with a voice of gentle promise. "And I'm glad you're here, My child. You are safe, you are loved, and you will always be with Me."

In that moment I felt a peace deeper than anything I had ever known, knowing that even though I didn't fully understand before, I was now exactly where I was always meant to be—forever in the arms of the One who had loved me from the very beginning. The next question that most naturally came was the one He most wanted to answer. "Why was my life on earth cut short," I asked—not from sorrow, for in His presence sorrow has no place, but from a deep, seeking wonder.

As He answered, it was as if He were unveiling a truth woven into the very fabric of the universe, a truth instilled since the beginning of time. "You and all those who cherished you could see only fragments of the whole, but I saw it all," He explained. And there, bathed in His radiant light, the brief narrative of my life…and death…was laid out before me—intertwined with the lives of hundreds, both those I loved dearly and many I had never met. It resembled an exquisite tapestry, revealing patterns and connections that earthly eyes could never have discerned. In that divine unveiling I saw His guiding hand gracefully weaving the intricate story of my existence, revealing a profound joy and meaning—especially in the love and unity of my family, the one constant I had always known.

When He allowed me to see the deep pain and suffering that surrounded my death—the heartbreak and the tears it caused in everyone around me—I asked, "But why did you allow such suffering?"

"For love," He said simply. "Love is not the absence of pain but the presence of purpose. There was purpose in both your life and your death. Purpose that only I can know, that will only be revealed when My glory is revealed. For that reason there is still a need for patience. But you see, I was there, working all things together for your good and My glory."

At that moment, I began to understand the magnificent tapestry of life, and the most amazing part was that every single thread bore God's touch. He showed me how every experience, including my sudden death, fit perfectly into the overall picture of my life. This picture was not ruined by the tragedy of my passing; instead, it became even more magnificent. This intricate tapestry was woven with beautiful threads of gold and silver, along with darker strands. All these threads shone with the same divine light that permeated everything where we stood.

Then in a very kind act God removed the dark threads that represented my death, and I saw the tapestry in only the sharper colors. To my surprise the tapestry lost much of its beauty without the darker fibers. Then with gentle care He slowly wove the dark threads back into the tapestry, restoring its perfect beauty. How clearly then I saw God's plan: He designed my life—and our entire world—to be understood only when we accept that sorrow has its place. Even the pain we experience is woven into a greater design that makes everything more beautiful than it would have been without it.

Suddenly I realized that the angel who had brought me here had appeared again and now stood silently nearby as if giving me space to absorb what I had seen. Finally he spoke. "Do you see now?"

"I see," I said, though my words felt feeble compared to the magnitude of what I meant. "I see how He worked all things for good, even when it did not seem possible. I see how His sovereignty is not a burden but a gift. And I see…I see that I belong here, not because of who I am but because of who He is and what He did."

The angel smiled, a smile that seemed to echo the smile of God Himself. "Then let us rejoice, for this is only the beginning." And so it was.

CHAPTER 25

SCRIPTURE TO SUPPORT MY IMAGINATION

1. THE INNOCENCE OF CHILDREN AND GOD'S LOVE FOR THEM

Matthew 19:14: But Jesus said, Suffer little children, and forbid them not, to come unto me: for of such is the kingdom of heaven.

Isaiah 40:11: He shall feed his flock like a shepherd: he shall gather the lambs with his arm, and carry them in his bosom, and shall gently lead those that are with young.

Deuteronomy 1:39: Moreover your little ones, which ye said should be a prey, and your children, which in that day had no knowledge between good and evil, they shall go in thither, and unto them will I give it, and they shall possess it.

2. THE AGE OF ACCOUNTABILITY AND
GOD'S GRACE COVERING THE INNOCENT

Romans 5:18: Therefore as by the offence of one judgment came upon all men to condemnation; even so by the righteousness of one the free gift came upon all men unto justification of life.

2 Samuel 12:23: : But now he is dead, wherefore should I fast? can I bring him back again? I shall go to him, but he shall not return to me. (David speaking after the death of his child)

3. THE ROLE OF ANGELS
AND THEIR CARE FOR US

Psalm 91:11–12: For he shall give his angels charge over thee, to keep thee in all thy ways. They shall bear thee up in their hands, lest thou dash thy foot against a stone.

Hebrews 1:14: Are they not all ministering spirits, sent forth to minister for them who shall be heirs of salvation?

4. THE TRANSITION FROM
EARTH TO HEAVEN AND THE
COMFORT OF GOD'S PRESENCE

2 Corinthians 5:8: We are confident, I say, and willing rather to be absent from the body, and to be present with the Lord.

Psalm 23:4: Yea, though I walk through the valley of the shadow of death, I will fear no evil: for thou art with me; thy rod and thy staff they comfort me.

5. THE VISION OF GOD'S THRONE
AND THE HEAVENLY WORSHIP

Revelation 4:2–6: And immediately I was in the spirit: and, behold, a throne was set in heaven, and one sat on the throne. And he that sat was to look upon like a jasper and a sardine stone: and there was a rainbow round about the throne, in sight like unto an emerald. And round about the throne were four and twenty seats: and upon the seats I saw four and twenty elders sitting, clothed in white raiment; and they had on their heads crowns of gold. And out of the throne proceeded lightnings and thunderings and voices: and there were seven lamps of fire burning before the throne, which are the seven Spirits of God. And before the throne there was a sea of glass like unto crystal.

Revelation 5:11–13: And I beheld, and I heard the voice of many angels round about the throne and the beasts and the elders: and the number of them was ten thousand times ten thousand, and thousands of thousands; saying with a loud voice, Worthy is the Lamb that was slain to receive power, and riches, and wisdom, and strength, and honour, and glory, and blessing.

Revelation 4:6–8: In the center, around the throne, were four living creatures, and they were covered with eyes, in front and in back. The first living creature was like a lion, the second was like an ox, the third had a face like a man, the fourth was like a flying eagle. Each of the four living creatures had six wings and was covered with eyes all around, even under its wings. Day and night they never stop saying: "'Holy, holy, holy is the Lord God Almighty,' who was, and is, and is to come"

Revelation 4:10–11: The four and twenty elders fall down before him that sat on the throne, and worship him that liveth for ever and ever, and cast their crowns before the throne, saying, Thou art worthy, O Lord, to receive glory and honour and power: for thou hast created all things, and for thy pleasure they are and were created.

Isaiah 6:1–3: In the year that king Uzziah died I saw also the Lord sitting upon a throne, high and lifted up, and his train filled the temple. Above it stood the seraphims: each one had six wings; with twain he covered his face, and with twain he covered his feet, and with twain he did fly. And one cried unto another, and said, Holy, holy, holy, is the Lord of hosts: the whole earth is full of his glory.

6. JESUS' SACRIFICE MAKING THE WAY FOR ALL, INCLUDING CHILDREN

John 14:6: Jesus saith unto him, I am the way, the truth, and the life: no man cometh unto the Father, but by me.

Romans 5:8: But God commendeth his love toward us, in that, while we were yet sinners, Christ died for us.

1 John 2:2: And he is the propitiation for our sins: and not for ours only, but also for the sins of the whole world.

7. GOD'S SOVEREIGN PLAN AND WORKING ALL THINGS FOR GOOD

Romans 8:28: And we know that all things work together for good to them that love God, to them who are the called according to his purpose.

Ecclesiastes 3:11: He hath made everything beautiful in his time: also he hath set the world in their heart, so that no man can find out the work that God maketh from the beginning to the end.

Jeremiah 29:11: For I know the thoughts that I think toward you, saith the Lord, thoughts of peace, and not of evil, to give you an expected end.

8. THE FEAR OF GOD AND THE AWE OF HIS PRESENCE

Isaiah 6:5: Then said I, Woe is me! for I am undone; because I am a man of unclean lips, and I dwell in the midst of a people of unclean lips: for mine eyes have seen the King, the Lord of hosts.

Revelation 1:17: And when I saw him, I fell at his feet as dead. And he laid his right hand upon me, saying unto me, Fear not; I am the first and the last:

9. THE PEACE AND WHOLENESS
FOUND IN GOD'S PRESENCE

Philippians 4:7: And the peace of God, which passeth all understanding, shall keep your hearts and minds through Christ Jesus.

Psalm 16:11: Thou wilt shew me the path of life: in thy presence is fulness of joy; at thy right hand there are pleasures for evermore.

CHAPTER 26

HE GETS THE LAST WORD

How God's ending rewrites our pain

You know how some movies end with a total emotional landslide—someone dies, a bombshell secret is revealed, the puppy runs away—and then boom, the screen flashes: *10 Years Later.* Suddenly the hero has a beard, a job in IT, and three kids who all seem suspiciously well-behaved. And you're sitting there thinking, "Wait... what just happened? Can we talk about the thing that wrecked me five minutes ago?"

Well, this is *that* chapter. Except it's my *Thirty Years Later.* And yes, I do have a beard. But I have reached a place where I can look back, not with all the answers but with some hard-earned conclusions. Not the final word, maybe—but the best word I've got right now.

So let me borrow some language from someone who *did* have the final word: Paul.

> **Romans 11:33–36**: Oh, the depth of the riches of the wisdom and knowledge of God! How unsearchable his judgments, and his paths beyond tracing out! "Who has

known the mind of the Lord? Or who has been his coun-
selor?" "Who has ever given to God, that God should repay
them?" For from him and through him and for him are
all things. To him be the glory forever! Amen

And if Paul were sitting next to us with a coffee in one hand and
a donut in the other, maybe he'd say it like this:

Oh, the depth of God's wisdom—it's bottomless. You
won't be able to Google your way to understanding. His
decisions? Way above our pay grade. I mean, we can't even
decide what to order at Chick-fil-A without second-guess-
ing ourselves. Who do we think we are giving God advice?

Who's ever done God a favor that put Him in our debt?

No one.

Because every single thing—everything you can name—
comes from Him, exists through Him, and exists for Him.
He is the source, the sustainer, the point, and the purpose. And when it's all said and done, He gets all the glory.
Not us. Not our cleverness. Not even our faith. Just Him.

IF WE ACCEPT GOD'S SOVEREIGNTY, WE HAVE TO ACCEPT ALL OF IT

Here's the fine print that nobody reads on the sovereignty contract:
God doesn't just reign over sunny days, hot coffee, and last-second
parking spots. He also reigns over cloudy days, cold diagnoses, and
seasons when your prayers bounce like gold balls in a tile bathroom.

His sovereignty covers:

- Promotions *and* layoffs
- Healing *and* heartache
- Marriage *and* miscarriage
- Celebration *and* grief

We're pretty okay with the God who blesses narrative. But the moment life punches us in the gut? That's when the questions start piling up like laundry we pretend isn't there.

Because honestly—we want to see the purpose before we experience the pain. We want a sneak peek at the last chapter before we get past the prologue. But that's not how faith works. Faith trusts that the Author knows what He's doing, even when we can't follow the plot.

WHEN WE CAN'T SEE THE END, HE'S ALREADY THERE

Here's one of the deepest (and hardest) truths I know: We may never get the explanation we want. But God already has the outcome. While we're stuck asking, "Why?" He's already standing at the end, nodding and saying, "Yes, this fits. It always fit."

Faith isn't about having all the facts. It's about knowing Who holds them.

"ALL THINGS" MEANS ALL THINGS

Paul writes, "From Him, and through Him, and to Him are all things." Let's underline that. ALL things.

Not just the wins. Not just the breakthrough moments. Not just the storybook endings.

All. Things.

The tear-stained nights. The deep disappointments. The divorce papers. The funeral. The unanswered prayers. The seasons where God seems silent—or worse, absent.

Romans 8:28 promises: "And we know that in all things God works for the good of those who love him, who have been called according to his purpose."

If He said *all*, then we trust *all*. Even the chapters that feel like footnotes. Even the sentences that don't make sense.

GOD ALWAYS HAS THE FINAL SAY

Here's the hope that anchors me: our lives often look like a length of rope someone tossed into a box—knots, frays, and loose ends everywhere. We try to tidy it, we tell ourselves stories to make sense of the tangles, but in the middle of the mess it's easy to imagine the loudest, meanest thing in the room has the final say—cancer, war, betrayal, a dream that simply dies. The gospel says something sturdier and kinder: those things shout, but they do not write the last line. God does. He will speak last, and when he does the fractured pieces will somehow fit together into a pattern we could not have sketched ourselves.

That doesn't make the pain smaller or the questions rarer. It simply refuses the bleak conclusion that suffering is final. Sometimes God's "good" looks like healing, yes; sometimes it looks like reunion; sometimes it looks like a faith that has been deepened by sorrow and made gentler by grief. In every case, his final word will reveal that nothing that is in his hands is meaningless. He will have the glory in the story's end—not because pain is erased from memory, but because love and wisdom have re-shaped it into something redeeming. He gets the glory. And we get the good.

EVEN IN THIS

It's easy to say, "God is in control." It's harder to say it with tears in your eyes. But that's when it means the most.

When the healing didn't come. When the loved one was taken too soon. When the dream crumbled. When the prayer wasn't answered how you hoped.

When Wade died. When _____ happened. Even in *that*.

Because "all things" includes *this thing* too.

I'll close with a poem that says it better than I can. John Oxenham wrote:

> He writes in characters too grand
> For our short sight to understand;
> We catch but broken strokes, and try
> To fathom all the reasons why
> Of withered hopes, of death, of life,
> The endless war, the useless strife,--
> But there, with larger, clearer sight,
> We shall see this—His way was right.[30]

And I believe that with every fiber of my being.

---

30. John Oxenham, "His Way Is Right," in *Bees in Amber: A Little Book of Thoughtful Verse* (London: Sampson Low, Marston & Co., 1913)

Because one day we'll see Him. And every chapter—even the one you're in now—will suddenly make sense.

Until then we trust the Author. And we keep reading.

ABOUT THE AUTHOR

Buddy Thigpen is a grandson of the Southland, a lover of God and family, a lifelong Bulldog fan, and a middle of the pack runner. For four decades, he has served churches in his beloved state of Georgia and as a missionary—first in Russia and now in Ukraine since the full-scale invasion by Vladimer Putin. Partnering with local congregations to care for widows, orphans, soldiers' families, and pastors. He also serves alongside Ukrainian military chaplains who minister to troops and their loved ones. He is the president of Frontline Fellowship International and "Big-Daddy" to his grandchildren.